Becoming Shakespeare

BY THE SAME AUTHOR

Samuel Johnson's Dictionary (editor)
Samuel Johnson's Insults (editor)

Becoming Shakespeare

The Unlikely Afterlife That Turned a Provincial Playwright into the Bard

Jack Lynch

Walker & Company
New York

Published by Walker & Company, New York

All papers used by Walker & Company are natural, recyclable products made from wood grown in well-managed forests. The manufacturing processes conform to the environmental regulations of the country of origin.

LIBRARY OF CONGRESS CATALOGING-IN-PUBLICATION DATA IS AVAILABLE.

ISBN-10: 0-8027-1566-4 (hardcover)
ISBN-13: 978-0-8027-1566-1 (hardcover)

Art credits Pages 2, 18, 29, 37, 52, 57, 69, 71, 72, 79, 106, 118, 128, 144, 162, 163, 175, 211, 219, 233, 242, 244, 249, 250, 255, and 265: courtesy of the Horace Howard Furness Memorial Library, University of Pennsylvania. Page 20: courtesy of the Edwin Forrest Collection, Rare Book and Manuscript Library, University of Pennsylvania. Pages 22, 47, 182, and 195: courtesy of Special Collections and University Archives, Rutgers University Libraries. Pages 26–27, 31, 60, 63, 65, 95, 100, 125, 134, 142, 155, 158, 217, 220, 223, 253, 257, and 263: courtesy of the Rosenbach Museum & Library, Philadelphia. Pages 35 and 36: courtesy of the Singer-Mendenhall Collection, Rare Book and Manuscript Library, University of Pennsylvania.

Visit Walker & Company's Web site at www.walkerbooks.com

First published by Walker & Company in 2007
This paperback edition published in 2009

Paperback ISBN-10: 0-8027-1678-4
ISBN-13: 978-0-8027-1678-1

1 3 5 7 9 10 8 6 4 2

Typeset by Westchester Book Group
Printed in the United States of America by Quebecor World Fairfield

Contents

A Note on Quotations

When I quote Shakespeare I normally use the Oxford Shakespeare of 1986, in which the editors, Stanley Wells and Gary Taylor, have modernized the spelling and punctuation (though I use the familiar traditional titles of the plays). When I quote other editions I say so. In most of the quotations from other authors, I've followed the original spelling and punctuation of my sources, with only minimal modernization. At first the older forms of the language may seem alien, but I hope the original spelling gives some of the flavor of the times. Besides, as Samuel Johnson wrote, "If phraseology is to be changed as words grow uncouth by disuse, . . . the history of every language will be lost; we shall no longer have the words of any authour."

A few tips will make it easy to decode the older quotations, and soon it will become second nature. First, until the middle of the nineteenth century, the spelling of Shakespeare's name was variable; it will be spelled many ways here, as *Shakespeare, Shakespear, Shakspeare, Shakspere,* and so on. (There were even early spellings like *Shagspere* and *Shaxberd;* the critic E. K. Chambers tallied eighty-three recorded spellings.) The same sort of variation occurred in other words, any of which might have had a half-dozen legitimate spellings, even in a single book. In the sixteenth and seventeenth centuries, the letters *U* and *V* were in some places interchangeable; ditto *I* and *J*—thus *vniuersal* sometimes appears for *universal,* and *John* is sometimes spelled *Iohn.* Consonants were often doubled willy-nilly, and silent *e*'s were more common than they are now. *Et cetera* was often abbreviated *&c* (the ampersand, *&*, was originally a scribal shorthand for the Latin *et*). Older rules for capitalization and italics were also different from ours. Decoding old handwriting is a little more complicated, since it often used abbreviations—*y*^{e} and *y*^{t}, for instance, for *the* and *that*. Note that all of these oddities affect just spelling, not pronunciation: *y*^{e} was pronounced "the," never "ye," just as *vniuersal* was pronounced "universal."

I did, however, make a few changes where the older typography threatened to pose real problems for comprehension. First, I changed the long *s*, the one that looks to modern eyes like an *f*, to the more familiar short form; I turned *VV* into a modern *W*; I eliminated "running quotation marks"; and I expanded a few abbreviations—some early sources omitted *n*'s after vowels, replacing them with marks over the vowels: *Gētlemē*, for instance, which I present as *Gentlemen*. And I print underscored passages in manuscripts as *italics*. Everything else, though, is presented as the authors wrote it, with the occasional clarification supplied in [square brackets].

Becoming Shakespeare

Introduction

On Thursday, 25 April 1616, William Shakespeare's mortal remains were laid to rest. It was a bright, warm spring afternoon in Stratford-upon-Avon; a few high clouds provided an ironically cheerful counterpoint to the melancholy mood below. Inside the Church of the Holy Trinity, crowded around a fresh grave, stood the playwright's many admirers, who had been following his career in London since he first arrived on the theatrical scene a quarter century earlier. Some in the back jockeyed for position to see what was going on. Closer to the front were some of the most distinguished theatrical men of the day: the actor Richard Burbage, the playwrights Philip Massinger and Thomas Heywood, and Shakespeare's partners in the King's Men theatre company, John Heminges and Henry Condell. By far the most important guest was Henry Wriothesley, third Earl of Southampton, Shakespeare's friend and patron from the beginning of his career. The mourners took turns reading passages from his poems and plays, their voices quivering with emotion. Ben Jonson even contributed a poem of his own to mark the sad occasion.

Or maybe not.

Maybe it was a cold, dark morning. Shakespeare had died suddenly, and few of his London friends had received the news that his end was imminent. Even fewer were able to make the trip to Stratford: the spring rains had washed out many of the roads from the capital. Only his local friends, including a few who had

Shakespeare was buried on 25 April 1616 in the Church of the Holy Trinity in Stratford-upon-Avon. This monument was erected not long thereafter. From Phoebe Dighton's Relics of Shakespeare.

known him since childhood, made it to the service. The center of attention was Anne Shakespeare, née Hathaway, her eyes red as she wept over her husband's casket and received comforting embraces from their daughters, Susanna and Judith.

Or maybe it was an uncommonly warm late April day, with a few mourners standing uncomfortably in the hot church, their eyes nervously scanning the entrance. The number of mourners was deliberately kept small because the priest reading the burial service was a crypto-Catholic. It was not long since England had officially embraced Protestantism, and Roman Catholicism was regarded as a serious threat to the nation. Many Catholics had been executed for their plots against Queen Elizabeth, and Shakespeare, a secret Catholic himself, had been a friend to many of them. In his final days he called on the local Catholic priest to read the last rites, and now he was being interred in secret in the old religion.

Or, once again, maybe not.

The fact is no one knows what William Shakespeare's funeral was like. Church records show that he died on 23 April 1616 and was buried two days later. After a very successful career as an actor, playwright, and theatrical shareholder in London, he had retired to the town of his birth, Stratford-upon-Avon. He had been living there with his wife and two daughters, probably since 1610 or 1611. But the cause of his death is a mystery. No record of who attended the funeral survives. No one knows what sympathies he might have had for Catholicism. This hasn't stopped people from speculating about all of these matters, but hard facts are frustratingly few. As the critic Paul Fussell writes, with only slight exaggeration, "What we actually know about Shakespeare as a person can go on a 3×5 card without crowding. But the writings confidently telling his life story and delineating his personality, morals, temper, and character would fill moving vans."

There were no newspapers to speak of in 1616; they wouldn't come into being for decades. But the Elizabethan and Jacobean ages were meticulous about record keeping, and plenty of letters and journals from the early seventeenth century survive. And yet not one contemporary scrap of paper contains anything about Shakespeare's death or his funeral. How can this be? How could it happen that the death of England's greatest writer created no public stir? The simple fact is that no one thought it was newsworthy.

Some people today think this silence is significant. There are those who suspect that Shakespeare wasn't really Shakespeare—that the man from Stratford was not the author of *Hamlet* and *Romeo and Juliet*—and that someone else deserves the credit for the finest plays in the English language. The first inklings that the Stratford man might not have been the author of the works attributed to him came in 1857, when an American ex-schoolteacher named Delia Bacon published *The Philosophy of the Plays of Shakespeare Unfolded*. That eccentric work suggested that the plays were actually written by her namesake Francis Bacon, in collaboration with Sir Walter Ralegh, Edmund Spenser, and others. The novelist Nathaniel Hawthorne was impressed enough to contribute a preface. Since then, the number of candidates proposed as the "true" Shakespeare has multiplied staggeringly. Some have suggested it was Christopher Marlowe, a rival playwright most famous for *Doctor Faustus*. Marlowe's death in a brawl at the beginning of Shakespeare's career—a knife wound above the right eye, an inch wide and two inches deep, ended his life in 1593—hasn't deterred "Marlovians" from attributing plays to him written nearly two decades later; he must have faked his own death and continued writing in secret. Some have even suggested Queen Elizabeth herself had a secret knack for writing plays and used a pseudonym to conceal her dramaturgical passion from the rest of the world.

The favorite candidate proposed by today's "anti-Stratfordians" is Edward de Vere, the seventeenth Earl of Oxford. The theory was first proposed by J. Thomas Looney in 1920 and given new life in 1984, when Charlton Ogburn published *The Mysterious William Shakespeare*. "Oxfordians" have shown considerable ingenuity in linking the plays with the earl—surely the line "That euery word doth almost fel [tell? spell?] my name" in *Sonnet* 76 is a coded reference to his own name, since "euery word" is *almost* a kind of anagram for Edward de Vere, and "envious silver" in *Hamlet* is *almost* an anagram of the Oxford family motto, *Nil vero verius*—although the earl's well-documented death in 1604, long before many of Shakespeare's plays were first produced, is a problem his supporters have struggled to explain in various ways. They also disagree over Oxford's relation to the Stratford man: some say he had an agreement with Shakespeare to use his name as a pseudonym on the plays, while others believe the Stratford man had nothing to do with the plays at all, and that Oxford's use of the name was just a coincidence. There is plenty of disagreement over the details, but all the anti-Stratfordians agree that the uneducated and untraveled commoner from the provinces, William Shakespeare, could not have written the masterpieces that now circulate under his name.

Fantasies about faked deaths and undercover noblemen certainly make for an exciting story, but there's nothing to them. Virtually no professional student of literature takes any of this seriously, and it's not because of some conspiracy among hidebound academics determined to maintain a unified front. Up-and-coming young critics adore taking potshots at their seniors and would like nothing more than to make their reputation with a revolutionary new thesis, but the evidence just doesn't support the case for anyone other than William Shakespeare of Stratford. Yes, there are gaps in the documentary record, gaps that are often infuriating for us today. There's every reason to assume Shakespeare went to the King's New School in Stratford, for instance, but the record books from the 1560s and '70s don't survive, so biographers can only guess about the kind of education he had. Almost nothing is known about his life during a seven-year stretch from 1585 to 1592. No one knows when he arrived in London or how he worked his way up the ranks from a bit-part actor to a major playwright and shareholder in the company. No letters he signed and no books he owned have been preserved.

But the surviving evidence, even with all its frustrating holes and mysteries, shows convincingly that William Shakespeare wrote the plays that bear his name, and the evidence for his authorship is at least as strong as that for any author of his era. There's no doubt that he was born in Stratford-upon-Avon, in the county of Warwickshire, shortly before 26 April 1564, the day on which church records show he was baptized. (It's customary to observe his birthday on 23 April, St. George's Day, but that's just a guess.) He married Anne Hathaway late in 1582, and she gave birth to the first of their three children, Susanna, around six months later. He moved to London in the late 1580s and became an actor, playwright, and shareholder in an acting company. His earliest plays, including some of the *Henry VI* cycle, had been acted by 1592. He had remarkable successes early in his career, including comedies, tragedies, and histories. (*The Taming of the Shrew*, *Titus Andronicus*, and *Richard III* were all early works.) An outbreak of plague closed the theatres in 1592 and '93, leading Shakespeare to try his hand at nondramatic verse. He published *Venus and Adonis* with a dedication to Henry Wriothesley, third Earl of Southampton. He began writing for the Lord Chamberlain's Men (later known as the King's Men) in 1594, producing works like *Romeo and Juliet* and *A Midsummer Night's Dream*. In the late 1590s came *The Merchant of Venice, Richard II*, and *Henry V*. His only son, Hamnet, died at the age of eleven on 11 August 1596, and in 1597 he bought New Place, probably the second-largest house in Stratford, demonstrating that he had already become a rich man. The early 1600s were marked by the great tragedies: *Othello, Hamlet, Macbeth, King Lear*. In 1609 there appeared *Shake-Speares Sonnets*, a collection of 154 poems he had written over the years. Late in his career he wrote "romances" like *The Tempest* and *The Winter's Tale*, around the time that the King's Men began performing in the upscale Blackfriars Theatre. At some point after 1609 or 1610 he stopped writing full-time and spent more time back in Stratford. He died there on 23 April 1616. We know these things as well as we know any fact about any Elizabethan author.

That's not to say every question about Shakespeare's authorship has been resolved. Experts continue to puzzle over how close the published plays are to Shakespeare's originals; the works that survive were almost certainly revised for performance, with actors and others adding and deleting passages to suit the dramatic occasion. It was also common in Shakespeare's day for playwrights to work with one another, and critics are now trying to figure out who else might have had a hand in the plays now attributed to Shakespeare. He probably collaborated with George Peele on *Titus Andronicus* and with George Wilkins on *Pericles*. He may also have contributed passages to plays by others; it may be his handwriting in a few scenes of the manuscript of *Sir Thomas More*, for instance, along with that of several other playwrights.

But insofar as anyone in the Elizabethan era can be said to have written plays, Shakespeare of Stratford wrote plays. As the critic Jonathan Bate has pointed out, the only mystery about Shakespeare's identity is why there's any mystery about Shakespeare's identity. We can say confidently that Shakespeare was really Shakespeare.

In another sense, though, the question of whether Shakespeare was really Shakespeare is more interesting, more profound. There's no reason to doubt that the man from Stratford wrote the plays. But was he really the great genius he's now made out to be?

His contemporaries didn't think so. That's not to say they didn't appreciate his work; his plays were very successful at every level of society, from the commoners who paid a penny to stand in the courtyard of the Globe to the monarchs who ordered Shakespeare's company to play before them. His *Venus and Adonis* was one of the most popular poems of the Elizabethan era. Several of his friends and colleagues wrote poetic tributes to his talents in the years after he died. But appreciating his skill as a popular poet and playwright isn't the same as worshipping him as a kind of secular deity—that happened much later.

An important milestone came seven years after the funeral: in 1623, two members of Shakespeare's company, Heminges and Condell, decided to collect his surviving plays and to publish them in a deluxe edition, in the large format usually reserved for serious literature. The result was the "First Folio," now the most famous book in the English language—and, after the Gutenberg Bible, probably the most famous book in the world. (Owning a First Folio moves a book collector into the big leagues; copies recently sold at auction have fetched more than three million pounds, or six million dollars.) Shakespeare's ephemeral popular entertainments had been given a lasting form and made available to new generations. And once the plays were available in a collected edition, people were able to start reading his works, editing them, annotating them, giving them scholarly attention, and eventually teaching them to young people. Actors were able to present them to new audiences born long after the author had died. These are some of the people who helped turn the Shakespeare of fact into the Shakespeare we know today. This "Shakespeare" isn't just the man from Stratford; Shakespeare is now an institution. Most books about Shakespeare stop, naturally enough, with that man's death in 1616. But while his grave is where one story ends, it's also where another story begins.

This book is therefore a kind of biography that begins with Shakespeare's death and runs to his three hundredth birthday, focusing especially on what happened to him between about 1660 and 1830. I hope that the selection of stories is illuminating for those who have never thought about what happened after the death of the immortal Bard. To say Shakespeare's greatness depends on the collective efforts of later generations takes nothing away from his own achievements. The man from Stratford wrote *Hamlet* and *King Lear* more or less on his own, but it took the combined efforts of countless actors, editors, scholars, readers, and teachers to turn Shakespeare, the provincial playwright and theatrical shareholder, into Shakespeare, the universal bard at the heart of English culture.

The result is a book about an afterlife, but there's nothing mystical about it. It's a book about sex comedies with no sex, about tragedies where everyone lives happily ever after, about a Shakespeare festival where not a line of Shakespeare was spoken. It's a book about a king's teenage mistress and a prudish doctor afraid of blood, about the almost religious adoration for a writer whose works were rewritten from top to bottom. It's about a classic of children's literature written by a murderess, a war fought in scholarly footnotes, and foreign affairs being conducted on the London stage. It's about a regicide and a forger contributing toward the production of a genius. It's about a provincial bumpkin who became the great portraitist of the human condition. It's only fitting that it should be a book about paradoxes, because it's about one of the greatest paradoxes in all of world literature: how Shakespeare became Shakespeare.

CHAPTER 1

Reviving Shakespeare

ONE OF THE CURIOUS THINGS about Shakespeare's afterlife is how long it took to get going. William Shakespeare died in April 1616. Seven years later his friends published his collected works; nine years after that a second edition came out; then—nothing, or nearly so. Shakespeareana slowed to a trickle. Productions of his plays became less common; of his three dozen recognized plays, only five were still appearing on the stage. There were no new collected editions of his works, and individual plays were published less and less often. This isn't surprising. By the 1630s, after all, Shakespeare's plays were old-fashioned, the sort of thing old-timers enjoyed, but not up-to-date, not on the cutting edge. Younger talents like John Webster, Philip Massinger, and John Fletcher were all the rage. Young people in 1635 didn't want to see plays written in 1595 any more than young people today want to hear forty-year-old popular music or watch forty-year-old television programs. This is the natural order of things. In 1642, though, Shakespeare presentations came to an abrupt end, and this was not at all a natural progression—it was part of a civil war. Only in 1660, a few years shy of Shakespeare's hundredth birthday, did things start to pick up again. And this long interval makes sense only against the background of the complicated politics of sixteenth- and seventeenth-century England.

The Catholike Faith

William Shakespeare was born in 1564, almost exactly between the Wars of the Roses, which ended in 1485, and the English Civil Wars, which began in 1642. Just as his life would be influenced by the earlier wars, so would his afterlife be influenced by the later ones. In fact his plays became a part of the disputes, and their survival depended on the outcome of the wars. In some of the bloodiest wars that ever took place on English soil, Shakespeare was an important battleground.

Politics and religion often go hand in hand, but in the sixteenth and seventeenth centuries they were inseparable. The Wars of the Roses brought the Tudors to the English throne, and the second Tudor king, Henry VIII, famously broke with the Roman Catholic Church in favor of a moderate brand of Protestantism. England had begun the Reformation. But before long the Protestant triumph was reversed as Henry's daughter Mary Tudor took the throne and converted the country back to Catholicism. The change came with the gruesome executions of Protestant heretics at Smithfield, memorably recorded (and turned into anti-Catholic propaganda) by John Foxe in his *Acts and Monuments*, better known as the *Book of Martyrs*. But with Elizabeth's accession to the throne in 1558, England was once again a Protestant nation, and Catholics were once again on the outs.

With all this turmoil and all these high-stakes shifts in power, it's no surprise that partisans on all sides were trying to pull England in contrary directions. Roman Catholics, horrified that the old faith had been abandoned, hoped another Catholic monarch would return to the throne and restore the true religion. On the other side, the more radical Protestants were convinced that the English Reformation had not gone far enough, and that many of the "impurities" of Catholicism remained—hence the name by which they are known, Puritans. They wanted England to embrace the most radical Protestant theologies on the Continent.

This is the world into which Shakespeare was born. Which side did he favor? No one knows for sure, even though his religious beliefs have prompted speculation for three hundred years. Warwickshire, his native county, was home to a number of prominent Catholic families, and some evidence suggests that Shakespeare's father remained a committed Catholic even after Elizabeth took the throne. Much of this depends on a document discovered in 1757 but published only in 1790, in which John Shakespeare avowed his adherence to Roman Catholicism: "I John Shakspear," he wrote, "do protest by the present writing, that I will patiently endure and suffer all kind of infirmity, sickness, yea and the paine of death it self [if I] should fall into any impatience or temptation of blasphemy, or murmuration against god, or the catholike faith." The document, however, disappeared soon after it was published, and hasn't turned up since, leading some experts to question its authenticity.

John Shakespeare's son William may also have admired the old faith; references in his plays to prayers for the dead and Purgatory, neither a part of Protestant theology, have led some to think he was a crypto-Catholic in an age when it was dangerous to express Roman Catholic sympathies publicly. But it's probably too simplistic to expect a yes-or-no answer to the question of whether Shakespeare was a Catholic. People had varying degrees of loyalty to the old faith and its rituals. Some sincerely proclaimed themselves Protestants without really giving up their Catholic beliefs, while others fought bitterly against changes they didn't understand. The critic James Shapiro puts it well in a recent book: "To argue that the Shakespeares were secretly Catholic or, alternatively, mainstream Protestants misses the point that except for a small minority at one doctrinal extreme or the other, those labels failed to capture the layered nature of what Elizabethans, from the queen on down, actually believed."

Whatever this religious strife meant during Shakespeare's lifetime, though, it became more important after his death. The tug-of-war between Catholics on the one hand and Puritans on the other, with moderate Anglicans trying to hold the middle ground, grew ever more intense and threatened to tear the country apart. This conflict was the background to England's Civil Wars, as an increasingly Protestant Parliament struggled against an increasingly Catholic-friendly monarch. And in these battles over the moral health of the nation, the theatre was often at the front line.

Pernitious Recreations

Everyone in England had reasons to be concerned about the success of the Puritans, but those whose livelihood depended on the theatre had more reason than most. There had been Puritans in England for decades, but they acquired more and more political power in the seventeenth century, and this was very bad news for the playwrights. Puritans had often objected to the immorality of the theatre, beginning not long after the first public playhouses opened. In 1577, for instance, when Shakespeare was thirteen years old, a preacher named John Northbrooke published *Spiritus Est Vicarius Christi in Terra* (*The Spirit Is Christ's Deputy on Earth*). The long subtitle shows Northbrooke's concerns: *A Treatise Wherein Dicing, Dauncing, Vaine Playes or Enterluds with Other Idle Pastimes &c. Commonly Vsed on the Sabboth Day, Are Reproued by the Authoritie of the Word of God and Auntient Writers: Made Dialoguewise by Iohn Northbrooke Minister and Preacher of the Word of God.*

Northbrooke attacked many popular pastimes—gambling with dice or cards, dancing, and so on—but he had a special animus against the newfangled "Stage playes and Enterludes which are nowe practised amongst vs so vniuersally in towne and country."

His book, cast as a dialogue between callow Youth and mature Age, lays out the case against the theatre. "What say you," asks Youth, "to those Players and Playes? Are they good and godly?" Not at all, says Age; "they are not tollerable nor sufferable in any common weale, especially where the Gospell is preached." He explains to his student that the theatres are places of sexual immorality, for "Satan hath not a more speedie way and fitter schoole to work and teach his desire, to bring men and women into his snare of concupiscence and filthie lastes of wicked whoredome." He therefore advises Youth that "those places and Players shoulde be forbidden and dissolued and put downe by authoritie, as the Brothell houses and Stewes [bathhouses] are."

Critics like Northbrooke had little effect during Shakespeare's lifetime; they were far outside the mainstream of public opinion, and playwrights often made fun of them. Ben Jonson, for instance, satirized Puritan scolds in *Bartholomew Fair*, in which a pompous and self-righteous Puritan improbably named Zeal-of-the-Land Busy makes a lot of noise and tries to shut down a puppet show, revealing himself at the same time to be a glutton and a hypocrite. Shakespeare too took some swipes at Puritans: the killjoy Malvolio in *Twelfth Night*, for example, is called "a kind of Puritan." Undeterred by the satires, though, the Puritans kept at it, and in the years after Shakespeare's death they were beginning to be heard. In 1625 a Puritan named Alexander Leighton published *A Short Treatise Against Stage-Playes*, in which he insisted that "Stageplayes are repugnant to the written Word and Will of Almightie God." They are, he argued, "dangerous to the eternall saluation both of the actours and spectatours," and they "procure the judgments of God to the whole kingdome": Leighton warned audiences that "sinne tollerated pourchaseth Gods wrath to the whole nation." An even more famous Puritan attack on the theatre came from William Prynne, a lawyer and pamphleteer. A work called *Histrio-Mastix*, or "Against Actors," was his magnum opus, and *magnum* it was—more than a thousand pages of densely argued syllogisms, every page crammed with dozens of Latin citations to the Bible, classical authors, and the church fathers. Today only the most devoted specialists can get through it. In 1633, though, it created a stir with its bitter denunciation of plays, playwrights, actors, theatres, and playgoers.

Plays, Prynne insisted, "are such sinfull, hurtfull, and pernitious Recreations, as are altogether vnseemely, and vnlawfull vnto Christians." After all, they "had their birth, and primary conception, from the very Deuill himselfe," and their style is "Heathenish, and Prophane." Their usual subject consists of the "*Actes, the Rites, the Ceremonies, Names, and Persons; yea, the very Rapes, Adulteries, Murthers, Thefts, Deceites, Lasciuiousnesse, and other execrable Villanies of Dung-hill, Idole, Pagan-gods, and Goddesses, or wicked men.*" The book lays out dozens of other charges against plays. Their plots are "*false and fabulous,*" made up of "merry, ludicrous, officious artificiall lies, to delight the eares of carnall Auditors." The wearing of costumes is unseemly, for plays "are usually acted and frequented in over-costly effeminate, strange, meretricious, lust-exciting apparell." Worst of all is the "lascivious mixt, effeminate Dancing on the Stage, not men with women onely, or rather *with Whores or persons more infamous, (for such are all those females . . . who dare dance publikely on a Theater;)* but even men with boyes in womans attire, representing the persons of lewde notorious Strumpets."

Prynne sounds strident, but, as the Puritans became increasingly powerful in the government, he had the ear of the right people. By 1642—twenty-six years after Shakespeare's death—such attacks on the morality of the theatre had a real effect, for the Puritans had finally secured enough political clout to enforce their will on the country. On 2 September of that year, the Parliament of England officially closed all the public theatres in the country. It marked an epoch in the history of the English stage.

The actors didn't go willingly. In a pamphlet of 1643 called *The Actors Remonstrance,* the anonymous author begged for one last chance. He insisted the players had now cleaned up their act and would no longer tolerate the sort of immorality that was once common. Besides, he warned, depriving actors of their livelihood would only drive them to even more immoral professions. If "we may be re-invested in our former Houses," he said, "and setled in our former Calling," he promised "never to admit into our six-penny-roomes those unwholesome inticing Harlots . . . nor any female of what degree soever, except they come lawfully with their husbands." And it wasn't just sexual immorality: "The abuses in Tobacco," he vowed, "shall be reformed." And the playwrights too would get the message: "For ribaldry, or any such paltry stuffe, as may scandall the pious, and provoke the wicked to loosenesse, we will utterly expell it with the bawdy and ungracious Poets."

But the time for compromise had passed. The Puritans, emboldened by their political successes, were becoming ever less tolerant of theatrical immorality. In 1644 the Globe was pulled down—not the original Globe, which was lost in 1613 when fire broke out during a performance of Shakespeare's *Henry VIII,* but another theatre on the same site. (It would not be rebuilt until 1997.) In 1648 came an act even stricter than the one of 1642, ordering that all the old playhouses should be demolished and all actors arrested and whipped. Those caught attending a play were to be fined five shillings, then a substantial sum. This isn't to say that drama disappeared altogether; private theatricals among noble families were still common, court masques continued among the royals, and students could present plays in universities (usually Roman plays in the original Latin). And a few companies put on plays secretly, hoping to avoid detection by the government. But without large paying audiences, the business that had sustained Shakespeare and his contemporaries shriveled up and nearly disappeared.

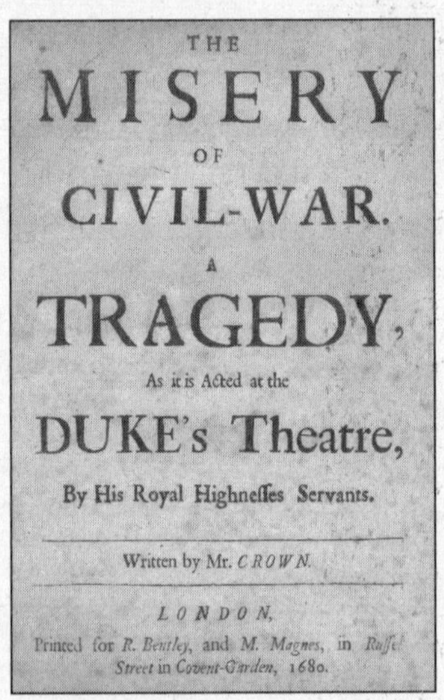
THE
MISERY
OF
CIVIL-WAR.
A
TRAGEDY,
As it is Acted at the
DUKE's Theatre,
By His Royal Highnesses Servants.

Written by Mr. *CROWN*.

LONDON,
Printed for *R. Bentley*, and *M. Magnes*, in *Russel Street* in *Covent-Garden*, 1680.

John Crown, writing in the aftermath of the English Civil Wars, adapted Shakespeare's 2 Henry VI *as* The Misery of Civil-War.

The theatre wasn't the Puritans' only enemy. Their biggest complaint was with King Charles I, and throughout the 1640s they conducted a series of civil wars against him, with parliamentarians on one side pitted against royalists on the other. The wars were bitter and often bloody, dividing the country against itself. Although things went back and forth for a while, the parliamentarians had their greatest success at the end of 1648, when they captured Charles. At the beginning of 1649 they tried him for exceeding his royal authority and executed him on 30 January. Most of the surviving members of the royal family fled to the Continent.

For the next decade, England was without a king. During this period, known as the Interregnum (between the kings), the country was ruled by a Protectorate, with Oliver Cromwell, a Puritan military hero, named Lord Protector in 1653. With the passing of the royal court—the main place where plays and masques had continued to appear after the closing of the public theatres—the

English drama was at a low ebb. Shakespeare's own fortunes also reached their nadir. Not one of his plays appeared on a public stage during the whole eighteen-year period from the closing of the theatres until 1660. Apart from a few short comic scenes adapted from Shakespeare, like *Merry Conceits of Bottom the Weaver* (from *A Midsummer Night's Dream*) and *The Grave Diggers' Colloquy* (from *Hamlet*), only three new printings of his works took place—*King Lear*, *Othello*, and his poem *The Rape of Lucrece* all appeared in 1655—and some unsold copies of *The Merchant of Venice* from 1637 were reissued, with a new title page, in 1652. This is less printing than in any other comparable period in the last four hundred years. Had history turned out only slightly differently, it's possible that Shakespeare's name would be largely forgotten today, known only to a few specialists.

Contented Enough to Be Thought His Son

But the situation didn't last forever. Oliver Cromwell's health declined and he died, at the age of fifty-nine, in September 1658. His son, Richard, took over the Protectorate for a short while, but with no great success. Richard Cromwell's lack of military experience gave him trouble with the army, and he inherited an administration deeply in debt. Even the Parliament began to turn on the son of their onetime champion. In April 1659 the army effectively took charge of the country, and Richard Cromwell was forced to resign the following month. The Protectorate, and the entire government of England, dissolved into chaos.

Royalist military leaders considered taking advantage of the political tumult by mounting an invasion to put a king back on the throne, but an assault proved unnecessary. A new Parliament, more sympathetic to royalist interests, took over in April 1660 and quickly resolved to bring back the king. The old king, Charles I, was beyond bringing back, since he was now in two pieces. But his son and heir, Prince Charles, had passed the danger years abroad. At the Parliament's invitation, he returned to London on 29 May 1660 and in a grand procession was declared Charles II. A new era in British history had begun; as the king had been restored to the throne, the age is known as the Restoration. And Charles's Restoration proved to be Shakespeare's as well.

This second Charles had been out of his country for a decade and a half, fully half his life, passing his time in Italy and especially in France. It stands to reason, then, that he and his courtiers would bring with them a number of French fashions. Louis XIV's passion for science, which led to the establishment of the Académie des Sciences in France, provided a model for Charles's patronage of the Royal Society, still Britain's preeminent scientific academy. French ideas about art, music, and architecture also influenced king and

King Charles II's restoration to the throne in 1660 inaugurated a new era in English theatre history.

court. Most important of all, though, Charles II brought back his taste for the theatre, which he'd been able to indulge in Paris. And one of his first public acts after the Restoration was the opening of the public theatres—for the first time in eighteen years.

The king settled on two theatrical impresarios, both with connections to the royal court and to the stage from before 1642: he called them "our trusty and well beloued Thomas Killigrew, esq., one of the groomes of our Bedchamber and . . . Sir William Davenant, knight." Charles appointed Killigrew to head a troupe called the King's Company and Davenant (or D'Avenant) to lead the Duke's Company under the patronage of the king's brother, James, Duke of York. These were interesting choices, picked as much for their political allegiance as for their artistic ability.

Thomas Killigrew was born in 1612, at the very end of Shakespeare's career. This means he never saw Shakespeare on the stage, but even as a child he seems to have loved the theatre. The great diarist of the Restoration era, Samuel Pepys, told the story of young Killigrew hanging around the Red Bull playhouse in Clerkenwell, hoping for bit parts. "When the man cried to the boys, 'Who will go and be a divell, and he shall see the play for nothing?' " wrote Pepys, "Then would he go in and be a devil upon the stage." As he grew older, Killigrew became a page of honor to Charles I, and Pepys described him as "a gentleman of great esteem with the King." But even as he moved in royal circles, he kept up his interest in the stage. In 1635 he wrote a play called *The Prisoners* for Queen Henrietta Maria, which was performed at Drury Lane by Her Majesty's Servants in the following year. Over the next few years he wrote three more plays, *Claricilla*, *The Princess*, and *The Parson's Wedding*.

Before the last of these plays could be produced or published, though, England's theatres were shut down, and soon the Civil Wars were in full swing. Killigrew, a prominent royalist, found his life in danger. After supporting the king's side for a while in England, serving as a messenger for the king and queen, he fled

Thomas Killigrew was authorized to open one of London's patent theatres in 1660. From John Genest's Some Account of the English Stage from the Restoration in 1660 to 1830.

for the Continent in the mid-1640s. By 1647 he had joined the exiled Prince Charles in Italy. He continued to write plays for the royal family but also served in more important roles: the king's special envoy in diplomatic matters, an attendant on the Duke of Gloucester, and a royal escort through the United Provinces in 1658. After the Restoration, the newly appointed Charles II remembered the support he had received from his ally, and rewarded him with a license to open a theatre in July 1660.

Sir William Davenant's loyalty to the king was similar to Killigrew's, but his early life was very different. Davenant, a little older than Killigrew, was born in 1606, around the time when *King Lear*, *Macbeth*, and *Antony and Cleopatra* were first staged. Unlike Killigrew, though, who grew up in a wealthy and titled family in

Hampton Court and London, Davenant was raised by a vintner and his wife in faraway Oxford. But if Killigrew could boast about his early association with the stage, Davenant went him one better. A legend circulated during Davenant's lifetime that he was illegitimate. Scurrilous accusations like that were common enough; what was odd about this one was that Davenant seemed to encourage the story—in fact, according to his friend and biographer John Aubrey, Davenant would spread the rumor himself. Another early biographer, Anthony à Wood, explained the reason for these aspersions on his own mother's virtue: Jane Davenant was "an admirer and lover of plays and playmakers, especially Shakespeare." And it happened that the Davenants' tavern was on the road between Stratford and London. As Aubrey recorded, "Mr. William Shakespeare was wont to goe into Warwickshire once a yeare, and did commonly in his journey lye at this house." Perhaps, Davenant hinted, Mr. William Shakespeare did also commonly lie with Mrs. Davenant? He was willing to have his mother thought a whore and himself a bastard because, as Aubrey wrote, "Sir William would sometimes, when he was pleasant over a glass of wine with his most intimate friends, . . . say that it seemed to him that he writt with the very spirit that did Shakespeare, and seemed contented enough to be thought his Son."

Tragedies Comedyes Playes Operas Musick Scenes

The date of the first post-Restoration performance of a Shakespeare play remains a mystery, but it was soon after the official opening of the theatres. It had certainly happened by 11 October 1660, when Davenant and Killigrew teamed up to present *The Moore of Venice*, their title for *Othello*, at the Cockpit in Drury Lane. Pepys saw it and found it "well done." He also noted, "A very pretty lady that sat by me, called out, to see Desdemona smothered." Other Shakespeare productions followed quickly. Just four weeks after *Othello* came Killigrew's production of *1 Henry IV* at the Theatre in Vere Street, and the next day the Vere presented *The Merry Wives of Windsor*.

For some time the two companies were operating on an informal basis; although they had the king's blessing, they needed legal documents to open their new theatres. In 1662–63, then, King Charles II issued formal patents, or charters, to the directors of the two companies, formalizing the agreement of 1660. Both of these documents survive: the one issued to Killigrew and the King's Company is now owned by the Theatre Royal at Drury Lane in London, while the one issued to Davenant and the Duke's Company crossed the Atlantic in 1927 and is now at the Rosenbach Museum & Library in Philadelphia. The two are very similar in content.

In one Charles declared that he would "grant unto the said Sir William Davenant his heires Executors Administrators and Assignes full power lycence and authoritie thatt hee . . . shall and may lawfullie peaceablie and quietlie frame erect new build and sett upp in Any place within our citties of London and Westminster or the Suburbs thereof . . . One Theatre or Playhouse." He went on to give his supporter the following rights and responsibilities:

1. He can build a theatre in or near London.
2. He can form an acting company.
3. "Tragedies Comedyes Playes Operas Musick Scenes and al other Enterteynments of the Stage whatsoever may bee shewen and presented" for "the honest recreation" of the audience.
4. He can charge money for these plays.
5. He can pay his actors.
6. He can eject "all scandalous and mutinous persons" from his theatre.

7. Only he and Killigrew are allowed to run theatres.
8. The two companies cannot hire actors from each other.
9. Anyone else who tries to open a theatre will "bee silenced and suppressed."
10. All "prophane obscene and scurrillous passages . . . offensive to Pietye and good manners" must be censored.
11. Actresses are allowed on the public stage.

Numbers 7 and 9 are especially important: only two companies were allowed to present plays. With this provision Charles not only was officially opening two new theatres but was also implicitly closing down those that were operating without his permission. "Wee are informed," said the patent, "thatt divers Companyes of Players have taken upon them to Act Playes publiquelie . . . without any authoritye for thatt purpose, We doe hereby declare our dislike of the same." Killigrew's and Davenant's companies, Charles ruled, could put on plays, but "none other shall from henceforth Act or represent Comedyes Tragedies Playes or Enterteynments of the Stage."

This exclusive right granted to the Duke's and the King's companies lasted, with only a few modifications, from 1660 until 1843; the two companies eventually found permanent homes in Drury Lane and Covent Garden, which were known as the "theatres royal." Not everyone was happy about this arrangement, since other managers hoped to capitalize on the new vogue for drama. Some theatres sprang up but were legally prohibited from presenting plays. A few simply ignored the prohibition, but others sought a way around the law. The patents prohibited the presentation of plays but not other sorts of entertainment—operas, lectures, even circuses. Many nonpatent theatres, therefore, introduced musical interludes into their plays, pretending that they were musical

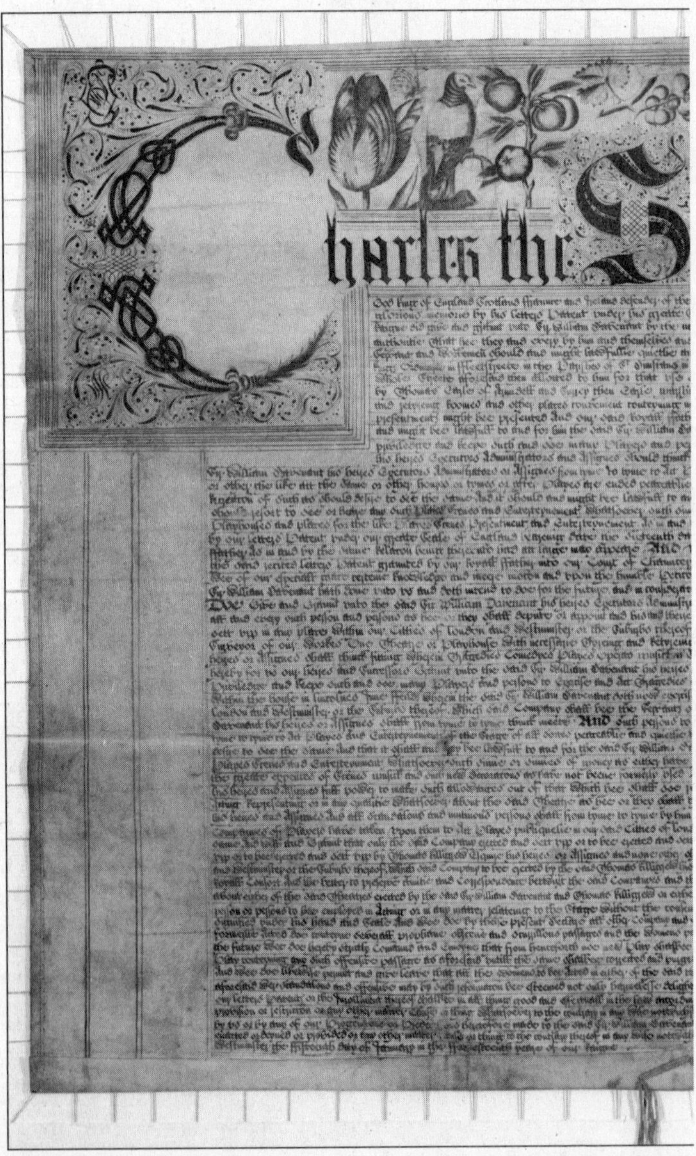
Charles the

Charles II issued this patent to William Davenant in 1663, authorizing him to open a new theatre.

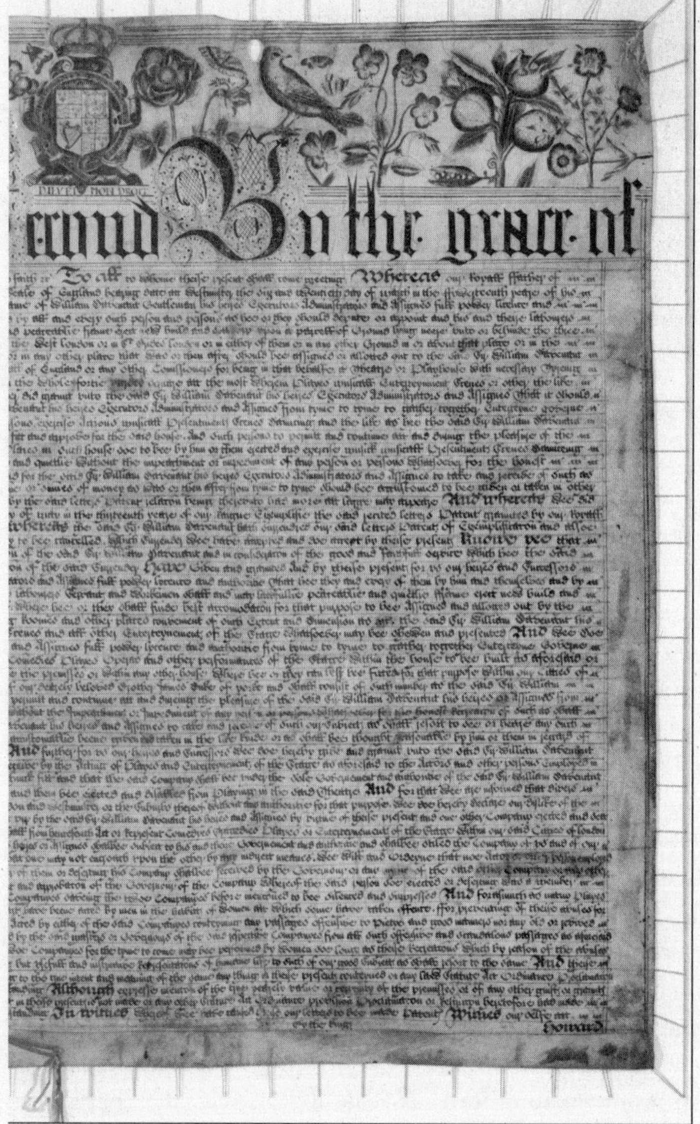

entertainments with only incidental dialogue. Not only did these "burlesques" (comic performances that made fun of serious works) and "melodramas" (sensational dramas accompanied by music) allow the unlicensed theatres to perform serious plays; they also planted the seeds for the musical theatre that continues to thrive. These legal requirements may have introduced a term still used today, almost two centuries after the patent system broke down: traditional dramas performed in licensed playhouses are known as the *legitimate theatre,* distinguishing them from musical comedies and other lighter fare.

The Old Stock of Actors

The new theatrical companies faced a number of problems in these early days. Real estate was their first and most pressing concern. Killigrew started in the Red Bull, an old theatre that had survived the demolition of 1648. But because the building was run-down, his company quickly moved to Gibbons's Tennis Court on Vere Street, which Pepys found "the finest playhouse . . . that ever was in England." Killigrew didn't think so, though, and a few years later he moved the King's Company into the purpose-built Theatre Royal on Bridges Street. Davenant too at first found himself in a tennis court, Lisle's, on Portugal Street in Lincoln's Inn Fields, and remained there until 1671, when he opened a new playhouse in Dorset Garden.

This wasn't the only problem Killigrew and Davenant faced; their new theatres were shut down almost as soon as they opened. Before the Civil Wars, London's theatres had often been closed during the periodic outbreaks of plague. The Puritans in Parliament were always glad to seize the opportunity to use concern about public health to shut down, at least for a while, the "pernitious recreations" they so disliked. Cynical leaders, after all, have long known how to manipulate a fearful public, and they have studied

After moving out of cramped quarters, Davenant's company performed in the Duke's Theatre at Dorset Garden.

how to exploit disasters to advance their agendas. But this time even the drama-friendly court of Charles II recognized that the threat was real and urgent. The Great Plague of 1665–66 was the worst since the Black Death of 1348–49—as many as a hundred thousand Londoners died—and so the Lord Chamberlain, recognizing that "it is thought dangerous that soe greate resort of people should be permitted at your theatre in this tyme of infection," directed Killigrew and Davenant to "forbeare acting any more playes until you shall receive future Order from me." Both patent theatres were closed from early June 1665 through late November 1666.

Even when the theatres were open, professionally trained actors were in short supply. A few of the players from before 1642 were still around and interested, but it had been nearly two decades since most of them had been on the stage. Actors who played romantic leads in 1640 were now limited to old-man roles. And it would be no small task to recruit new actors; since a whole generation had grown up without seeing a play, how could they be expected to perform in one? Killigrew and the King's Company were more successful in lining up the older and more experienced actors, while Davenant and the Duke's Company had to make do almost entirely with newcomers. Lacking the established talent, Davenant's company competed by putting on lavish spectacles with elaborate special effects. These rivalries could be expensive, and both companies took great financial risks in the hopes of luring audiences to see their increasingly grand shows. The competition eventually became more than the market could bear: from 1682 to 1695, the two companies, the King's and the Duke's, were folded into one united company.

But the most pressing problem for the newly instituted companies was that they had no new plays to perform, since virtually nothing had been written for the stage in decades. Doubtless new plays would be written again, but that would take time, and the theatrical managers were eager to start making money right away. For now, their only option was to turn to the old repertoire. Ben Jonson, Francis Beaumont, John Fletcher—all were beneficiaries of this need for scripts. But no one benefited more than William Shakespeare.

"What eager Appetites from so long a Fast," exclaimed the actor and playwright Colley Cibber, "must the Guests of those Times have had, to that high and fresh Variety of Entertainments, which *Shakespear* had left prepared for them?" The two companies competed for the rights to the old plays, and it's clear that Shakespeare's works were becoming hot property, more popular than they had been in decades. Killigrew, the leader of the new King's Company, asserted his right to all the plays owned by the old King's Men, but the Lord Chamberlain eventually assigned nine of Shakespeare's plays, including *The Tempest*, *Romeo and Juliet*, *Twelfth Night*, *Henry VIII*, *King Lear*, *Macbeth*, and *Hamlet*, to Davenant.

To the Reader.

This *Figure*, that thou here ſeeſt put,
It was for gentle *Shakeſpeare* cut;
Wherein the *Graver* had a ſtrife
With *Nature*, to out-doe the *Life*:
O, could he but have drawn his *Wit*
As well in *Braſſe*, as he has hit
His *Face*; the *Print* would then ſurpaſſe
All, that was ever writ in *Braſſe*.
But ſince he cannot, *Reader*, look
Not on his *Picture*, but his *Book*.

B. J.

M^R. WILLIAM
SHAKESPEAR'S
Comedies, Hiſtories, and Tragedies.
Publiſhed according to the true Original Copies.
The third Impreſſion.
And unto this Impreſſion is added ſeven Playes, never before Printed in Folio.
viz.
Pericles Prince of *Tyre.*
The *London Prodigall.*
The Hiſtory of *Thomas* L^d. *Cromwell.*
Sir *John Oldcaſtle* Lord *Cobham.*
The *Puritan Widow.*
A *York-ſhire* Tragedy.
The Tragedy of *Locrine.*

LONDON, Printed for *P. C.* 1664.

The revised title page of the Third Folio boasts of "seven Playes, never before Printed in Folio."

Another sign of Shakespeare's growing popularity is the number of new editions of his works that appeared in the years after the Restoration. No new collected edition of his works had been printed since the Second Folio of 1632, but now Shakespeare was becoming fashionable again. Publishers were eager to take advantage of his newfound popularity. And so in 1663 there appeared the Third Folio. This book appeared in two "issues," one being mostly a straightforward reprint of the Second Folio, but the other being a new and improved version. The second issue of the Third Folio featured seven plays omitted from the earlier folios:

> M^R. WILLIAM SHAKESPEAR'S Comedies, Histories, and Tragedies. Published according to the true Original Copies. *The third Impression*. And unto this Impression is

> added seven Playes, never before Printed in Folio. *viz.* *Pericles* Prince of *Tyre*. The *London Prodigall*. The History of *Thomas* L[d.] *Cromwell*. Sir *John Oldcastle* Lord *Cobham*. The *Puritan Widow*. A *York-shire* Tragedy. The Tragedy of *Locrine*.

If some of these titles sound less than familiar, it's because they're not really Shakespeare's. Of this group of "seven Playes, never before Printed in Folio," only *Pericles* is now believed to be mostly by Shakespeare (probably with the collaboration of another playwright, George Wilkins). The other six had been published in small, cheap editions early in the seventeenth century, some of them under Shakespeare's name or initials, but without any real justification; it was probably just a marketing gimmick on the part of the publishers, hoping to cash in on the increasingly valuable Shakespeare brand name.

This Tempest (Suppos'd to Be Rais'd by Magick)

While the theatres were open again, and some degree of continuity with the great age of the English drama was restored, many other things had changed. The physical space of the new playhouses, for instance, was very different. In Shakespeare's day, the Theatre, the Curtain, the Rose, the Swan, and the Globe were all round courtyards open to the air. (Blackfriars, which housed Shakespeare's company beginning in 1609, was a smaller rectangular indoor space.) There was no artificial lighting, only daylight. Scenery was minimal, and props were few. By some estimates the Globe held as many as three thousand spectators, and actors had to project their voices powerfully if they wanted audiences to hear them. But the physical space was fairly small, and even the back rows were no more than seventy feet from the stage. Prices were also low. To stand in the open courtyard at the Globe cost only a penny, well within the means of most people, and the more comfortable indoor halls cost sixpence—still quite a bargain.

All of this changed after 1660. Though theatres grew over time, the early Restoration theatres were small, and audiences were smaller than in Shakespeare's day: instead of three thousand spectators at the Globe, the tennis courts probably held only around four hundred, and the first theatres in Bridges Street and Lincoln's Inn Fields around seven hundred. To make a profit with smaller crowds, the prices had to go up. Even the cheap seats in the galleries cost a shilling, twice the cost of the most expensive seats at the Globe and fully twelve times what the groundlings paid. The best seats in the private boxes cost four shillings—forty-eight pence—compared to the sixpence of Shakespeare's era. On days when new plays opened, these charges might be doubled. Even accounting for a few decades of inflation, this was a steep increase, and it meant the social profile of the theatres changed. Where they were once accessible to all but the poor, the Restoration theatres were necessarily more genteel. Even the king himself began frequenting the public theatres. Earlier monarchs who enjoyed the drama could see command performances at their palaces, but Charles enjoyed sitting in the royal boxes at both of the patent playhouses.

The physical design of the building was also different. Instead of a round courtyard open to the air, the theatres were rectangular and enclosed, relying on artificial lighting. The stage at the Globe jutted out into the audience, and only a small recess in the back was concealed by a curtain, but the new stages had what's called a proscenium arch with a deep forestage, or apron. These new theatrical spaces made possible the first popular "spectaculars," or "machine plays," grand dramas that made use of expensive scenery, costumes, and special effects. Davenant played a large part here; even before the Restoration, he dreamed of theatres with impressive machinery that could create stunning illusions. As he and

Killigrew were racing to open the two competing patent theatres, he knew that the King's Company had the more impressive actors. Davenant therefore made a calculation that having impressive scenery would give him a competitive edge, and it would be worth the extra time it would require. His theatre at Lincoln's Inn Fields opened in June 1661 and was notable for its use of movable scenery: painted flats that sat in grooves along the back of the stage, and could be slid in and out as needed. This kind of scenery, once reserved for court masques and private theatricals, became commonplace.

We have only a few rough illustrations of the Restoration theatres, and only sketchy descriptions, but it's possible to get a sense of what they might have looked like. The stage directions from a production of *The Tempest* from 1676 explain that, as the great orchestra plays an overture, the curtain rises to reveal "a noble Arch, supported by large wreathed Columns of the *Corinthian* Order; the wreathings of the Columns are beautifi'd with Roses wound round them, and several *Cupids* flying about them." Painted scenery adds to the effect, with a backdrop of "a thick Cloudy Sky, a very Rocky Coast, and a Tempestuous Sea in perpetual Agitation. This Tempest (suppos'd to be rais'd by Magick) has many dreadful Objects in it, as several Spirits in horrid shapes flying down amongst the Sailers, then rising in the Air." The special effects are even more shocking as the ship goes down: "a shower of Fire falls upon 'em," accompanied by "Lightning, and several Claps of Thunder." Davenant's *Macbeth* was another audience favorite. The most popular part of the play was the witches, who flew around the stage supported by wires—a gimmick without Elizabethan precedent, and one that amazed audiences. Joseph Addison's *Spectator* paper included this description of a fashionably airheaded woman at a performance: "A little before the rising of the Curtain, she broke out into a loud Soliloquy, *When will the dear Witches enter*; and immediately upon their first Appearance, asked a Lady that sat three Boxes from her . . . if those Witches were not charming Creatures."

The Woman Playes Today

One other development on the Restoration stage deserves attention. In Shakespeare's day and in the decades that followed, all actors on the public stage were male. Women had appeared in private theatricals, court masques, and some religious pageants, and they sometimes sang or had nonspeaking parts in plays. A few Continental troupes featuring actresses had toured England to mixed reviews. But the stages at the Theatre, the Rose, the Curtain, the Globe, and Blackfriars were, for the most part, all-male spaces. Women's parts were played by boys whose voices had not yet changed.

It's worth bearing this in mind when thinking about how Shakespeare's plays looked to their original audiences. The love scenes in *Romeo and Juliet*, for instance, containing some of the most beautiful love poetry in the language, were probably first played between a man and a prepubescent boy. And some of the cross-dressing comedies gain a new level of complexity when they're presented in something like their original staging. In *Twelfth Night*, the lady Olivia falls in love with the boy Cesario, who is actually the woman Viola in disguise. If this isn't complicated enough, remember that the original audiences watched a boy dressed as a woman falling for a boy dressed as a woman disguised as a boy. The gender-bending could become mind-bending.

Shakespeare poked fun at the tradition, as when Cleopatra imagines herself the subject of some future play and laments, "I shall see / Some squeaking Cleopatra boy my greatness." He also suggested that the boys were eager to graduate from female to male roles. In *A Midsummer Night's Dream*, a group of amateur performers is to present the story of the lovers Pyramus and Thisbe. Peter Quince, the head of the troupe, is giving out the roles to each member of the cast: "Flute, you must take Thisby on you." The young Francis Flute, unfamiliar with the play, asks, "What is Thisby? a wandering knight?" No such luck: "It is the lady that Pyramus must love." "Nay, faith," complains the disappointed Flute, "let me not play a woman; I have a beard coming." But Flute and his kind were often stuck with women's roles—and audiences were stuck with boys in most women's roles for a long time.

Charles and his court, though, had spent many years in France, where actresses were the norm, and they were eager to import this Continental tradition into the newly Frenchified England. It's not known when the first professional actress appeared on the English public stage, but it was certainly by December 1660, when a woman was performing as Desdemona in *Othello*. It was enough of a novelty that the politician Andrew Newport wrote to a friend, "Upon our stages we have women actors, as beyond seas." The prologue to a production of *Othello* on 8 December 1660 put it this way:

> The Woman playes today, mistake me not,
> No Man in Gown, or Page in Petty-Coat.

The Protestant Whore

The most famous—or infamous—of the new actresses was Eleanor "Nell" Gwyn (sometimes spelled Gwynn or Gwynne). Hard facts about her early life are scant, though rumors, legends, and scandalous gossip are plentiful. She was probably born around 1650, making her only ten years old when Charles II returned to England and the theatres were opened. Pepys records a story that she was "brought up in a bawdy-house to fill strong water to the guests," while others hint that as a child she swept London's streets or sold herrings. Beginning in 1663, though, when she was around twelve years old, she worked in the theatre—not, at first, as an actress but as an "orange girl," selling refreshments to the audience. Within two years she had somehow managed to find her way from the pit to the stage, taking bit parts in plays around the age of fourteen. Before long she was among the most popular actresses in London. John Doran, who wrote a history of the English stage in 1864, captured something of her charm. "For tragedy," he acknowledged, "she was unfitted." But when "she assumed comic characters, stamped the smallest foot in England on the boards, and laughed with that peculiar laugh," then "she fairly carried away the town, and enslaved the hearts of city and court."

Eleanor "Nell" Gwyn was famous both as an actress and as mistress to King Charles II. From a painting by Sir Peter Lely.

The first heart to be enslaved belonged to Charles Sackville, Lord Buckhurst, who took Gwyn as a mistress when she was about sixteen. When that didn't work out, she returned to London, and this time caught the eye of Charles II himself: Pepys reported that in January 1668 "the King did send several times for Nelly." Not long afterward she became a royal mistress, living in lavish houses and receiving extravagant payments—four thousand pounds a year beginning in 1674, increased to five thousand pounds two years later, and this at a time when a middle-class family could live comfortably on less than fifty pounds a year. A sinecure post as Lady of the Privy Chamber came in 1675. All the while she continued acting, leaving the stage only long enough to bear Charles several illegitimate children.

Her behavior was often considered shocking in aristocratic circles—not because mistresses were unusual but because her origins were far from the court, and her manners retained a rough edge her whole life. Doran noted that she "could curse pretty strongly," and Bishop Gilbert Burnet called her the "indiscreetest and wildest creature that ever was in court." But Charles was smitten. "The King," one royal-watcher observed, loved her "more for her wit than the attractions of her person . . . It was difficult to remain long in her company without sharing her gaiety." Her only frustration was that Charles had more than a dozen mistresses, and Gwyn's main rival for his affection was Louise de Kéroualle, the Duchess of Portsmouth, a Catholic born in France. When the king asked Gwyn for advice on how to deal with Parliament, she told him a good place to begin would be to "hang up . . . the French bitch." According to another story, when an angry mob surrounded Gwyn's coach, thinking she was Kéroualle, she told the crowd, "Pray good people be silent, I am the *Protestant* whore." Her down-to-earth wit was enough to save her from the violence of the mob.

Nell Gwyn was beloved by many, and the story of her fairy-tale rise from the streets to the palace was widely recounted. As one anonymous satirist put it around 1687,

> I sing the story of a scoundrel lass
> Rais'd from a Dung-hill to a King's embrace.

And though the "scoundrel lass" was not known for Shakespearean parts, she became the archetype of the superstar actress whose offstage life was every bit as fascinating as her onstage roles. The king remained committed to her until the very end. According to legend, as Charles lay dying, he asked his brother, the Duke of York, soon to be James II, "Let not poor Nelly starve." Although she did not starve, she did not long outlive her royal lover: Charles died in 1685, and she followed him two years later, around thirty-seven years old.

This Spacious Land Their Theater Became

Charles had many reasons to care about the theatre, and his fondness for beautiful actresses like Nelly was only one of them. He enjoyed the company of his courtiers, who started making the theatre a kind of second home. He was also known for a hearty sense of humor and liked not only watching plays but trading jests with the players. The actor Colley Cibber recalled one of these exchanges in his memoirs. Although women were allowed on the stage beginning in 1660, in the early days trained actresses were in short supply. "There was still a Necessity," wrote Cibber, "for some time, to put the handsomest young Men into Petticoats." Charles arrived at one of these performances a little early and "found the Actors not ready to begin." Kings, of course, are not accustomed to being kept waiting, so His Majesty "sent to them, to know the Meaning of it." The manager responded to the royal summons and, deciding that "the best Excuse for their Default, would be the true one," he "fairly told his Majesty, that the Queen was not *shav'd* yet." Charles laughingly "accepted the Excuse, which serv'd to divert him, till the male Queen could be effeminated."

But the king had another reason to be devoted to the theatre. Charles developed his taste for drama during his exile in France, where he also developed a new conception of regal power. Whereas England had a long tradition of balancing the interests of the Crown with those of the people, France was an absolute monarchy, and Charles grew fond of the unchecked royal prerogative and splendor he saw in the court at Paris. When he returned to England, he knew that the stage could be a very effective tool in shoring up his own kingly powers. As the critic Paula Backscheider writes, "In this time before mass literacy and a well-developed press and propaganda network, the best means of mass communication available was public spectacle." As a result, it became nearly impossible to separate plays from politics, because Charles and his court often used the one to promote the other.

The first and most obvious political message to come from the theatres was simply that they existed—that Charles and his forces had triumphed over the theatre-hating Puritans. The very act of putting on a play was an insult to the losing side. But the political significance of the theatre could be more involved than that. This was the era that saw the beginning of modern party politics, and public affairs were increasingly seen as a series of skirmishes in which both sides constantly struggled for power. These wars were not fought on battlefields, though, but in the forum of public opinion, and for that, propaganda was essential. Charles thought of politics in theatrical terms and thought of theatre in political terms; for him, the nation and the stage were one. The poet John Denham bore that in mind when he welcomed the king back to the theatre in 1660 and linked the stage with the monarchy, the poet's laurel with the king's crown. "Greatest of Monarchs," he declared, "welcome to this place / Which *Majesty* so oft was wont to grace / Before our Exile." He then praised His Majesty for making theatrical culture possible once again:

> This truth we can to our advantage say,
> They that would have no *KING*, would have no *Play*.
> The *Laurel* and the *Crown* together went,
> Had the same *Foes*, and the same *Banishment*.

Later in the poem he made it clear that the stage and the country were inseparable: "This spacious Land their Theater became."

This association of statecraft with spectacle was a mixed blessing. At its worst, it reduced literature to the crudest kind of propaganda and turned poets and playwrights into partisan political hacks. At its best, though, it linked literature with the English nation as a whole in an unprecedented way. Literature, especially drama, was becoming vital to the health of the nation. And Shakespeare, more than any other old writer, benefited from this development: he started to become the national poet. Even now, Shakespeare is tightly bound up with the idea of "Englishness." Royal patronage had once again made the theatre respectable. The playwright had been saved from oblivion and was on his way toward becoming a national institution. Shakespeare was back.

CHAPTER 2

Performing Shakespeare

IN TODAY'S HIGHLY LITERATE CULTURE, most people probably get their first exposure to Shakespeare through print, and it feels perfectly natural to study him in school. That hasn't always been the case. Before literacy became widespread, people who wanted to experience his plays had to see them on the stage, not the page. It took real men and women to bring his words to life.

The Saturnalian License of the Rabble

Although the post-Restoration theatres had become more upscale venues than in Shakespeare's day, their moral profile had improved little. Puritans had railed against the immorality of the drama in the late sixteenth century, and there seemed to be even more to complain about in the late seventeenth. The critic Philip H. Highfill argues that this reputation was unearned, and that the lasciviousness of real-life theatre people was overstated. "Much recent pecksniffian bridling at the people of the stage," he writes, "has been either hypocritical or ignorant. Sexual scandals involving actors occurred; they were scandalous because they became known; they became known because they involved prominent persons." He's right, and there's no reason to assume actors and actresses were any more wicked than anyone else. In the public mind, though, they were notorious sinners, living lives of bacchanalian riot, and the many surviving accounts of the bizarre antics of both the players and their audiences only add to the impression that the theatre was often a scene of bedlam.

The early theatre historian John Downes, for instance, recorded a performance of *Romeo and Juliet* at Lincoln's Inn Fields in 1662. During a struggle between the Capulets and the Montagues, Lady Capulet was to enter and try to break up the fight, but she succeeded only in breaking up the audience. The actress, Downes wrote, "enter'd in a Hurry, Crying, O my Dear *Count*! She Inadvertently left out, O, in the pronunciation of the Word *Count*! giving it a Vehement Accent, put the House into such a Laughter, that *London* Bridge at low-water was silence to it."

Even when actresses were not bellowing obscenities at the audience, the seventeenth- and eighteenth-century theatre could be a boisterous place. Prostitutes and pickpockets prowled the area. Henri Misson, who visited the London theatres in the 1690s, reported that "Men of Quality, particularly the younger Sort, some Ladies of Reputation and Vertue, and abundance of Damsels that hunt for Prey, sit all together in [the pit], Higgledy-piggledy, chatter, toy, play, hear, hear not." The actors were often the last thing on the spectators' minds; being seen in the right company was far more important. In 1778 Frances Burney made fun of such people in her novel *Evelina*, where the foppish Mr. Lovel admits, "I seldom listen to the players: one has so much to do, in looking about, and finding out one's acquaintance, that, really, one has no time to mind the stage." Then, "most affectedly fixing his eyes upon a diamond-ring on his little finger," he asks his companions after the production, "pray—what was the play to-night?" His acquaintance, the gruff Captain Mirvan, is astonished: "Why, what the D——l," he cries, "do you come to the play, without knowing what it is?" "O yes, Sir," says Lovel, "yes, very frequently; I have no time to read play-bills; one merely comes to meet one's friends, and shew that one's alive."

Small wonder people like Lovel didn't know what play was being performed, considering how much was going on in the audience. More than a hundred years before Burney satirized such characters, Pepys the diarist watched one of the *Henry IV* plays in November 1667, where "a gentleman of good habit, sitting just before us, eating of some fruit in the midst of the play, did drop down as dead, being choked." Fortunately, the woman who sold the oranges—"Orange Moll," Pepys called her—"with much ado . . . did thrust her finger down his throat, and brought him to life again." Not all the disasters, though, were so satisfyingly averted. One contemporary reported on a performance of *Macbeth* from 1675: "At the Acting of this Tragedy, on the Stage, I saw a real one acted in the Pit." A fight broke out between two men, and Sir Thomas Armstrong stabbed one Mr. Scroop, who "died presently after he was remov'd to a House opposite to the Theatre."

Sometimes the whole theatre was ready to collapse into anarchy. In his *History of the Theatres of London and Dublin*, Benjamin Victor told the story of a drunken earl who in 1721 was seated on the side of the stage. "Seeing one of his Companions on the other Side," noted Victor, "he crossed over the Stage among the Performers, and was accordingly hissed by the Audience." The manager, John Rich, confronted the boorish nobleman: "I hope your Lordship will not take it ill, if I give Orders to the Stage-Door Keeper, not to admit you any more." But the earl did take it ill: "My Lord saluted Mr. *Rich* with a Slap on the Face, which he immediately returned; and his Lordship's Face being round and fat, made his Cheek ring with the Force of it." In the ensuing tussle the earl and his friends threatened Rich's life, but the actors teamed up to drive the drunken troublemakers out the stage door into the street. Things didn't end there, though, for the rowdies soon stormed back in: "They then sailed into the Boxes with their Swords drawn, and broke the Sconces, cut the Hangings (which were gilt Leather finely painted) and continued the Riot there." Finally, one of the actors "came round with a Constable and Watchmen, and charged them every one into Custody." After the king heard about the scuffle, he ordered that military guards should be posted every night at both of the patent theatres—a tradition that lasted for well over a century.

The Last of Our Tragedians

This is the raucous background against which the players had to try to make Shakespeare live. With the boorishness of the audience it's surprising that the actors were able to do a thing, and yet they managed to excite audiences as never before. Many performers became national, even international, celebrities, achieving a degree of fame that no one in Shakespeare's day could have imagined. The star system was being born.

The first actor to achieve stardom under the new dispensation was Thomas Betterton, who gained a reputation as the greatest player since Shakespeare's day. He was born in 1635, before the closing of the theatres, but was probably too young to have seen any drama before the Puritan takeover. His background is largely unknown, though his family apparently had royalist connections during the Civil Wars. (One biography published in 1741 plays up these royalist sentiments, saying that he fought on the king's side at the Battle of Edgehill—an exciting story, but one that becomes considerably less plausible when we remember that Betterton was all of seven years old at the time. Seven-year-olds, even passionate and dedicated seven-year-old royalists, were probably of little use to the king's forces.) He was playing with John Rhodes's company at the Cockpit Theatre in 1659, even before the Restoration made dramatic performances legal again. In the next year, when the two patent companies were licensed, Betterton teamed up with Sir William Davenant in what proved to be a good career move for both men. Because Killigrew's rival company had more of the big-name actors, the competition inside Davenant's company was less intense, and it was easier for a talented actor to achieve real prominence. Betterton quickly made his way up the ranks and soon became the leading figure in the Duke's Company.

While he could neither sing nor dance, Betterton had a stirring voice and piercing brown eyes, and he was admired for his wide range. Early in the eighteenth century, a friend wrote, "*Betterton* was an Actor, as *Shakespear* was an Author, both without Competitors!" Samuel Pepys would have agreed, for Betterton was his favorite performer. Over the course of his long career he probably played a total of around two hundred characters, and many of his most successful were Shakespearean. He not only played grand, serious roles like Hamlet, Lear, and Othello, but also distinguished himself as Falstaff, Sir Toby Belch in *Twelfth Night*, and Mercutio in *Romeo and Juliet*. After Davenant's death in 1668, Betterton moved into management, where he encouraged young actors and playwrights and served as a mentor for them in the same way Davenant had helped him. He also continued acting until he was seventy-five, although his health suffered at the end of his life. As an early biographer put it, he was "long troubled with the Stone and the Gout," and the "repellatory Medicines" given to him for his gout "prov'd so fatal as in a few Days to put an End to his Life." He died in 1710, fifty years after the opening of the theatres, and was buried with honor in Westminster Abbey. The critic Charles Gildon published the first biography of Betterton a few months later. "As it was said of *Brutus* and *Cassius*," wrote Gildon, "that they were the last of the *Romans*; so it may be said of Mr. BETTERTON, that he was the last of our *Tragedians*."

Betterton, of course, was not the last of the tragedians, though he was one of the last major players to have been born before the closing of the theatres. None of the actors who came to prominence after 1700 had any firsthand experience of the old regime, and as the Restoration turned into the eighteenth century, a new age began. The period isn't remembered for its original drama—apart from John Gay's *Beggar's Opera*, Oliver Goldsmith's *She Stoops to Conquer*, and Richard Brinsley Sheridan's *School for Scandal*, few plays from the era have survived in the modern repertoire—but it was undeniably a great age for acting. Playgoing was at the center of London social life from September through May every year.

The next big celebrity performer was the oddly named Colley Cibber, who described himself in his autobiography, the equally oddly named *Apology for the Life of Colley Cibber, Comedian*, as "A Man who has pass'd above Forty Years of his Life upon a Theatre, where he has never appear'd to be himself." He thought that he "may have naturally excited the Curiosity of his Spectators to

Colley Cibber was the most famous comic actor of the early eighteenth century. From John Genest's Some Account of the English Stage from the Restoration in 1660 to 1830.

know what he really was, when in no body's Shape but his own," and so published his *Apology* in order "to give the Public This, as true a Picture of myself as natural Vanity will permit me to draw." Plenty of readers noted a superabundance of that "natural Vanity" in Cibber, which made him a favorite target for the London satirists. Alexander Pope eviscerated him in his mock-epic poem *The Dunciad*, and Henry Fielding, best known today as the author of *Tom Jones*, took aim at "Conny Keyber" in his early satire *Shamela*. The satirists became even more flustered when Cibber was named poet laureate in 1730, despite an indifferent body of writing.

But even his enemies recognized his talent as an actor, and the success of his *Apology* shows that the spectators really were curious to know about him. In that work Cibber gave an account of his early ventures onto the stage. "The first Thing that enters into the Head of a young Actor," he recalled, "is that of being a Heroe." But it was not to be: "In this Ambition I was soon snubb'd, by the Insufficiency of my Voice; to which might be added, an uninform'd meagre Person . . . with a dismal pale Complexion." But after a few successful performances he began receiving applause, "which you may be sure, made my Heart leap." His heart leaped even higher when he overheard a more experienced player say, "If he does not make a good Actor, I'll be d——n'd!" The praise "almost took away my Breath, and (laugh, if you please) fairly drew Tears from my Eyes!" Before long he was the leading actor in London, and he played many Shakespearean roles: Gloucester in *King Lear*, Osric in *Hamlet*, Shallow in 2 *Henry IV*, and Wolsey in *Henry VIII*. Cibber was fond of writing his own adaptations of Shakespeare's plays, and one of the advantages of sharing the writing credits with the Sweet Swan of Avon was that he could take all the best parts for himself. In his version of *Richard III* he played the lead, and in his version of *King John* he played Cardinal Pandulph. He also became a theatre manager at

Drury Lane, where his wife Catherine, his son Theophilus, and his granddaughter Jennie were members of the company. (Theophilus may be best remembered for playing Romeo to his fourteen-year-old daughter Jennie's Juliet.)

The Cibbers were thus the descendants of Killigrew's King's Company, but the rival company at Covent Garden, descended from Davenant's Duke's Company, had its own superstar, James Quin, the most successful tragic actor of the early eighteenth century. He first appeared on the Dublin stage around 1713, but two years later he moved to England and had his London debut in 1715. His reputation grew slowly, but he eventually secured the leading place among the tragic players in eighteenth-century London. His most successful roles were Othello, Macbeth, Lear, and Brutus in *Julius Caesar*.

If the rumors are to be believed, as a young man Quin lived a wild life, filled with plenty of eating, drinking, and love affairs. The rumors about the eating, at least, were true: late in life he swelled to nearly three hundred pounds. He also had a hot temper, engaging in many high-profile quarrels with other men of the theatre. Things came to a head in 1718 when he ran into William Bowen, a rival actor twice his age, with a similar temper. The outcome was that Quin killed Bowen in a duel and was found guilty of manslaughter. He somehow escaped punishment for the crime, under circumstances that aren't clear, and was able to stay on the stage without too great an interruption of his career.

Cibber and Quin were theatrical giants in the 1730s, but both watched their reputations decline rapidly in the early 1740s—not because they left the stage, not because they chose bad roles, but because they were eclipsed by a much greater talent. No actor in the eighteenth century—perhaps no actor at any time—had a higher profile than David Garrick, who ruled the London theatre world for decades.

A Theatrical Newton

Garrick was born in 1717, the grandson of a French Protestant refugee named David de la Garrique. He spent much of his early life in Lichfield in the English Midlands, and for a short while studied at Edial School, where he was one of the few pupils of the great critic Samuel Johnson. Garrick was mischievous in his early days; he and his schoolmates, wrote Johnson's biographer James Boswell, "used to listen at the door of [Johnson's] bed-chamber, and peep through the key-hole, that they might turn into ridicule his tumultuous and aukward fondness for Mrs. Johnson." Much later Garrick remembered his naughty peeping on the love life of his teacher, for Boswell—who met Garrick more than a quarter century after these episodes—recorded, "I have seen Garrick exhibit her, by his exquisite talent for mimickry, so as to excite the heartiest bursts of laughter."

Despite Garrick's fondness for mischief, he and his teacher came to London together in March 1737. Both were without money and without real prospects. Garrick's father intended him for a career in law, but Garrick showed no interest. He therefore entered the family business as a wine merchant in a partnership with his brother Peter. His heart, though, wasn't in that either; as he later wrote to Peter, "My Mind (as You must know) has been always inclin'd to ye Stage." While he was still in the wine business, he wrote a few short plays, which enjoyed some modest success. More daringly, he also ventured onto the stage himself, but not yet in the big commercial theatres in London. He may have appeared in an amateur production of Henry Fielding's play *The Mock Doctor* late in 1740, and he was probably in a pantomime in March 1741; but these were small affairs. According to Thomas Davies, his first biographer, "Mr. Garrick's diffidence with-held him from trying his strength at first upon a London theatre; he thought the hazard was too great, and embraced the advantage of commencing noviciate in acting with a company of players then ready to set out for Ipswich." And so, in 1741, he appeared on the stage in Ipswich as Aboan in Thomas Southerne's play *Oroonoko*. He served a valuable apprenticeship, however brief, in the provincial theatre, for as Davies said, "The Clown, the Fop, the Fine Gentleman, the Man of Humour, the Sot, the Valet, the Lover, the Hero, nay, the Harlequin, had all been critically explored, and often rehearsed and practised by him in private." He concealed his identity, appearing under the pseudonym of Mr. Lyddal.

Davies wrote that "our young player's applause was equal to his most sanguine desires," but Garrick couldn't expect to find fame in Ipswich, which was too far from the mainstream. On 19 October 1741, there appeared an advertisement for a production of *Richard III* that night at the unlicensed Goodman's Fields Theatre in London, with "The Part of King Richard by a GENTLEMAN (*who never appear'd on any Stage*)." The mysterious "gentleman," even though he played before a sparse audience, was a hit. The next day's newspaper reported that his "Reception was the most extraordinary and great that was ever known upon such an Occasion," and soon the news of the talented newcomer spread through London. The play was repeated seven times in the next eight nights, each time to a larger audience; crowds were flocking to see the new sensation. So successful was he at Goodman's Fields, said Davies, that "the more established theatres of Drury-Lane and Covent-Garden were deserted."

Garrick knew he was a success from the very first night; more than that, he knew his life had changed. The morning after his first performance he wrote to his brother, announcing his determination to leave the wine trade. He worked hard to make a convincing case. For one thing, he explained, he wasn't showing much promise as a businessman. "I have made an Exact Estimate of my Stock of wine & What Money I have out at Interest," he wrote, "& find that Since I have been a Wine Merchant I have run

William Hogarth painted one of the most famous images of David Garrick, shown here in his role as Richard III.

out near four hundred pounds." He saw no prospect that things would improve. Besides, he had always longed to appear on the stage, "so strongly so that all my Illness & lowness of Spirits was owing to my want of resolution to tell You my thoughts."

Garrick was aware his brother would have reservations about his entering such a morally dubious profession, so he tried to reassure him: "I hope when You shall find that I may have y[e] genius of an Actor without y[e] Vices," he wrote, "You will think Less Severe of Me & not be asham'd to own me for a Brother." But he had finally had a taste of public adulation, and he liked it: "Last Night," he wrote, "I play'd Richard y[e] Third to y[e] Surprize of Every Body & as I shall make very near £300 p Annum by It & as it is really what I doat upon I am resolv'd to pursue it." Three hundred pounds a year was very good money, but Peter was still unhappy with the news—the more so when, by the end of

November, his brother's anonymity was gone, and the family name was bruited about the West End.

David Garrick eventually succeeded in winning Peter over, but he also had to win over the theatrical establishment. In particular he had to overcome the comparisons with other Richards. As Davies put it, "An actor, who . . . undertakes a principal character, has generally . . . the prejudices of the audience to struggle with, in favour of an established performer." Garrick was taking on a part that others had succeeded in, and he knew he'd have to be at least as good as his predecessors. Colley Cibber had been very successful as Richard III, and Quin too had played the role. But Garrick distinguished himself from the competition with a new natural style of acting, a departure from the usual formal declarations that had long dominated the stage.

It was still conventional for interpretations to be handed down from generation to generation, and innovation was frowned upon. But now a young upstart was introducing a radically new approach to acting: one that seemed *genuine*, one that relied less on mannered postures and more on subtle intonations, realistic expressions, believable reactions. Actors before Garrick studied poses and declamation designed to elicit the right emotions from the audience. Garrick appeared to abandon the techniques and instead to *feel* the emotions he was portraying. To modern eyes, accustomed to method acting and the kind of intimacy the big screen makes possible, Garrick would probably have looked terribly stilted and artificial. To eighteenth-century eyes, though, he was a revelation.

At first this new approach baffled audiences as much as it fascinated them. As Davies reported, "Mr. Garrick's easy and familiar, yet forcible style in speaking and acting, at first threw the critics into some hesitation concerning the novelty as well as propriety of his manner. They had long been accustomed to an elevation of the voice, with a sudden mechanical depression of its tones, calculated to excite admiration, and to intrap applause." They didn't know what to make of "the just modulation of words, and concurring expression of the features from the genuine workings of nature." But soon, Davies noted, they caught on and came to appreciate Garrick's real brilliance: "after he had gone through a variety of scenes, in which he gave evident proofs of consummate art, and perfect knowledge of character, their doubts were turned into surprize and astonishment; from which they relieved themselves by loud reiterated applause." One contemporary wrote, "He is the only Man on any Stage where I have been, who speaks Tragedy truly and natural." Garrick, a master of moving the emotions, brought about an acting revolution. Davies even likened him to another revolutionary, England's greatest scientific genius, the recently dead Sir Isaac Newton, when he said that he "shone forth like a theatrical Newton; he threw new light on elocution and action, he banished ranting, bombast and grimace, and restored nature, ease, simplicity and genuine humour."

A New Religion

No actor had ever achieved Garrick's level of stardom. So famous was this "theatrical Newton" that he featured in a number of novels of the period. In Henry Fielding's *Tom Jones*, written fairly early in Garrick's career, Tom and his friend Partridge go to see *Hamlet*. Tom admires Garrick in the lead role, but the naïve Partridge admits that he preferred the actor who played the king. Another of the party is shocked: "You are not of the same Opinion with the Town," she says; "for they are all agreed, that *Hamlet* is acted by the best Player who was ever on the Stage." Partridge, though, wasn't impressed with Garrick. "He the best Player!" he exclaims. "Why I could act as well as he myself. I am sure if I had seen a Ghost, I should have looked in the very same Manner, and done just as he did." No, it wasn't the realistic Garrick who deserved the prize, but "the King for my Money; he speaks all his Words distinctly, half as loud again as the other.—Any Body may see he is an Actor." The joke is obvious: Garrick's natural style of acting doesn't look like *acting* to a rube from the country. *Real* acting, he thinks, is the sort of stylized declamation that Garrick had rendered obsolete. Frances Burney's character Evelina, far shrewder than Partridge, is duly impressed when she sees Garrick thirty years later, praising him breathlessly: "Such ease! such vivacity in his manner! such grace in his motions! such fire and meaning in his eyes!" The young theatregoer continues in the same rapturous strain, declaring that "every word seemed spoke from the impulse of the moment," and that "His action—at once so graceful and so free!—his voice—so clear, so melodious, yet so wonderfully various in its tones—such animation!—every look *speaks*!"

Inevitably the young upstart, with his new approach to performing, acquired enemies. Quin watched his reputation decline as Garrick's rose, and wasn't happy with it. "If the young fellow was right," said Quin, everyone else—including him—"had been all wrong." He didn't like the prospect. He called Garrick "a new religion" but remained convinced that it was just a fad and that the crowds "would all come to church again." Others found things to ridicule in Garrick's performances. Legend has it that he had a special wig constructed for his performances of *Hamlet*: when the ghost vows that his story will cause "each particular hair to stand on end," Garrick supposedly pumped a hidden pneumatic bulb that caused the hair on the wig to stand up. As the critic Joseph Roach puts it, "On the line 'Look, my lord, it comes,' the hairs of this remarkable appliance rose up obligingly at the actor's command. Hamlet, Prince of Denmark, flipped his wig." The satirist Samuel Jackson Pratt ridiculed Garrick in a poem called *Garrick's Looking-Glass; or, The Art of Rising on the Stage*, with a mischievous description of the effect:

> One minute marks a start, at most,
> But, if on entrance of a ghost, . . .
> 'Twere well indeed, if, when *it's* come,
> With dext'rous dash of hand, or thumb,
> You caus'd the hair, to stand an end.

Colley Cibber, too, thought that Garrick didn't measure up to his own son Theophilus. Not everyone in the acting establishment, though, resented Garrick. Anne Bracegirdle, a star actress who had long been retired from the stage, was impressed by the young man. "Come, come," she said to Cibber, "tell me, if there is not something like envy in your character of this young gentleman. The actor who pleases every body must be a man of merit." Cibber was forced to admit she was on to something: "Bracey," he conceded, "I believe you are right—The young fellow is clever."

The clever young fellow also aroused envy closer to home. He and his old schoolmaster, Samuel Johnson, came to London together in 1737, but Garrick was a sensation on the stage by 1741, while Johnson toiled in obscurity until the 1750s. This may have contributed to Johnson's lifelong ambivalence toward his most talented pupil; he took every opportunity he could to poke fun at him. When Johnson was asked his opinion of one of Garrick's poems, he complained, "I got through half a dozen lines, but I could observe no other subject than eternal dulness. I don't know what is the matter with David." James Boswell once tried to defend Garrick, but Johnson snapped, "The next subject you talk to him of, 'tis two to one he is wrong." But as a friend pointed out, Johnson "always abused Garrick himself, but when anybody else did so, he fought for the dog like a tiger."

Garrick played hundreds of roles over the course of his career from dozens of playwrights, and many of the best were Shakespearean. His Richard III was legendary from his first appearance on the London stage in 1741. Later in the same season, in March

1742, he played King Lear; according to some reports the performances were interrupted by weeping in the audience. In January 1744 he first played Macbeth, a role he gave up only in 1768, when Hannah Pritchard, who played opposite him as Lady Macbeth, retired from the stage. In February 1745 he took on King John, and just a few weeks later he appeared as Othello—one of his few unsuccessful roles, so four years later he took on the more comfortable part of Iago. He was also successful in comic parts, among which Benedick in *Much Ado About Nothing* was an audience favorite.

Not every Garrick performance was a dignified success. One hot and humid night Garrick was playing Lear, in a performance that went with its customary propriety for the first four acts. But when, in the fifth act, he was supposed to cry over Cordelia, his face suddenly changed its character—he was trying to stifle a

David Garrick played Macbeth with Hannah Pritchard for nearly a quarter century. From a painting by Johann Joseph Zoffany.

laugh. The others on stage joined in the snickering, and the dying Cordelia even opened her eyes to see the source of the hubbub. Soon the whole cast ran off stage. A butcher seated in the front row of the pit had brought his dog along with him. As one news account recorded it, the dog, "being accustomed to sit on the same seat with his master at home, naturally supposed he might enjoy the like privilege here," and so the mastiff sat on the butcher's lap and rested his forepaws on the orchestra rail. The butcher, for whom a visit to the theatre was an exciting night out, was dressed in his best clothes and wig but was unprepared for the sultry climate in the theatre. The account continued, "Our corpulent *Slaughter-man* . . . found himself much oppressed by the weight of a large and well-powdered Sunday periwig, which for the gratification of cooling and wiping his head, he pulled off, and placed on the *head* of his *mastiff*." When Garrick, at the most pathetic and touching moment in the play, looked up from Cordelia's body and saw a periwigged dog sitting attentively in the front row, he lost his composure.

Eclipsed the Gaiety of Nations

Late in his life Garrick's health, never very good, turned very bad. Gout and arthritis caused him much discomfort, and at night he was plagued by bouts of "the bile." He suffered from kidney stones throughout much of his life, and his illnesses sometimes caused him to leave London for the spa at Bath. In his late fifties he'd had enough. Garrick's reign came to an end in spring 1776, when he retired from the stage after a third of a century at the top of his profession. A series of farewell performances packed the house. Garrick lived another three years, but his health at last got the better of him. In Davies's words, "He died on Wednesday morning, January the 20th, at eight o'clock, without a groan. Mr. Garrick's disease was pronounced . . . to be a palsy in the kidneys."

(An autopsy revealed that he had been born with only one kidney, which makes his long history of problems more understandable.)

After more than thirty years of presenting some of London's grandest spectacles, Garrick had one great performance left in him after his death. On the first of February his funeral procession set out from his house in the Adelphi and took more than an hour to reach Westminster Abbey. More than fifty coaches and two dozen leading actors participated in the funeral, accompanied by what Davies called "persons of the first rank; by men illustrious for genius, and famous for science; by those who loved him living, and lamented his death." At three o'clock they reached Westminster Abbey, where the bishop of Rochester, the dean of Westminster, and the hooded choir "preceded the corpse up the center ayle, during which time the full organ and choir performed Purcel's grand funeral service." As they reached Poets' Corner, the part of the abbey marked by the Shakespeare monument, "the bishop performed the last sacred ceremony of the church; the choir sung another solemn strain, and the remains were deposited in a grave, doubly hallowed by a nation's grief, and the copious tears of private friendship." Garrick's old friend Samuel Johnson was part of the crowd of mourners, and in his last major work, *Lives of the Poets*, he recorded a more private expression of grief: "I am disappointed by that stroke of death, which has eclipsed the gaiety of nations, and impoverished the publick stock of harmless pleasure."

Tragedy Personified

However impoverished Garrick's friends were, though, the nations didn't take long to recover from his death, because the next few decades brought a long train of great actors. The most important came from the Kemble clan, the leading theatrical dynasty of the late eighteenth and early nineteenth centuries. The family

Sarah Siddons, the greatest tragic actress of the late eighteenth century, was the first of the Kemble family to achieve fame on the stage.

patriarch, Roger Kemble, was a minor actor in a touring company who did not want his children to follow his example. The wish was for nought: eight of the twelve Kemble children became actors, and several more followed in the next generation. Two in particular, daughter Sarah and son John Philip, were universally regarded as the greatest performers of their age.

Sarah Kemble—better known by her married name, Mrs. Siddons—was the first of the Kemble children to make the stage her profession. Her debut came at the age of just eleven, when she played Ariel in *The Tempest*. Through her teens she continued acting in the provinces, all the while being courted by a fellow actor, William Siddons. The two married in 1773, when she was eighteen. Two years later she played Rosalind in *As You Like It*, prompting one spectator, the Reverend Henry Bate, to note, "[Her face was] one of the most beautiful that ever I beheld." He did, however, object that "her big belly . . . entirely mars for the present her whole shape." Siddons was then very pregnant with her second child but remained on the stage for as long as she could.

Her London debut came at the end of 1775, when she played

Portia in *The Merchant of Venice*. For many major actors their London debut was their chance to shine—but not so for Siddons, whose performance was disastrous. Accustomed to the smaller provincial theatres, she was not prepared for the huge space at Drury Lane, and her voice did not reach the back rows. The reviews were harsh; the *Morning Chronicle*, for instance, reported that she had "vulgarity in her tones" and "no comedy in her nature." This hostile reception drove her from London back to the provinces, and she passed six more years in Liverpool, Manchester, and York. In 1778 she found herself in Bath, which was becoming the most fashionable city in England outside London. While there she came to know Johnson's friend Hester Thrale, Frances Burney, and Georgiana, Duchess of Devonshire.

In 1779, while still outside London, she originated some of her most famous roles, including Constance in *King John* and Queen Katherine in *Henry VIII*. But her Lady Macbeth became the stuff of legend, and it was a role she would play for decades thereafter. As the essayist Charles Lamb wrote in 1812, the year of Siddons's retirement from the stage, "we speak of Lady Macbeth, while we are in reality thinking of Mrs S." The essayist William Hazlitt, writing in 1817, was equally mesmerized by her performance, admitting that he could "conceive of nothing grander. It was something above nature. It seemed almost as if a being of a superior order had dropped from a higher sphere to awe the world with the majesty of her appearance." This genius from another world seemed to Hazlitt to be "tragedy personified."

She may have had all the talent she needed in Bath, but celebrity would have to await her return to London. Richard Brinsley Sheridan, the manager at Drury Lane since Garrick's retirement, was convinced that Siddons was ready to try the metropolis again, but she had been so shaken by her early failure that it took nearly two years of coaxing before she could be persuaded to take the chance. When she finally consented in October 1781, though, her performances were electrifying. Her biographer James Boaden commented on her ability to arouse "sobs and shrieks among the tenderer part of her audiences"—and not only the tenderer part. Men too "at first struggled to suppress" those tears, "but at length grew proud of indulging" them. "The nerves of many a gentle being," Boaden said, "gave way before the intensity of such appeals, and fainting fits long and frequently alarmed the decorum of the house, filled almost to suffocation."

Despite the professional triumphs, though, her personal life remained difficult. In the space of two weeks she suffered a miscarriage and watched the death of her six-year-old daughter. She began experiencing health problems of her own and eventually discovered that they were caused by a venereal disease passed on to her by her unfaithful husband. And Sheridan neglected to pay her salary promptly; by 1800 he was more than two thousand pounds in arrears.

Still, she was England's most famous actress for an entire generation, so powerful that she seemed to be almost a force of nature. A visiting Frenchman, Jacques-Henri Meister, wrote in 1799 that "if Garrick was the greatest actor, Mrs. Siddons is the greatest actress the English stage could ever boast of."

Sarah's brother John Philip also began acting at a young age: he appeared in a professional production of *The Tempest* at ten. He went on to surpass even his sister in fame, becoming the brightest star in an acting dynasty that dominated the end of the eighteenth century and the beginning of the nineteenth. Like his sister, Kemble began his career not in London, but in a company in Liverpool. This meant that real stardom would have to wait, but the provincial apprenticeship allowed him to hone his craft. In just over a year starting in June 1777, Kemble played dozens of roles, including Lear, Brutus, Shylock, Posthumus (from *Cymbeline*), Othello (opposite a Desdemona played by his sister), and Laertes (this time his sister played Hamlet in a "trouser role," where

John Philip Kemble was London's leading tragedian as the eighteenth century turned into the nineteenth. Francesco Bartolozzi based this engraving on a painting by William Hamilton.

women dressed as men, a reversal of the older system where boys played women).

Kemble first tried the role of Hamlet in Dublin in 1781, and when, two years later, he had his London debut, Hamlet was the obvious choice. His performance created a stir in the London press: Thomas Davies, Garrick's biographer, included some observations on this "new Hamlet" in his *Dramatic Miscellanies*, noting that "his particular emphases, pauses, and other novelties in acting, have surprised the public and divided the critics; some of whom greatly censure, while others as warmly extol, his peculiarities." Davies counted himself among the supporters: "I congratulate the public on the prospect of much rational entertainment."

He advised audiences to "encourage the industry of every young stage-adventurer, who, by a deep search into character, finds out new methods of pleasing." Kemble was happy to have the encouragement and went on to become the most important actor on the stage for decades. His only rival for the title of greatest performer was his sister, and the two were happy to share the spotlight. They often played together, as in the 1783 performance of *King John* and, most famously, the 1785 performance of *Macbeth*.

Kemble's acting was not for everyone. It was said to be stilted and declamatory rather than understated and naturalistic. One satirist complained about his pompous style:

> With the lineal brow, heavy, dismal, and murky,
> And shoulders compress'd like an over-truss'd turkey.

Though he was ill suited to comedy, his tall, graceful, and powerfully built frame made him a natural tragedian. "No actor," wrote an anonymous supporter in 1789, "ever derived greater advantages from nature . . . A majestic form, and a countenance marked with uncommon expression, raise this tragedian in natural endowments above the rest of his contemporaries . . . There is a certain melancholy visible in his countenance that peculiarly fits him for the filial and grief-worn Hamlet." Over the course of his career he played almost every tragic role in the Shakespeare canon, and his histrionic style was well suited to the ever-expanding theatres. The tennis-court playhouses of the Restoration held only around four hundred people, none of whom was more than forty-five feet from the stage; by the 1790s, when Kemble's fame was at its height, the Theatre Royal at Drury Lane seated around thirty-six hundred, with the cheap seats as much as seventy-five feet away. It took someone with Kemble's stature and power to compete with the other entertainments that were showing up in the theatres, including hippodromes and even circuses.

Fanny Kemble, the niece of Sarah Siddons and John Philip Kemble, achieved fame on both sides of the Atlantic. Thomas Sully painted this portrait in the 1830s.

The Kemble dynasty continued for another generation with Fanny Kemble, niece of Sarah and John Philip, and daughter of Charles Kemble. Although she grew up in a theatrical family, she had little interest in making the stage her profession. But when, in 1829, the family's finances were beginning to suffer, her father convinced her to try it. She had little time to prepare; after just three weeks' rehearsal she made her first appearance on a public stage, playing Juliet at Covent Garden. As she stood in the wings, waiting for her entrance, her nerves nearly got the better of her, until another actor gave her this advice about the audience: "Never mind 'em, Miss Kemble, never mind 'em. Don't think of 'em any more than if they were so many rows of cabbages." She finally had to be pushed onto the stage and later recollected that she was "stunned by the tremendous shout" and "stood like a terrified creature at bay, confronting the huge theatre full of gazing human beings." But soon she began to relax and even boasted that she lost herself in the part when she reached the famous balcony scene: "I did not return to myself," she told a friend, "till all was over."

No longer "an insignificant schoolgirl," as she once had called herself, she was now an instant theatrical celebrity. Her tall and slender figure, with a long, graceful neck and dark eyes, made her a favorite subject of portraitists. And yet she never really liked acting—or, more precisely, "I do not think it is the acting itself that is so disagreeable to me," she wrote, "but the public personal exhibition, the violence done . . . to womanly dignity and decorum in thus becoming the gaze of every eye and theme of every tongue." Still, she was a very thoughtful actress and recorded in her diaries lengthy meditations on what makes various characters tick. Her father's performance of Hamlet, for instance, led her to contemplate his madness. She never could understand "anybody's ever questioning the real madness of Hamlet," she admitted. Hamlet was really "of a thoughtful, doubtful, questioning spirit, looking with timid boldness from the riddles of earth and life to those of death and the mysterious land beyond it; weary of existence on the very threshold of it, and withheld from self-destruction by religious awe; in love, moreover, and sad and dreamy in his affections." Surely his insanity was genuine, for "if these do not make up as complete a madman as ever walked between heaven and earth, I know not what does."

After a successful early career in London, at the age of twenty-five she moved to Philadelphia. It was an obvious choice: in 1834 Philadelphia was the theatrical capital of North America. It had been the home of the first American professional troupe of stage actors in 1749 and the site of the first permanent theatre in America, the Southwark, in 1766. In 1820 the actor Edmund Kean included Philadelphia in his North American tour, followed by

William Charles Macready's tour of 1827; Lorenzo Da Ponte, Mozart's most famous librettist, brought an Italian opera company to Philadelphia in 1823. Later the city would be the home base of Edwin Forrest and the Barrymore dynasty. Fanny Kemble quickly took to her new home, where she married and found new fame. Four years later she moved briefly to Georgia, where she lived on her husband's plantation. Though she was there for only a few months, the exposure to the horrors of slavery affected her profoundly, and she wrote a passionate attack on the institution—one that would remain unpublished, because of her husband's objections, until the 1860s. But as America's Civil War began, she finally published her conviction "that the national character produced and fostered by slaveholding is incompatible with free institutions . . . It is slavery that has made the Southerners rebel against their government, traitors to their country, and the originators of the bloodiest civil war that ever disgraced humanity and civilization."

Although other kinds of writing occupied much of her life—plays, poems, a novel—and although acting was never her passion, she did make a living for herself for fifteen years, traveling through England and America giving dramatic solo readings from Shakespeare. She retired from this in 1863 and passed the rest of her long life traveling between London, Philadelphia, and Lennox, Massachusetts. She died in London in 1893 at the age of eighty-three.

A Laughing Devil in His Sneer

By the end of the eighteenth century, the acting profession had shaken some of its reputation for moral turpitude, and the notorious associations with drunkenness and prostitution became less common after upstanding men and women like David Garrick, John Philip Kemble, and Sarah Siddons had been on the stage. But the public was still hungry for scandalous gossip about the players and eagerly bought works like Joseph Haslewood's eight-hundred-page

Secret History of the Green Rooms: Containing Authentic and Entertaining Memoirs of the Actors and Actresses. And some of the actors seem to have done their best to ensure that their profession should never achieve real respectability.

Two actresses, for instance, came to prominence late in the eighteenth century with remarkably similar careers. They performed in the same company, they played many of the same roles, they received very similar reviews—and they were both royal mistresses, one to George, Prince of Wales, who would later become George IV; the other to his brother, Prince William Henry, Duke of Clarence, who would later become King William IV.

The first of these was Mary Robinson, "a Lady of beautiful person and accomplished manners." That "beautiful person"—a pretty face, green eyes, and pouting lips—would eventually attract the attention of some of England's best painters, including Thomas Gainsborough, Sir Joshua Reynolds, and George Romney. She had prominent supporters: Georgiana, Duchess of Devonshire, was her patron, and Garrick personally prepared her for her first big role as Juliet at Drury Lane and watched her debut from the orchestra. Known for her acute fashion sense, she took great care that her costume should be just right, wearing a dress of "pale pink satin, trimmed with crape, richly spangled with silver . . . My head was ornamented with white feathers, and my monumental suit [the one worn in the Capulets' monument] for the last scene, was white satin and completely plain, excepting that I wore a veil of the most transparent gauze." The attention paid off, and the reviews were encouraging. London's *Morning Post*, for instance, wrote that "Her person is genteel, her voice harmonious, and admitting of various modulations;—and her features, when properly animated, are striking, and expressive." That was a promising beginning to a career that in the next year gave her the parts of Ophelia in *Hamlet*, Lady Anne in *Richard III*, and Lady Macbeth. But over time she discovered that her real strength was

Mary "Perdita" Robinson threatened to blackmail her lover, George, Prince of Wales, who later became King George IV. From Memoirs of the Late Mrs. Robinson, Written by Herself *(1801).*

comic roles, and she achieved her greatest success as Viola in *Twelfth Night*, Rosalind in *As You Like It*, and, above all, Perdita in *The Winter's Tale*. She was so firmly associated with this, her signature role, that she was known universally as "Perdita" Robinson.

She caught Prince George's eye in 1779 and later described her "embarrassment, owing to the fixed attention with which the prince of Wales honoured [her]." But the embarrassment passed quickly, and the two began a flirtatious correspondence, she adopting the name Perdita, he the name of Perdita's lover, Florizel. Soon the two were inseparable, playing their private Shakespearean romance together. Robinson adored her time with the prince but particularly adored the new standard of living she had achieved. She probably adored it a little too much, for she spent recklessly and was soon deeply in debt. To make matters worse, the prince's affection was intense but short-lived: just a year after they met, he abandoned her.

Robinson did not take her dumping lightly and began to drop hints that the prince's love letters might find their way into the newspapers if she weren't treated well. The crisis was averted only when Robinson's new lover, Lord Malden, brokered a deal between the prince and the actress. In September 1781 Robinson agreed to turn over all the prince's indiscreet letters in exchange for a cash payment of five thousand pounds and the promise of an annuity. After this she was independent and became a successful author, writing in a wide variety of forms: poems, plays, novels, an autobiography, and miscellaneous journalism, sometimes in support of the French Revolution. She later had a fifteen-year affair with Sir Banastre Tarleton, who fought for the British in the War of American Independence.

Robinson's story has some interesting parallels with Dorothy Jordan's. Jordan, described by one contemporary critic as "an admirable Comedian in the characters of the *Romp* kind," had successes in a number of Shakespearean roles, including Rosalind in *As You Like It*, Viola in *Twelfth Night*, and Anne in *Richard III*, where she played opposite John Philip Kemble. Appearing at Drury Lane in 1790, Jordan attracted the notice of the Duke of Clarence, who was soon smitten with her. He set her up in a house and supported her with one thousand pounds a year, even as she continued to act. But the money caused trouble. Clarence's father, King George III, never got along very well with his son, and he thought little of his son's new mistress. The king therefore proposed cutting this allowance in half. According to a widely circulated story, Jordan tore off the bottom part of a playbill reading "No money returned after the rising of the curtain" and returned it to His Majesty.

But Mary Robinson and Dorothy Jordan, for all their high-profile royal affairs and even blackmail, never managed to equal Edmund Kean's ability to generate scandal. Kean was indisputably

Dorothy Jordan, mistress to the Duke of Clarence, never received the approval of the king. From a painting by George Romney, reprinted in James Boaden's Life of Mrs. Jordan *(1831).*

a great tragic actor, but his offstage life was legendary, and few of the legends were complimentary. Kean's family background is more than usually colorful. His mother, Ann Carey, was descended from a seventeenth-century nobleman, George Savile, the Marquess of Halifax. But the descent was illegitimate, and she didn't benefit from her aristocratic forebears. Alternately an actress and a prostitute, she was not at all pleased when she gave birth to Edmund in 1787. Unwanted by his mother, he was bounced from family to family, until he came to settle with his aunt Charlotte Tidswell—he called her "Aunt Tid"—an actress at Drury Lane. She introduced him to the theatre, and soon he was spellbound.

Even as a child he played small roles, and a playbill from 1801 suggests Kean (known here by his mother's surname) was accounted a prodigy: it features "The Celebrated Theatrical Child,

Edmund Carey, not eleven years old," though he was already at least thirteen. By 1804 he had become a professional actor. He was eager to take on leading tragic roles, and his chiseled features, serious brow, and penetrating black eyes spoke in his favor. But his physical type—he was short and thin—made it difficult for him to be taken seriously. Sarah Siddons saw him in a performance early in his career; afterward she patted him on the head, saying, "You have played very well, sir, *very* well. It's a pity, but there's too little of you to do any thing." For a long time others agreed, and he was restricted to supporting parts. In 1812, though, Kean finally got the chance to play a number of serious leading roles—Macbeth, Richard III, Hamlet, Othello—but they were in a provincial theatre, not in London. Finally, in January 1814 came the turning point in his career, when he played Shylock at Drury Lane.

Edmund Kean was one of the most fiery actors of the nineteenth century. He is shown here in the role of Gloucester from King Lear.

The effect was stunning. The *European Magazine* reported that "the evening of this day added a very bright star to the dramatic hemisphere . . . We have rarely seen a performer on the stage who appeared to copy less from others in his mode of acting." Jane Austen saw his Shylock in March 1814 and wrote to her sister, "I cannot imagine better acting." Many others had played the role before, including the great Kemble, but Kean eclipsed all his predecessors and made Shylock his own. "We wish we had never seen Mr. Kean," William Hazlitt wrote, tongue in cheek. "He has destroyed the Kemble religion and it is the religion in which we were brought up." The next month saw him as Richard III, the role that had been a star vehicle for James Quin, Colley Cibber, David Garrick, and Kemble. He had nearly equal success in the part. The poet Lord Byron, who was once "seized with a sort of convulsive fit" when he watched Kean, praised the power of his Richard III in a poem:

> There was a laughing devil in his sneer,
> That raised emotions of both rage and fear;
> And where his frown of hatred darkly fell,
> Hope withering fled, and Mercy sigh'd farewell!

Another great Romantic poet, Samuel Taylor Coleridge, declared of Kean, "To see him act, is like reading Shakespeare by flashes of lightning."

March 1814 brought him the part of Hamlet, and May, Othello. Macbeth followed in November, then Romeo in January 1815, and Richard II in March. Not all the roles were received equally enthusiastically—his Hamlet and his Romeo, for instance, were not equal to the rest—but in a short period he had revealed himself to be the leading tragic actor of the generation after Kemble. His great charisma and his resonant voice combined to make him a huge draw, and soon he was earning an unprecedented salary. He also became well known for his many eccentricities, like keeping a pet lion, which he would walk through the streets of London.

Some of his power as an actor came from his ability to harness his personal demons. As the *Oxford Dictionary of National Biography* puts it, "Inner fury, amounting frequently to paranoia, fuelled his finest performances and made them dangerous to a degree unrivalled on the English stage." But that fury and paranoia sometimes got the better of him. After his rise to stardom he became a victim of his own celebrity, for he suffered from a self-destructive streak. Drunkenness ran in the family, and he continued the tradition by founding a drinking society called the Wolves Club in 1815. He also took refuge with prostitutes: one of his contemporaries recorded in his diaries that Kean would have sex with actresses or prostitutes before a play, after a play, and sometimes even during the intervals between acts as well. But all the drinking and whoring eventually caught up with him. Drunkenness began to interfere with his performances and sometimes even kept him from the stage altogether. Worse still, he contracted a venereal disease, and when a jealous husband discovered Kean's long-term affair with his wife, he filed a suit of "criminal conversation" against Kean. Kean lost the suit and was fined eight hundred pounds. In the process he lost his own wife.

The public scandals, helped by a series of attacks in the *Times* of London, turned the public against him. Years earlier he had undertaken a tour of America, which, although successful at first, turned sour when he petulantly refused to play before half-empty houses. Now he once again fled to America, performing in cities from Charleston to Montreal. He succeeded in raising a good deal of money, but the tour as a whole did not go smoothly. Riots broke out in Boston, and he once again returned to London in frustration.

Kean's end was as sad as his beginning. His old habits of drunkenness and dissipation led to gallstones, gastritis, and gout.

Some speculate he also suffered from syphilis; late in life he had great trouble memorizing his lines, and one of the side effects of the mercury treatment for syphilis is memory loss. His debut of a new role in 1830, Henry V, was disastrous when he found himself unable to remember his lines. He went through several retirements and revivals, but never with any success. He finally died in 1833, and supporters petitioned to have him buried in Westminster Abbey beside David Garrick. The application was denied.

CHAPTER 3

Studying Shakespeare

THE OPENING OF THE THEATRES had brought Shakespeare back to life. It also breathed life into the publishing industry, because Shakespeare's rise coincided with a great rise in literacy. The ability to read, once the province of a tiny privileged minority, was becoming widespread, even commonplace, and all these new readers longed for things to read. To meet the demand for new reading material, publishers created a new world of print culture in which Shakespeare was a giant. This is an odd fate for a playwright. As the critic Laurie Maguire notices, "When we read Shakespeare's plays, we are reading something that was never meant to be read: the primary destination of drama is performance, not print." Whether or not he was meant to be read, though, it was books that spread the Shakespearean gospel around the country and around the world.

Fraught with Improbabilities

Shakespeare himself never bothered to publish his plays and probably never had any thought of their appearing in print. But as he assumed a larger and larger place in the culture of the English-speaking world, reading his works became ever more common. In 1700 virtually every literate family could be expected to own two books, the Bible and John Bunyan's *Pilgrim's Progress*. By 1850 Shakespeare's plays had joined them on the shelf. But it didn't happen all at once. The first question was whether Shakespeare was worth reading at all. Although he'd later be read and celebrated by virtually everyone, Shakespeare wasn't always above criticism.

In his own lifetime, Shakespeare had to withstand attacks from other writers. In *Greenes Groats-Worthe of Witte*, for instance, a contemporary playwright took aim at his rival in 1592, complaining about "an vpstart Crow, beautified with our feathers." This newcomer, "with his *Tygers hart wrapt in a Players hyde*, supposes he is as well able to bombast out a blanke verse as the best of you." Worse still, the young playwright thinks of himself as the "onely Shake-scene in a countrey." The "Tygers hart wrapt in a Players hyde" echoes a line from Shakespeare's *3 Henry VI*, which mentions a "tiger's heart wrapped in a woman's hide." If anyone missed the reference, the name "Shake-scene" should leave little doubt about the identity of this conceited "upstart crow."

A hundred years later another critic was still hammering on Shakespeare's reputation. In 1692 the poet and playwright Thomas Rymer published *A Short View of Tragedy: It's Original, Excellency and Corruption, with Some Reflections on Shakespear, and Other Practitioners for the Stage*. Rymer was impatient with English plays in general, but he singled out Shakespeare as the worst of English playwrights and *Othello* as the worst of his plays.

Rymer's complaints about Shakespeare were many. Shakespeare lifted his plot for *Othello* from an Italian writer, Giraldi Cinthio. That wasn't unusual, since recycling old stories was a common practice. Rymer's objection wasn't that Shakespeare borrowed a plot, but that he borrowed it badly: "*Shakespear* alters it from the Original in several particulars, but always, unfortunately, for the worse." His verdict was uncommonly harsh: "Nothing is more odious in Nature than an improbable lye; And, certainly, never was any Play fraught, like this of *Othello*, with improbabilities . . . In the *Neighing* of an Horse," he said, "there is . . . more humanity, than many times in the Tragical flights of *Shakespear*."

The racial issues Shakespeare explores in *Othello* gave Rymer the most trouble. He had a hard time believing the Venetians could pick a black man for a position of military honor: "shall a Poet," he asked, "fancy that they will set a Negro to be their General; or trust a *Moor* to defend them against the *Turk*?" But if a black hero was improbable, a black lover was inconceivable. The thought that a black man could romance a white woman—and a rich and beautiful white woman at that—was beyond Rymer's comprehension. "With us," he wrote, "a *Moor* might marry some little drab [slut], or Small-coal Wench: *Shake-spear*, would provide him the Daughter and Heir of some great Lord." True, he's a war hero; true, he tells exciting stories of his exploits—but in Shakespeare's play, it's as if these tales were "sufficient to make the Black-amoor White, and reconcile all, tho' there had been a Cloven-foot into the bargain." Rymer fretted that Shakespeare didn't even bother to make this love between a white angel and a black devil plausible, though it would have been easy to do with just a few hints: "He might have helped out the probability," Rymer suggested, "by feigning how that some way, or other, a Black-amoor Woman had been her Nurse, and suckl'd her: Or that once, upon a time, some *Virtuoso* [scientist] had transfus'd into her Veins the Blood of a black Sheep." A mad scientist might have made the story believable, but without black milk in her stomach or black blood in her veins, Rymer insisted, there was no way a beautiful white woman could ever have fallen for the Moor. He was convinced the play was worthless, and if he had his way, Shakespeare's works would never again see print.

Complaints like Rymer's, though, were becoming less common as the seventeenth century came to a close. Shakespeare was starting to be regarded not only as a great playwright but as the greatest,

John Dryden, shown here in a print from 1851, declared his passion for Shakespeare in an early milestone of English literary criticism, An Essay of Dramatick Poesie *(1668).*

and not only as the greatest playwright but as the greatest writer in the language. In 1668 the poet and playwright John Dryden published his *Essay of Dramatick Poesie*, in which he sought "to vindicate the honour of our English Writers, from the censure of those who unjustly prefer the French before them." Dryden considered the four superstars of the Elizabethan and Jacobean theatre: Ben Jonson, Francis Beaumont, John Fletcher, and William Shakespeare.

In the 1660s Shakespeare had some passionate defenders, but most common readers would have placed him last on this list. Not that they disliked him, but few would have put him in the very first rank. Beaumont and Fletcher (who often worked together as a team) were by far the most popular: as Dryden noted, "Their Playes are now the most pleasant and frequent entertainments of the Stage; two of theirs being acted through the year for one of *Shakespeare's* or *Johnsons*." And if Beaumont and Fletcher were the people's favorites, Ben Jonson was the critics' choice; he was regarded as the most "correct" playwright of the age, who knew how to construct a "regular" plot and to observe all the rules of dramatic propriety. The critic Edward Phillips (John Milton's nephew) found Jonson "the most learned, judicious and correct, generally so accounted, of our *English* Comedians." Shakespeare, on the other hand, was sloppy. He lacked a university education. His flights of fancy sometimes passed the bounds of plausibility. He improperly mixed serious and frivolous scenes.

In spite of all this, though, Dryden had some very kind things to say about Shakespeare, calling him "the man who of all Modern, and perhaps Ancient Poets, had the largest and most comprehensive soul." He did have to admit that Shakespeare had his faults: "I cannot say he is every where alike . . . He is many times flat, insipid; his Comick wit degenerating into clenches [puns]; his serious swelling into Bombast." But, said Dryden, "he is alwayes great, when some great occasion is presented to him." In fact, while Jonson was "the more correct Poet," Shakespeare was "the greater wit." Jonson may have had the edge on propriety but, as Dryden confessed, "I admire him, but I love *Shakespeare*." And although Dryden was early to declare his admiration, he was not alone. That love was soon to take over, pushing Shakespeare to the top of the roster among both the critics and the public at large. Soon everyone would be reading Shakespeare.

There's the Point

Reading Shakespeare, though, isn't as simple as it sounds. Few people realize how much effort has gone into clarifying the texts they read. A comparison of several modern editions of the plays will reveal any number of differences. Consider a passage from *Hamlet*. In the Pelican Shakespeare, the ghost promises to tell Hamlet a story that will make

> Thy knotted and combinèd locks to part,
> And each particular hair to stand an end
> Like quills upon the fearful porcupine.

In the Oxford Shakespeare, on the other hand, the tale will make

> Thy knotty and combinèd locks to part,
> And each particular hair to stand on end
> Like quills upon the fretful porcupine.

And the ghost in the Oxford School Shakespeare will make

> Thy knotted and combined locks to part,
> And each particular hair to stand an end,
> Like quills upon the fretful porpentine.

Are the locks *knotted* or *knotty*, *combinèd* or *combined*? Do the hairs *stand an end* or *stand on end*? Is it a *fearful porcupine*, a *fretful porcupine*, or a *fretful porpentine*? (And what's a porpentine anyway?) The differences may not be big—not much seems to ride on whether the *e* has an accent—but surely it should be possible to read the play as Shakespeare wrote it.

Some variants can be more meaningful. Consider another passage from the same play. In the Oxford Shakespeare, Hamlet soliloquizes:

> O that this too too solid flesh would melt,
> Thaw and resolve itself into a dew.

The Norton Critical Edition, though, is different:

> O, that this too too sallied flesh would melt,
> Thaw, and resolve itself into a dew.

And the Pelican Shakespeare differs from both of them:

> O that this too too sullied flesh would melt,
> Thaw, and resolve itself into a dew.

So which is it? Should the word be *solid, sallied* (besieged), or *sullied* (dirty)? This is one of Hamlet's most important speeches; the answer presumably matters. And there are hundreds of problems like this in every single play, some of which can make for very different interpretations. Why all the confusion?

The difficulty is that all the plays survive only in imperfect texts, riddled with errors. No handwritten draft of any of Shakespeare's works survives, and the author didn't oversee the printing of any of his plays. He cared about the publication of his poems—*Venus and Adonis*, for example, got careful scrutiny as it went through the press—but his plays were meant for performance, not for reading. He couldn't be bothered with publishing them, and that fact has made life difficult for Shakespeare's editors and commentators ever since.

About half of Shakespeare's surviving plays appeared during his lifetime in the small, cheap format known as "quartos" (abbreviated as "Q"—"Q1" for the first quarto edition of a play, "Q2" for the second, and so on). The texts in these editions range widely in reliability. Some are clear and reliable, probably based on Shakespeare's original drafts, but a number of them are now called "bad quartos" from the poor quality of the text they give. Here, for instance, is the first instance in print of the most famous speech in the English language, as it appeared in the first quarto edition (Q1) of *Hamlet*, printed in 1603:

> To be, or not to be, I there's the point,
> To Die, to sleepe, is that all? I all:
> No, to sleepe, to dreame, I mary there it goes,
> For in that dreame of death, when wee awake,
> And borne before an euerlasting Iudge,
> From whence no passenger euer retur'nd,
> The vndiscouered country, at whose sight
> The happy smile, and the accursed damn'd.

We recognize these lines as garbled because we know the more familiar text from other, better, versions. But sometimes all the available evidence is little better than nonsense. Consider these lines from the second quarto edition (Q2) of *Hamlet*:

> the dram of eale
> Doth all the noble substance of a doubt
> To his own scandle.

What's a "dram of eale," and what does it do to "all the noble substance of a doubt"—to say nothing of how it does it "to his own scandle"? A dram is an eighth of a fluid ounce, but there's no sign of the word *eale* in the other literature of Shakespeare's day. Maybe a "dram of eale" is really a "dram of ale" or a "dream of ease," but that's just guesswork, what scholars call "conjectural emendation." If these lines ever made sense they don't anymore, and if there's a misprint it's not obvious what it should have been. Critics have to work to recover sense from the nonsense, and figure out what Shakespeare wrote before they can even start to ask what he meant.

Fretful Porcupine? Fearful Porpentine?

The process began early. Seven years after Shakespeare's death, two members of his company, John Heminges and Henry Condell, decided to collect all his plays into one volume. The result is the famous "First Folio" (F1), the most important source for almost all of Shakespeare's plays and, for eighteen of them, the only source.

One problem facing those who try to edit Shakespeare's works is the many differences between the quarto and the folio versions. Sometimes it's clear that, in compiling the First Folio, Heminges and Condell worked directly from the earlier quartos, cleaning up the errors (or what they regarded as errors). In other cases, though, the differences suggest they were working from another text—maybe Shakespeare's original draft; maybe a version revised for the acting company; maybe a version tidied up by the prompters in the theatre. Theories abound on how to account for the differences and, in case matters weren't complicated enough already, no two plays have exactly the same story. Since there's little agreement over why the versions differ, editors continue to quarrel over exactly what to print.

It's no easy matter. Imagine an editor confronted with the passage where the ghost speaks to Hamlet. On the desk in the British Library or the Folger Shakespeare Library are two early versions of the play: Q2, which reads, "Thy knotted and combined locks to part . . . Like quils vpon the fearefull Porpentine," and F1, which reads, "Thy knotty and combined locks to part . . . Like Quilles vpon the fretfull Porpentine." Which should appear in the edition? Why? Is it acceptable to mix readings from the two, or if you choose one text, must you stick with it all the time? Some experts think one text represents Shakespeare's first draft, the other a revised version for the theatre, probably the result of collaboration. If that's true (and it's a big if), which one is better? Should an editor opt for authorial "purity," favoring Shakespeare's original conception before he was forced to compromise for the theatre, or would it make more sense to print the version that people might actually have seen on the stage? And *knotted* or *knotty, fearefull* or *fretfull* are only the beginning; editing a play requires thousands of tiny changes. Some are uncontroversial. In Shakespeare's day *combined* was often three syllables—*com-bye-ned*—so many editors print a mark over the *e* to remind modern readers of how it was pronounced. The punctuation in the quartos and folios looks erratic to modern eyes, so most editors feel justified in changing it to suit modern practice. And early modern spelling can be confusing. Is it okay to change *vpon* to *upon* and *quils* or *Quilles* to *quills*? (Virtually all editors do.) What about changing *porpentine,* an obsolete form of *porcupine,* to its modern form? (Some do.) Shakespeare often wrote *murther* where moderns would write *murder*—is that a separate word from *murder,* or is it just a difference in spelling, which justifies updating it to *murder*? (A few do.) What about changing *doth* to *does,* or even *wherefore* to *why*? Editors face literally thousands of such decisions in every play, which is why no two editions are exactly the same, even before they get to the complicated business of writing footnotes and explaining the difficult passages.

The Injuries of Former Impressions

Hamlet is unusually complex, but all the plays pose similar problems. And it was in the eighteenth century that people first came to see how formidable a task it would be to recover Shakespeare's words. All of the playwright's early editors and publishers agreed that they'd have to make many changes to the printed plays because of the sorry state of the text, but they agreed on little else, and they have been willing to go to war over them. It may seem odd to think about reading Shakespeare—reading anyone, for that matter—as the subject of a "war." But the eighteenth century saw the first serious disputes over how the works should be interpreted. The stakes were high, for the winners of this battle would determine how readers should understand the greatest writer in the language and, by implication, how they should approach all English literature. As it happens, the outcome of this war has affected both the publishing industry and the shape of education for three centuries.

Collected editions of the plays appeared four times in the seventeenth century in the four folio editions of 1623, 1632, 1663–64, and 1685. But F2 just reprinted F1; F3 reprinted F2; F4 reprinted F3. There was no real editorial labor. After all, Shakespeare's plays weren't considered serious works of literature, but popular entertainment. Scholars were interested only in important authors, those who published in Latin and Greek, and couldn't be expected to waste time on the vernacular.

The first person to take the task at all seriously was Nicholas Rowe, whose edition of the plays appeared in six volumes in 1709. (Another publisher rode his coattails by issuing "Volume the Seventh," featuring Shakespeare's poems, the next year, but Rowe had nothing to do with it.) Rowe was a successful poet and dramatist whose plays were often inspired by Shakespeare. (His *Jane Shore* was "Written in imitation of Shakespear's style.") He therefore struck a group of publishers as an obvious candidate for editing the plays, and Rowe was glad for the chance to make sense of the works he admired so much. "I have taken some Care," he said, "to redeem [Shakespeare] from the Injuries of former Impressions [printings]." But he admitted that all he could do was "to compare the several Editions, and give the true Reading as well as I could from thence"—in other words, he had no coherent principles to guide his choices, just an intuition about what made sense to him. Still, he seemed proud of his success; he said he had "render'd very many Places Intelligible, that were not so before."

He did correct some of the more obvious typos in the folios, but his other contributions were minor. Rowe was a playwright and a poet, not an academic. He was not well versed in sixteenth-century literature, and he knew little about the history of the language. He wrote almost no explanatory notes. And though he claimed "to compare the several Editions," he didn't have the patience to sort systematically through all the variants; he looked at only a few early editions. For the most part he gave the world a spruced-up version of the Fourth Folio of 1685, with a few new touches of his own. He added the "Dramatis Personae," or list of characters, to the beginning of each play; he clarified some of the more inconsistent stage directions and speech prefixes; and he modernized the spelling, capitalization, and punctuation.

Rowe's most lasting contribution was "Some Account of the Life, *&c.* of Mr. *William Shakespear*," the first substantial biography of the playwright. This forty-page work is the source of many of the famous stories about Shakespeare's early days—"He had, by a Misfortune common enough to young Fellows, fallen into ill Company; and amongst them, some that made a frequent practice of Deer-stealing, engag'd him with them more than once in robbing a Park that belong'd to Sir *Thomas Lucy*"—but Shakespeare had been dead for nearly a century when Rowe published his biography. Rowe was working with little more than hearsay, often second- or third-hand hearsay, and critics have learned to be very cautious with his claims. But many of Rowe's stories were reprinted and recycled so often that they have passed into legend.

Rowe did an important service in cleaning up the folio text, and for this he is regarded as the first modern editor of Shakespeare's works. But his work was cursory at best. He didn't compare the quartos and the folios; he didn't provide interpretive notes; he didn't clarify the more complicated passages in the plays. The editorial problems remained, awaiting another editor better qualified for the job.

The Dull Duty of an Editor

The next one to answer the call was Alexander Pope. This strange creature was an outsider religiously, politically, emotionally, physically, even spiritually. He was a Roman Catholic at a time when that excluded him from most positions in public life, and a supporter of the Tory party after it had fallen from power. He was physically deformed; Pott's disease, tuberculosis of the bones, had stunted his growth and left him a hunchback, standing only around four feet six inches tall. It also caused cardiac and respiratory problems for his whole life. In the words of his biographer Maynard Mack, Pope was "a dwarf and cripple."

But that twisted body housed a brilliant poet. Early works like *An Essay on Criticism* and *The Rape of the Lock* attracted some attention, but real fame came with his translation of Homer's *Iliad*, published in a deluxe edition of six volumes. It sold for the exorbitant price of six guineas (six pounds and six shillings), equivalent to several thousand dollars today. Pope was also a master of marketing and managed to earn the modern equivalent of around £250,000, or $500,000, the first time a professional author had earned that sort of money from his writing.

In the 1720s Pope was at the top of his game, one of the brightest literary celebrities in England, so it's no surprise that a publisher contracted with him in 1721 to produce a new edition of Shakespeare's plays. He moved quickly: the first five volumes appeared in 1723, and the sixth and last was published two years later. The edition opens with a preface that goes even further than Dryden in claiming Shakespeare as the greatest writer in the language. "Of all *English* Poets," Pope wrote, "*Shakespeare* must be confessed to be the fairest and fullest subject for Criticism"—not only for his "Beauties" but also for his "Faults." But the beauties far outweighed those flaws, leading Pope to declare, "I cannot however but mention some of his principal and characteristic

Excellencies, for which (notwithstanding his defects) he is justly and universally elevated above all other Dramatic Writers." What Pope most prized in Shakespeare was his originality—he was the poet of nature. "If ever any Author deserved the name of an *Original*," wrote Pope, "it was *Shakespeare. Homer* himself drew not his art so immediately from the fountains of Nature." Heaven spoke directly to Shakespeare: "he is not so much an Imitator as an Instrument of Nature; and 'tis not so just to say that he speaks from her as that she speaks thro' him." So Pope's appreciation for Shakespeare seems sure. His ability to undertake what he called "the dull duty of an Editor," though—to make sense of a messy pile of quartos and folios—was less certain. Pope was a great poet but, like Rowe, he was no scholar. Though he insisted that he proceeded "without any indulgence to [his] private sense or conjecture," he had little more than "private sense" to guide him. And the cavalier way he treated Shakespeare's text can be surprising, even shocking, to modern eyes. He found some passages inferior to what he expected from the great playwright, and so these "suspected passages which are excessively bad," he said, "are degraded to the bottom of the page"—more than fifteen hundred lines are relegated to footnotes. He applied the same logic to choosing among readings from the quartos and folios: whatever seemed best to him went in. If he didn't like it, it stayed out. Whenever anything seemed wrong with the text, he felt comfortable substituting something better.

A simple guiding principle is behind all such changes: whatever is imperfect cannot be Shakespeare's. If a passage in the early editions seems flawed—an inconsistency, a grammatical fault, a mixed metaphor, a sloppy bit of verse—someone else must have been the culprit; the error must have occurred somewhere between Shakespeare's pen and the printing of the book. The actors must have changed and debased the original, or the printer misread the handwriting, or censors must have demanded a change—any explanation that allows him to lay the blame on someone else. The critic Alfred Harbage called this "the myth of perfection," and the rise of this myth tells us a lot about what was happening to Shakespeare's reputation. He was becoming not only a great writer but the greatest, and therefore incapable of making a mistake. Many of the eighteenth-century editors declared their determination to save Shakespeare, whether from actors, printers, censors, or earlier editors. The talk was never of *changing* but of *restoring* Shakespeare's text, and even those who introduced the most bizarre emendations themselves could still chide their rivals for recklessly altering the sacred text. *Sacred* is the right word; Pope professed "a religious abhorrence of all Innovation." But he was ill prepared to deal with complicated textual puzzles. Whenever he came across a passage he couldn't understand or didn't like, he relied on his taste, rather than on historical knowledge or coherent critical principles, to decide what to do with it.

Rooting Out That Vast Crop of Errors

People noticed Pope's inadequacies at the time, above all a critic named Lewis Theobald. Theobald attacked Pope in a book called *Shakespeare Restored* (1726), a bitter two-hundred-page attack on Pope's editorial skills—and, as it happens, the first book-length work of Shakespeare criticism ever published. The full title of his book, in all its eighteenth-century glory, leaves no doubt where Theobald stood: "*SHAKESPEARE* restored: OR, A SPECIMEN OF THE Many ERRORS, AS WELL *Committed*, as *Unamended*, by Mr. *POPE* In his Late EDITION of this POET. DESIGNED Not only to correct the said EDITION, but to restore the True READING of *SHAKESPEARE* in all the *Editions* ever yet publish'd." As the arrogant tone suggests, Theobald could be an insufferable prig. He certainly should have known better than to pick a fight with the most talented satirical poet in England. Pope responded to *Shakespeare Restored* by making Theobald one of the "heroes" of his mock-epic poem *The Dunciad,* where Theobald is crowned the king of the Dunces. But the fact remains that he was a much better editor than Pope, and in his stated goal of "retrieving, as far as possible, the *original Purity* of his *Text,* and rooting out that vast Crop of *Errors*" introduced by his rival editor, he was largely successful.

The contrast between the two is especially clear in their treatment of a famous textual puzzle, a passage in *Henry V*. Falstaff—the beloved character in the *Henry IV* plays and the center of *The Merry Wives of Windsor*—has been rejected by his former friend, once Prince Hal, now King Henry V. At the beginning of the new play, Falstaff's friend and companion Bardolph reports on the old man's death and says (in the First Folio), "Would I were with him, wheresomere hee is, eyther in Heauen, or in Hell." The Hostess replies, "Nay sure, hee's not in Hell: hee's in Arthurs Bosome, if euer man went to Arthurs Bosome." She goes on to recount the circumstances of his death: "after I saw him fumble with the Sheets, and play with Flowers, and smile vpon his fingers end, I knew there was but one way: for his Nose was as sharpe as a Pen, and a Table of greene fields."

"A Table of greene fields"? What's "a Table of greene fields," and how could Falstaff's nose be as sharp as one? No one had an answer. The Second, Third, and Fourth folios reprinted the text of the First Folio without comment, and Rowe, in his edition, just updated the spelling. Pope, though, saw that the line was a problem, and decided to fix it. His reading was ingenious: he noticed that "and a table of green fields" didn't appear in the old quarto editions, only the folios. He therefore hypothesized that the passage began as a stage direction. "This nonsense," he explained, "got into all the following editions by a pleasant mistake of the Stage-editors, who printed from the common piecemeal-written

Parts in the Play-house." On one of these parts, said Pope, was scribbled a stage direction, and the printer inadvertently picked it up as part of the text: "A Table was here directed to be brought in, (it being a scene in a tavern where they drink at parting;) and this direction crept into the text from the margin." That explains the table; why "greene fields"? "*Greenfield*," he declared, "was the name of the Property man in that time who furnish'd implements, *&c.* for the actors. *A Table of Greenfield*'s." It's a very clever theory—this is where the actors were supposed to bring in Mr. Greenfield's table—and it seems to solve the mystery. The only problem is that there was absolutely nothing to it. How did Pope know, for instance, that "*Greenfield* was the name of the Property man"? There's no evidence for it anywhere. Pope simply made up facts to suit his theory.

It was the pedantic but brilliant Theobald who first objected that "it never was customary in the Promptor's Book . . . to add the Property-man's Name," the sort of thing only a real scholar would know. Theobald was no poetic genius like Pope, but he had read many hundreds of old plays, and he knew Pope's explanation was inadequate. "*Greenfield*'s Table," therefore, "can be of no Use to us for this Scene." Having demolished Pope's reading, he went on to provide his own. Theobald had read not only printed plays from Shakespeare's age but documents of every sort, and he was familiar with the older styles of handwriting. That led him to note that "a table of green fields" could easily be a misreading of the original manuscript. As he explained in his own edition of Shakespeare's works, published in 1733, "It has certainly been observ'd (in particular, by the Superstition of Women;)" that feverish "People near Death" often suffer from delirium and begin to ramble: "they have their heads run on *green Fields*." Then they *babble*: "To *bable*, or *babble*, is to mutter, or speak indiscriminately . . . like dying Persons, when they are losing the Use of Speech." By reading the folio's *a* not as the indefinite article but as a common form for *he*, and by realizing that in sixteenth-century handwriting *babble* or *bable* looked an awful lot like *table*, Theobald made sense out of a passage that had been nonsense for nearly a century and a half: not "his nose was as sharp as a pen, and a table of green fields," but "his nose was as sharp as a pen, and *a'* [that is, *he*] *babbled of green fields*." The change was utterly convincing, and every edition since Theobald's has accepted it as the correct reading.

The battle between Pope and Theobald ended with a strange distribution of the spoils. Pope is famous today as one of the greatest poets in the language and one of the most talented satirists who ever lived. Works like *The Rape of the Lock* and *An Essay on Criticism* are still read around the English-speaking world, and some of Pope's more famous lines—"Fools rush in where angels fear to tread," "Hope springs eternal in the human breast," "A little learning is a dang'rous thing"—are known to all. Lewis Theobald, if he's known at all, is merely the butt of some of Pope's nastier satires, remembered by posterity as a mean-spirited pedant who got his comeuppance. But it was Theobald who, in the long run, won the battle of the editors. And even modern readers who rejoice in Pope's satirical jabs at the surly Theobald have to admit that Theobald's was the way to go—gentlemanly appreciation couldn't stand up to professional labor. As the critic Laurie Maguire puts it, "Shakespeare editing changed its spiritual location, from the poet in the coffeehouse to the academic in the university."

Any One Who Shall Attack Our Property

Theobald had shown the world that the way to understand the great poetic genius was through serious application. Shakespeare was being converted from an entertainer to a classic, and it was no longer enough to appreciate him; one had to *study* him. Whole industries have emerged as the result of that shift in emphasis, and much of the modern educational system, where students are now expected to study great works of English literature in school, has emerged from the canonization of Shakespeare.

By the middle of the 1740s, as more knowledge about Shakespeare and his age had accumulated, readers felt the need for an even more reliable text of Shakespeare's works, one with explanatory notes to make sense of all the dense and complicated passages. In April 1745, therefore, a publisher printed a proposal for a new edition of the plays, along with a "specimen" of the kind of criticism that would appear in the notes. The pamphlet of sixty-four pages was called *Miscellaneous Observations on the Tragedy of Macbeth*, and it was accompanied by a two-page flyer, "Proposals for Printing a New Edition of the Plays of William Shakespeare, with Notes Critical and Explanatory."

The publisher of the proposals was Edward Cave. The son of a shoemaker, Cave worked odd jobs in London until he became an apprentice printer. He also took on some copy-writing responsibilities and may have worked with Daniel Defoe, now famous for *Robinson Crusoe* and *Moll Flanders*, on his journalism. After a while he started his own printing house, which specialized in cheap pamphlets and broadsides. In January 1731 he started a monthly publication that would long outlive him. Since his periodical was a collection of miscellaneous writing, he named it after a storehouse or armory, or *magazine*, and he was therefore the first to use that word in its modern sense. The *Gentleman's Magazine* ran from 1731 to 1833, and every magazine in the last three centuries has paid implicit tribute to Cave's innovation.

Even more interesting than the publisher Cave, though, was the author of the *Miscellaneous Observations*. No name appeared on the title page, and the reason is obvious: the author, a man of thirty-six who had recently arrived in London from his hometown of Lichfield, had done nothing of public note. His name would have meant nothing to most readers, and there was no point advertising it. But the writer of the proposals was Samuel Johnson, who would eventually become England's most celebrated man of letters and its most distinguished critic.

The planned edition came to nothing. After such luminaries as Rowe, Pope, and Theobald had produced their editions of Shakespeare, an unknown schoolmaster from the Midlands didn't sound like a good bet. It probably didn't do much for public confidence that the title page of the hastily printed *Miscellaneous Observations* promised "a New Edition of *SHAKESHEAR*." But the real reason the edition was abandoned was that the most powerful publisher in London, Jacob Tonson, threatened a lawsuit against Cave and Johnson for violating his copyright.

The whole idea of copyright, the notion that someone can own words, is fairly new in cultural history. The world's first copyright

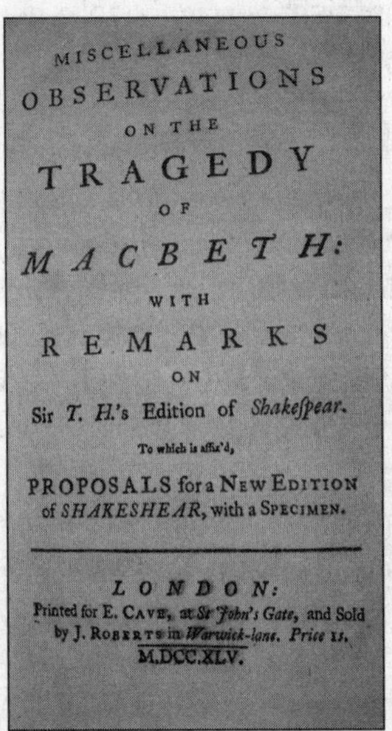

MISCELLANEOUS
OBSERVATIONS
ON THE
TRAGEDY
OF
MACBETH:
WITH
REMARKS
ON
Sir *T. H.*'s Edition of *Shakespear.*
To which is affix'd,
PROPOSALS for a New Edition
of *SHAKESHEAR*, with a Specimen.

LONDON:
Printed for E. Cave, at *St John's Gate*, and Sold
by J. Roberts in *Warwick-lane. Price 1s.*
M.DCC.XLV.

Samuel Johnson's proposals for a new edition of the plays were marred by an embarrassing printing error.

act, passed in Great Britain in 1710 (with the help of Tonson and other publishers), declared that authors had a monopoly on the right to reproduce their words. They might sell this right to a bookseller in exchange for publication, but no one could profit from a writer's labor without his or her permission. The idea was to encourage writers to keep writing and publishers to keep publishing, free from fear of literary piracy. Similar things were going on in early America in the eighteenth century. The word *right* appears in the Constitution of the United States only once before the ratification of the Bill of Rights: in article 1, section 8, the legislative branch is charged with passing laws "To promote the Progress of Science and useful Arts, by securing for limited Times to Authors and Inventors the exclusive Right to their respective Writings and Discoveries."

It wasn't only the author's and publisher's rights, though, that were at issue. Copyright is a monopoly, but one with a limited term: it originally lasted fourteen years after first publication, a term that could be extended to twenty-eight. After the monopoly expired a work would enter the public domain, and anyone could legally reprint it. This balanced the interests of authors and publishers with the interests of the wider public, which is served by the free flow of ideas. As more people are able to edit and publish Shakespeare, the public receives more accurate and cheaper editions. Publishers have naturally worked to tip the balance in their own direction, since the longer the copyright term, the more valuable their property becomes.

This desire to protect its own interests lay behind the Tonson house's threat against Johnson. It was the elder Tonson who commissioned Rowe to edit Shakespeare's works in 1709, and the younger Tonson, Jacob, who contracted with Pope in 1721. The Tonson house therefore claimed the sole right to print the works not only of Shakespeare, but also of John Milton, John Dryden, and other literary greats, because it was determined to hold on to this increasingly valuable property. Whether it actually had a legal right to Shakespeare's works is unclear, since the real implications of the copyright act of 1710 weren't settled in the courts until 1774. What is obvious, though, is that the Tonson house was willing to fight. Jacob Tonson wrote to Cave to warn him off the project, threatening a lawsuit in the Court of Chancery if Cave and Johnson went ahead. In the words of the critic Andrew Murphy, it was "a letter in which politesse and threat were mixed in equal measure." Tonson invited Cave, "a man of character," to sit down and discuss things like gentlemen, since he would "rather satisfy you of our right by argument than by the expence of a Chancery suit, which will be the method we shall take with any one who shall attack our property in this or any other copy that we have fairly bought and paid for." Cave and Johnson relented, realizing that they couldn't afford a court battle with Tonson. Johnson turned his attention to another project instead: the year after *Miscellaneous Observations* appeared, he signed a contract for *A Dictionary of the English Language*, a project on which he spent the next nine years.

The Dignity of an Ancient

While Johnson was busy with his lexicographical labors, the commentary on Shakespeare continued to accumulate. After Theobald's edition came Sir Thomas Hanmer's in 1744 and William Warburton's in 1747, but neither produced the kind of definitive edition that readers longed for. And so, after he finished his *Dictionary*, once again Johnson turned his attention back to Shakespeare. In June 1756 he published another pamphlet, the eight-page *Proposals for Printing, by Subscription, the Dramatick Works of William Shakespeare, Corrected and Illustrated* [annotated] *by Samuel Johnson*. This time he worked with, not against, Jacob Tonson, who served as the publisher.

"Subscription" was a common method of undertaking big publishing projects in the eighteenth century, and it marked a transitional phase between old-fashioned patronage, where one wealthy aristocrat agreed to foot the bill in return for a flattering dedication, and the modern literary marketplace, where sales alone determine the author's income. The idea behind subscription was that the author would approach people to pay for a book before it was written; this money would support the author while he or she wrote the book. When it finally appeared, a list of subscribers' names would appear prominently at the beginning. The system offered benefits to all parties: publishers didn't have to pay risky advances, authors were supported without depending on the whims of aristocrats, and subscribers had their vanity gratified by seeing their names in print and imagining themselves as patrons without paying the extravagant sums that real patronage demanded.

The system often worked well, but it wasn't foolproof. Johnson was notoriously sloppy with paperwork. When Tonson asked Johnson for the total number of subscriptions he had taken in, Johnson replied he could not give it. Why not? "I have lost all the names," he admitted, "and spent all the money." In Andrew Murphy's apt euphemism, "Johnson does seem to have been less than completely efficient when it came to the business of handling subscriptions." Charles Churchill, one of the most famous satirical poets of the day, was less reserved:

> He for *Subscribers* baits his hook
> And takes your cash—but where's the Book?

Others complained that the project was taking much longer than expected. Johnson's energy was legendary, but he had a habit of promising things much faster than he (or anyone) could deliver them. He said his *Dictionary* would be published in three years; it took nine. Things were even worse with the Shakespeare edition. Johnson promised in June 1756 "that the work shall be published on or before Christmas 1757," but 1757 came and went—then 1758, and 1759, and 1760. By the early 1760s subscribers were growing antsy, and Tonson was growing frustrated.

Despite the delays, and despite the mismanagement of the subscriptions, the edition finally appeared in eight attractive volumes on 10 October 1765. Twenty years earlier, when he first proposed his Shakespeare edition, Johnson was an unknown; it's not surprising that nothing came of it. But by this time he was famous as England's most distinguished man of letters, and probably the most qualified man in England to do the job. He was renowned for having a prodigious memory; he could recite thousands of lines of poetry by heart, and he recalled all sorts of historical trivia that helped to make sense of the plays. But Johnson's most important qualification was his knowledge of the history of the English language, better than that of almost any of his contemporaries, which came from his experience with the *Dictionary*. The most popular author in that book, by a large margin, is Shakespeare, who is quoted some ten thousand times.

So it made perfect sense that, after he finished his great *Dictionary*, he turned his attention to England's greatest writer. Johnson's deep scholarship was on display in his edition, which was packed with learned footnotes explaining all the difficult passages. The revolution Theobald had begun was continuing: a minute knowledge of the English language, an understanding of sixteenth- and seventeenth-century customs, and a knowledge of the whole history of English literature were now requisite to understanding Shakespeare, who "may now begin to assume the dignity of an ancient, and claim the privilege of established fame and prescriptive veneration. He has long outlived his century, the term commonly fixed as the test of literary merit." A new, paradoxical category was being born: the "modern classic."

Since Shakespeare was now a classic, he deserved the same kind of treatment previously reserved for the Greek and Roman classics. Johnson's edition uses a style of editing that was almost unprecedented with mere English authors—only the greats of the ancient world had merited it. It's known as a "variorum edition," from the Latin phrase *cum notis variorum editorum*, "with the notes of the various editors." The footnotes in Johnson's edition, in other words, contained not only his own comments but also those of all his predecessors. Among English authors, only Milton had received similar treatment before. Readers could turn to Johnson's Shakespeare edition and see not only what Johnson thought about a confusing passage, but also what Pope and Theobald and Warburton and Hanmer had to say. It's not merely an edition but a virtual library of Shakespeare criticism.

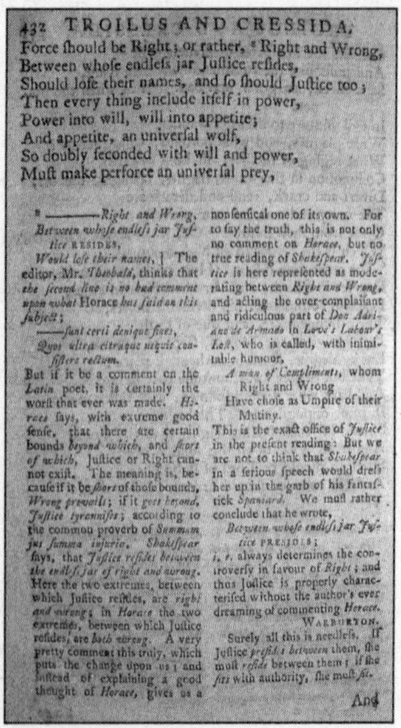

432 TROILUS AND CRESSIDA.

Force ſhould be Right; or rather, * Right and Wrong,
Between whoſe endleſs jar Juſtice reſides,
Should loſe their names, and ſo ſhould Juſtice too;
Then every thing include itſelf in power,
Power into will, will into appetite;
And appetite, an univerſal wolf,
So doubly ſeconded with will and power,
Muſt make perforce an univerſal prey,

* ——*Right and Wrong,*
Between whoſe endleſs jar Juſtice RESIDES,
Would loſe their names,] The editor, Mr. *Theobald*, thinks that *the ſecond line is no bad comment upon what* Horace *has ſaid on this ſubject;*

——*ſunt certi denique fines,*
Quos ultra citraque nequit conſiſtere rectum.

But if it be a comment on the *Latin* poet, it is certainly the worſt that ever was made. *Horace* ſays, with extreme good ſenſe, that there are certain bounds *beyond which*, and *ſhort of which*, Juſtice or Right cannot exiſt. The meaning is, becauſe if it be *ſhort* of thoſe bounds, *Wrong prevails*; if it *goes beyond*, *Juſtice tyranniſes*; according to the common proverb of *Summum jus ſumma injuria*. *Shakeſpear* ſays, that *Juſtice reſides between the endleſs jar of right and wrong*. Here the two extremes, between which Juſtice reſides, are *right and wrong*; in *Horace* the two extremes, between which Juſtice reſides, are *both wrong*. A very pretty comment this truly, which puts the change upon us; and inſtead of explaining a good thought of *Horace*, gives us a nonſenſical one of its own. For to ſay the truth, this is not only no comment on *Horace*, but no true reading of *Shakeſpear*. *Juſtice* is here repreſented as moderating between *Right and Wrong*, and acting the over-complaiſant and ridiculous part of *Don Adriano de Armado* in *Love's Labour's Loſt*, who is called, with inimitable humour,

A man of Compliments, whom Right and Wrong
Have choſe as Umpire of their Mutiny.

This is the exact office of *Juſtice* in the preſent reading: But we are not to think that *Shakeſpear* in a ſerious ſpeech would dreſs her up in the garb of his fantaſtick *Spaniard*. We muſt rather conclude that he wrote,

Between whoſe endleſs jar Juſtice PRESIDES;

i. e. always determines the controverſy in favour of *Right*; and thus Juſtice is properly characteriſed without the author's ever dreaming of commenting *Horace*.

WARBURTON.

Surely all this is needleſs. If Juſtice *preſides between* them, ſhe muſt *reſide* between them; if ſhe *ſits* with authority, ſhe muſt *ſi-*

And

The footnotes have nearly crowded Shakespeare's text off the page in Samuel Johnson's edition of the plays (1765).

Too Little Ceremony

Johnson's edition obviously didn't put an end to the production of new knowledge about Shakespeare. In a way, though, this is perfectly fitting, because Johnson's Shakespeare wasn't intended to end debates, but rather to continue them.

A variorum edition turns many critical commonplaces upside down. In most editions, the longest notes appear on the passages that are best understood. In a variorum, though, the most commentary appears on the passages where there is the least agreement, because every editor has weighed in with his or her own suggestions. In other words, it highlights critical disagreements rather than critical consensus. And there were plenty of disagreements among Shakespeare's readers. The tiniest questions of spelling and punctuation could produce vehement personal attacks, delivered in the sort of language usually reserved for the grossest perversions. The tone could be so harsh that it seemed the security of the nation depended on the placement of a comma.

Samuel Johnson—or, as he was styled after he received an honorary doctorate of laws in 1765, "Doctor Johnson"—was by the time he published his Shakespeare the alpha male of the critical establishment, and every would-be critic had to show his mettle by going head-to-head with him. One of the fiercest attacks came from William Kenrick—in the words of *A Biographical Dictionary of Actors . . . & Other Stage Personnel in London, 1660–1800*, "a querulous, publicity-seeking, lying, drunken, mischief-making playwright and pamphleteer who had attacked nearly every successful writer in London." Shortly after Johnson's edition appeared, the mischief maker launched a verbal assault and, though Johnson maintained a dignified silence, Kenrick kept at it in a series of increasingly strident and vitriolic attacks.

Other editors and critics could be just as crabbed and grouchy. Joseph Ritson's behavior is all too typical of the kinds of rancor that Shakespeare could generate among the scholarly classes. Ritson was an eccentric: a strict, even evangelical, vegetarian when such a thing was nearly unheard of in England, and a political radical who expressed his contempt for George III's administration by praising both the old Stuarts and the new French Revolutionaries. A more literary eccentricity shows up in his "entire new system of spelling." But Ritson was also a serious scholar with a passionate interest in old ballads and medieval romances. He planned to put his antiquarian knowledge to good use by producing his own complete edition of Shakespeare's plays, but all he ever produced was a few pages of a sample of *The Comedy of Errors*.

Still, if he couldn't create an edition of his own, he could at least tear others' editions down. In a work called *The Quip Modest* (the title comes from *As You Like It*) he admitted, "I must not pretend to be ignorant that I have been accused of treating the most eminent Editors, Commentators, and Critics, with too little ceremony." He certainly earned that reputation, attacking Isaac Reed's edition of Shakespeare as incompetent and noting of Johnson that "no one was ever more ignorant of the manners either of Shakspeares age or of the ages preceding it." A few years later he published *Cursory Criticisms on the Edition of Shakspeare Published by Edmond Malone*, in which he called the great scholar Malone a liar, a thief, a "literary prostitute," a "most despicable character," "cowardly," and "malignant," all in the space of a paragraph. Two pages later he spelled out his mission: "I wish to rescue the language and sense of an admirable author from the barbarism and corruption they have acquired in passing through the hands of this incompetent and unworthy editor. In a word, I mean to convict and not to convince him."

But all the tussles and all the wrangling, while they may have been rough on the editors and critics, served the public well, because it meant more ideas about Shakespeare were in circulation. This is something Johnson's edition helped to encourage. By collecting many commentaries in one place, the variorum Shakespeare showed the world that disagreements could be fruitful because they pointed the way toward further study.

After Johnson, the flood. Critical works on every aspect of Shakespeare—his life, his works, his world—came pouring forth. And many went beyond the fundamental question of what Shakespeare wrote, and tried to take on the more complicated questions about how his works should be interpreted. Titles like *Observations and Conjectures upon Some Passages of Shakespeare, An Essay on the Writings and Genius of Shakespear, A Philosophical Analysis and Illustration of Some of Shakespeare's Remarkable Characters,* and *The Morality of Shakespeare's Drama Illustrated* all tried to make sense of the now-classic works of genius, as did Samuel Taylor Coleridge's series of lectures on Shakespeare, which drew large crowds in the early nineteenth century.

Women of the First Quality and Fashion

Shakespeare criticism wasn't all about competition among alpha males. In fact the very first published critical essay on Shakespeare was written by a woman, Margaret Cavendish, the Duchess of Newcastle, who initiated the tradition of feminist Shakespeare criticism as early as 1664: "*Shakespear*," she wrote, "did not want [lack] Wit, to Express to the Life all Sorts of Persons, of what Quality, Profession, Degree, Breeding, or Birth soever." His miraculous ability to take on so many voices led her to "think he had been Transformed into every one of those Persons he hath Described." What's more, he could write both male and female parts with equal skill: "One would think that he had been Metamorphosed from a Man to a Woman, for who could Describe *Cleopatra* Better than he hath done, and many other Females of his own Creating, as *Nan Page*, Mrs. *Page*, Mrs. *Ford*, the Doctors Maid, *Bettrice*, Mrs. *Quickly, Doll Tearsheet*, and others, too many to Relate?"

Other women were influential in Shakespeare's reception, though they are only now beginning to attract the kind of attention they deserve. The Shakespeare Ladies Club, for instance, was formed in London in 1736, making it the first of many clubs and societies devoted to the playwright. As the *Daily Journal* noted at the time, its members were "women of the first quality and fashion," who worked together to increase public interest in Shakespeare. In 1737 the playwright Francis Lynch argued that Shakespeare would be grateful for the female attention:

> And *Shakespear* smiles to be with tender Care,
> Old as he is, supported by the Fair.

These women pressured theatre companies to increase the number of his works in their repertoire, and soon one out of every four performances on the London stage was a Shakespeare play—never before had one playwright been so dominant. They also campaigned to have a statue of Shakespeare erected in Westminster Abbey, a monument that still stands.

An even more important female contribution to Shakespeare studies came from Elizabeth Montagu. She was known as the "Queen of the Blues" for her part in the "Bluestocking Circle," a group of friends who met to discuss literature, history, philosophy, and social issues. Among the people who could be seen at their gatherings were some of the most distinguished men in England: Samuel Johnson, the actor David Garrick, the painter Sir Joshua Reynolds, the political philosopher Edmund Burke, and the wealthy gadabout Horace Walpole. And it's said that the group took its name from another man, the botanist Benjamin Stillingfleet, known for his eccentric blue socks. But all the most important figures at the center of the Bluestocking Circle were women who worked to create an English equivalent of the Parisian salons, where intellectual women could engage in serious conversation. *Bluestocking* would later become a term of abuse directed at learned women, those who neglected the feminine graces when they presumed to exercise their minds. ("I have an utter aversion to *blue-stockings,*" said William Hazlitt in 1822. "I do not care a fig for any woman that knows even what an *author* means.") But the original Bluestockings were proud of their intellect, and prouder still of the contributions they made to the society and learning of the day.

The most important work of Bluestocking Shakespeare criticism was Montagu's *Essay on the Writings and Genius of Shakespear*, which appeared in 1769. There she picked fights with a few big-name commentators, including her sometime friend Samuel Johnson and the great French man of letters Voltaire. Voltaire in particular erred by mindlessly judging Shakespeare by the "rules" of the drama, when he should have realized that Shakespeare transcended all rules. Montagu was pleased to defend "our poet" against "the presumptuous invasions of our rash critics, and the squibs of our witlings." But she was kinder to critics than many, since she believed that "more learned, deep, and sober critics" in recent days had finally succeeded in making the plays comprehensible. "Shakespear's felicity," she wrote, has therefore "been rendered compleat in this age."

Wilhelm Shakespeare

Both men and women kept reading and studying Shakespeare in London, and soon the habit spread across the world. It's no surprise that, as the British Empire expanded to America, Canada, India, Australia, New Zealand, and South Africa, Shakespeare's works came along. Less expected is the boom in Shakespeare studies outside the English-speaking world. While Shakespeare was still alive, English companies played in Germany and Holland. *Titus Andronicus*, *Hamlet*, *King Lear*, *Romeo and Juliet*, and *The*

Merchant of Venice were all played in some version on the Continent in the seventeenth century. While the East India Company's ship the *Dragon* sat off the coast of Sierra Leone in 1607, the sailors put on performances of *Hamlet* and *Richard II*. And alongside the performances came translations, editions, and studies. Germany was introduced to Shakespeare during his lifetime; by the end of the eighteenth century, the great English poet had been transmuted into a classic of German literature in A. W. Schlegel's influential verse translations.

Shakespeare looms large in the works of Germany's most beloved writer, Johann Wolfgang von Goethe, who, in an essay called "On Shakespeare's Day," announced, "The first page I read of him made me his own for the rest of my life, and as I finished the first play I stood like one who has been blind from birth being

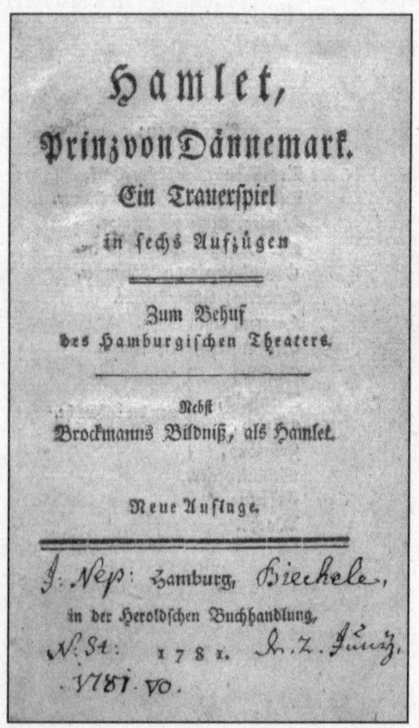

Hamlet,
Prinz von Dännemark.
Ein Trauerspiel
in sechs Aufzügen
Zum Behuf
des Hamburgischen Theaters.
Nebst
Brockmanns Bildniß, als Hamlet.
Neue Auflage.
Hamburg,
in der Heroldschen Buchhandlung,
1781.

German translations of Shakespeare's plays abounded in the eighteenth and nineteenth centuries. This version, Hamlet, Prinz von Dännemark, *appeared in Hamburg in 1781.*

given the gift of sight by a miraculous hand." For the first time, "I felt in the liveliest way how my existence extended to infinity, everything was new to me, unknown, and the unaccustomed light hurt my eyes." Goethe wrote his own drama in the Shakespearean mode called *Goetz von Berlichingen*, and Shakespeare's plays feature in his great novel *Wilhelm Meisters Lehrjahre* (Wilhelm Meister's Apprenticeship). And Goethe wasn't alone in this passion. For the writers associated with the late eighteenth-century Sturm und Drang (storm and stress) movement, he was "Wilhelm Shakespeare," an honorary German. Goethe described the spell he cast on the members of that circle, "so that in the same way that men come to know the Bible, we came to know Shakespeare." In 1827 Christian Dietrich Grabbe published *Über die Shakespearomanie* (On Shakespeare-mania). The mania has been long-lived in Germany, and not only in times of celebration. In 1844, during an era of national crisis and indecision, the poet Ferdinand Freiligrath wrote a poem called "Deutschland ist Hamlet." And even in the depths of the Nazi era, Shakespeare inspired a kind of passion. In the run-up to the Second World War, all English cultural products were frowned on by authorities, and all plays written in enemy nations were banned—except for Shakespeare, who was officially considered a German author. As a high-ranking figure in the Nazi ministry of culture wrote in 1939, "In view of the present circumstances, you are strongly discouraged from performing works written by Anglo-Saxon, American, or Russian playwrights . . . An exception is made for Shakespeare."

Not everyone on the Continent admired Shakespeare with the same fervor. Voltaire was of two minds: on the one hand, he did much to bring Shakespeare's works to the attention of his French contemporaries, and his translation of the "To be, or not to be" speech was Shakespeare's first appearance in French. On the other hand, though, he complained about Shakespeare's irregularity and lack of taste. "*Shakespeare* boasted a strong, fruitful genius," Voltaire admitted in his *Letters Concerning the English Nation*, but he "had not so much as a single spark of good taste, or knew one rule of the drama . . . The great merit of this dramatic poet has been the ruin of the *English* stage." As the critic John Pemble puts it, Voltaire "was shocked and even disgusted by what he saw in the plays of Shakespeare—a Moor strangling his wife; mad royalty; a prince, his mother, and his stepfather drinking together; gravediggers digging a grave while quaffing and singing rude vaudeville songs; a crowd of Roman plebeians haranguing patricians; Roman conspirators washing their hands in the blood of a murdered dictator." The result is that the English drama was left in what Voltaire called "a grossly infantile state." But other French critics were more forgiving. The novelist Victor Hugo, for example, praised Shakespeare as the supreme master of the theatre. "Shakespeare," he wrote, "c'est le drame"; Shakespeare *is* drama. Although Hugo spoke no English, he came to know the works through French translations, including some done by his son. He also conducted a series of séances in which the great dramatist spoke to him from heaven—and *le Barde* was thoughtful enough to speak *en français* when he contacted living Frenchmen.

By the end of the nineteenth century Shakespeare was speaking virtually all the languages of the world. The major European languages came early—Shakespeare could be had in German, Spanish, French, and Italian in the eighteenth century—but he was becoming almost universally available in the late nineteenth century. *Hamlet* was translated into Welsh in 1865, *Othello* could be read in Hebrew in 1874, *Julius Caesar* was available in Japanese in 1883, and fourteen of Shakespeare's plays were translated into Hindi between 1880 and 1900. (The translation of *Hamlet* into Klingon took a little longer, appearing only in 1996.) There are now at least twenty different verse translations of *Hamlet* in Polish. Browsing a library shelf turns up titles like *Foreign Shakespeare, European Shakespeares, Four Hundred Years of Shakespeare in Europe,*

Shakespeare Goes to Paris, Shakespeare und der deutsche Geist, Shakespeare en España, Poland's Homage to Shakespeare, Shakespeare and South Africa, India's Shakespeare, Shakespeare in Egypt, Shekspir v ukrains'kii, Meiji no Shekusupia, and *Shakespeare in der Türkei.* And now that Shakespeare is a world author rather than an English author, the quarrels over how to interpret him have gone international. The fights among commentators continue across national boundaries, with critics taking potshots at one another in footnotes of editions and scholarly articles, and occasionally daring to eviscerate one another in lecture halls and professional conferences.

Every generation finds and fights its own battles. Many of the disputes are between old-guard critics and au courant theorists, as those who would study Shakespeare's Christian theology and images of light and darkness go head-to-head with the Marxists and queer theorists. Inevitably the young Turks become the old guard and find themselves defending as orthodoxy what was once radical. (It's telling that the most retrograde criticism today—the old-fashioned kind of scholarship that the avant garde is most eager to beat up on—is called "the New Criticism," a name adopted when it was still the up-and-coming movement.) And many of the disputes are still over the same things that got Rymer, Theobald, and Ritson worked up, whether it's as important as race relations or as trivial as the positioning of a comma. At their worst, these arguments are little better than childish squabbles. And yet, while they may not show individual critics in their best light, their willingness to argue so fervently shows how an author who has been dead for nearly four hundred years can continue to arouse passion.

CHAPTER 4

Improving Shakespeare

DAVID GARRICK GOT HIS FIRST taste of fame in a wildly successful production of *Richard III*. Thomas Davies, Garrick's first biographer, recounted one of the highlights of the performance:

> When news was brought to Richard, that the duke of Buckingham was taken, Garrick's look and action, when he pronounced the words,
>
> ———Off with his head!
> So much for Buckingham!
>
> were so significant and important . . . that several loud shouts of approbation proclaimed the triumph of the actor and satisfaction of the audience.

It sounds like a powerful moment—except that the line "So much for Buckingham" appears nowhere in Shakespeare's *Richard III*, neither in the quartos nor the folios. What happened? Did Davies's memory fail him?

In another great Shakespearean moment, the ardent young lover asks, "What Light is that which breaks through yonder Shade?" as he gazes at his beloved on the balcony above. "Oh!" he cries, " 'tis my Love!" And then he listens breathlessly as she parts her ruby lips and speaks:

> O Marius, Marius! wherefore art thou Marius?
> Deny thy Family, renounce thy Name.

Surely that's no error of memory: a Romeo by any other name doesn't sound as sweet.

Cleared of Some Part of Its Rubbish

These performances seem odd because modern readers expect Shakespeare's plays to be made up of Shakespeare's words; but for much of the last four hundred years, they were rarely presented as he wrote them. Editors and critics savaged one another in their quest for Shakespeare's true text, down to the last semicolon, but most people couldn't be bothered with such minutiae. They were content to publish, perform, watch, and read his plays in thoroughly rewritten versions. Garrick, for example, was performing not Shakespeare's *Richard III* but an adaptation by Colley Cibber. Little of Shakespeare's text survived Cibber's popular revision, which presumed to "improve" the messy original. And the second passage comes not from Shakespeare's *Romeo and Juliet* but from Thomas Otway's *Caius Marius*. Otway, one of the leading playwrights of the late seventeenth century, wasn't plagiarizing *Romeo* but "fixing" it, giving it to audiences as they wanted it—cleansed of its many "imperfections." The critic and novelist Eliza Haywood praised *Caius Marius* as the "same play" as *Romeo and Juliet*, "only modernized and cleared of some part of its rubbish." She was convinced that, had Shakespeare lived to see this improved version, he "would have been highly thankful and satisfied with it." That sort of rewriting seems unthinkable to us—an insult to Shakespeare's ghost.

Cibber's and Otway's audiences, though, were grateful; they adored these "improved" versions and made them more popular than Shakespeare's originals. As the critic Jean Marsden writes, "theater-goers may have venerated the idea of Shakespeare—but not his text."

All plays undergo some revision for the stage. Directors always have to make cuts and changes to their scripts, whether to suit the actors on hand or to squeeze the play into the time available. (An uncut *Hamlet* runs to more than four hours.) Most people find nothing offensive about that, nor about works "based on" or "inspired by" Shakespeare, like *West Side Story* or *Rosencrantz and Guildenstern Are Dead*. The difference is that modern culture draws a sharp line between works "inspired by" Shakespeare and works "by" Shakespeare. Other ages didn't. As the critic Michael Dobson writes, "Shakespeare's plays belonged to the theatre more significantly than they belonged to Shakespeare," and all were fair game for rewriting.

At some point in their history, nearly all of Shakespeare's plays have been reworked. The process began as early as 1662, when William Davenant blended *Measure for Measure* with *Much Ado About Nothing* to create *The Law Against Lovers*. Soon the practice was nearly universal. In the 1660s, for instance, one company performing *Romeo and Juliet* alternated between the original tragic conclusion and a new happy ending every other night. *Richard III* was rewritten from top to bottom, leaving only the outline of the story intact. Falstaff, the eternal bachelor, was married off. Characters from *A Midsummer Night's Dream* wandered into *As You Like It*'s Forest of Arden and spoke lines from *Much Ado About Nothing*. John Dryden, England's poet laureate, transfigured three of Shakespeare's plays, and David Garrick's version of *Romeo and Juliet* cut much of the supposedly inappropriate humor—the bawdy joking of Gregory and Sampson, for instance, and the dark humor of Mercutio's "Ask for me tomorrow, and you shall find me a grave man"—and aged Juliet from a cradle-robbing fourteen to a more respectable seventeen years old. Audiences, far from being outraged, generally approved.

Without Any Moral Purpose

Sometimes the changes were minor and arose from an attempt to make sense of Shakespeare's old-fashioned language. Shakespeare's vocabulary and syntax can be difficult, even for experts. In the folio text of *Macbeth*, for instance, one of the witches says,

> A Saylors Wife had Chestnuts in her Lappe,
> And mouncht, & mouncht, and mouncht:
> Giue me, quoth I.
> Aroynt thee, Witch . . .

Mouncht seems to be an old form of *munched*, and *giue* is just an old spelling of *give*—that much is easy. But to this day, no one knows for sure what *aroynt* means. In printed editions, editors can offer their best guesses in footnotes (the *Oxford English Dictionary* says "In *aroint thee!* . . . meaning apparently: Avaunt! Begone!"), but on the stage it's impossible to stop and explain. So when William Davenant decided to adapt *Macbeth* for the theatre in the 1660s and came across *aroynt*, a word he didn't understand, he simply changed it into one he did: *anoint*. It doesn't make much sense in the passage, but at least it's a real word. And sometimes it's clear Davenant knew what a difficult word meant but was worried that his audience might not. Shakespeare gives us Macbeth's fears about blood on his hand:

> This my Hand will rather
> The multitudinous Seas incarnardine,
> Making the Greene one, Red.

The verb *incarnadine* (to redden) isn't exactly obvious, and it's unlikely the typical playgoer would have known it. Davenant decided the best way to be clear was to rewrite the lines altogether:

> No, they would sooner add a tincture to
> The Sea, and turn the green into a red.

No ambiguity there. Not much Shakespeare, either, but no ambiguity.

Not all of the changes had to do with clarity, though, and not all of them were minor. Sometimes new lines, even whole new scenes, were written to take advantage of the new actresses. Other changes had to do with Shakespeare's violation of the rules of propriety and decorum, his occasional lapses into bad taste. The less agreeable passages were cleaned up to suit modern tastes: Davenant found Hamlet's line "To grunt and sweat under a weary life" a little indelicate, so he replaced *grunt* with *groan*. And many critics expected all plays to observe the "three unities," supposedly authorized by Aristotle: the "unity of time," which says a play has to happen in less than twenty-four hours; the "unity of place," which says a play should happen in one location; and the "unity of action," which says a play should focus on one story, with no subplots. Shakespeare made mincemeat of these rules; *Antony and Cleopatra*, *The Winter's Tale*, and *Pericles*, for instance, take place over the course of years and in many countries, and most of his plays have complicated subplots. As John Dryden complained, Shakespeare was often "deficient" in "the mechanick beauties of the plot, which are the observation of the three unities, time, place, and action." When he turned *Antony and Cleopatra* into *All for Love*, he condensed the original fifteen years into a single day, and the whole ancient Mediterranean into a single city.

Shakespeare had the bad habit of mixing comic and tragic scenes, and critics lined up to attack his fondness for puns, an example of what the eighteenth century called "false wit." Samuel Johnson, for instance, wrote about how "quibbles" (puns) affected Shakespeare like a will o' the wisp—"A quibble is to *Shakespeare*, what luminous vapours are to the traveller; he follows it at all adventures, it is sure to lead him out of his way, and sure to engulf him in the mire"—or, to switch metaphors, a dangerous seductress: "A quibble was to him the fatal *Cleopatra* for which he lost the world, and was content to lose it." And, perhaps most damningly, Shakespeare didn't care enough about poetic justice: "He sacrifices virtue to convenience," wrote Johnson, "and is so much more careful to please than to instruct, that he seems to write without any moral purpose . . . He makes no just distribution of good or evil, nor is always careful to shew in the virtuous a disapprobation of the wicked." All of these things had to be addressed.

Problems like these were on Davenant's mind as he worked on *Macbeth*. One of the most troublesome scenes in that play was the one where, shortly after Duncan's murder, the porter staggers in to open the door. He's drunk and makes a number of bawdy jokes about the effects of alcohol on a man's libido (too much wine "makes him stand to and not stand to"). This low comic relief at a moment of serious dramatic intensity bothered many readers. Davenant therefore simply eliminated it—the porter is gone. He would not return to the stage for a century and a half.

What Davenant was doing wasn't looked on as an outrageous violation of dramatic propriety, but as a helpful tidying-up. For most of the twentieth century critics looked back on these adaptations in horror and disgust, offended at the very thought that mere mortals would presume to cheapen Shakespeare. But these "improvements" seem to have answered a real need. Instead of assuming that some epidemic of bad taste broke out in the 1660s, then, it's important to understand what these rewriters were doing and why.

Success to the Innocent Distrest Persons

The most notorious rewriting is a version of *King Lear*. To judge by the treatment *Lear* received in the seventeenth and eighteenth centuries, it might seem that audiences disliked the play. In Shakespeare's original, Lear asks his daughters how much they love him; to eighteenth-century audiences, Cordelia's terse response seemed harsh and unmotivated. The Fool and his low jokes detracted from the dignity of the tragedy. The Gloucester subplot drew attention away from the main story, and his imagined leap from Dover Cliff was preposterous. The scene in which his eyes are put out was simply disgusting. Gloucester's son Edgar pretended to be insane, but without any apparent motivation; his rant about "the foul fiend Flibbertigibbet" just evoked uncomfortable tittering in what was supposed to be a tragedy. Lear's own demented raving was sometimes obscene: lines like "Let copulation thrive!" had no place in the works of England's greatest genius. Worst of all, Lear and Cordelia die in the end; this was a serious violation of poetic justice. (About the ending, Samuel Johnson famously wrote, "I was many years ago so shocked by Cordelia's death, that I know not whether I ever endured to read again the last scenes of the play till I undertook to revise [edit] them.")

These were not minor blemishes that might be overlooked, but defects so serious that many found Shakespeare's play unwatchable. Critics said as much: Johnson thought "the extrusion of *Gloucester*'s eyes" was "an act too horrid to be endured in dramatick exhibition"; his friend Joseph Warton regretted the "considerable imperfections" that destroyed "the unity of the fable [plot]"; and Thomas Davies found the tragic conclusion so excessive as to border on farce ("The slaughter of characters in the last act . . . too much resembles the conclusion of Tom Thumb").

And yet, for all its flaws, there was something irresistible about *King Lear*, and for all its faults it remained a masterpiece. Johnson noted, "There is perhaps no play which keeps the attention so strongly fixed; which so much agitates our passions and interests our curiosity," and Davies said it was "universally esteemed to be one of Shakspeare's noblest productions." As the eighteenth century turned into the nineteenth, the veneration became even more extravagant. The poet Samuel Taylor Coleridge included it among "the Plays w[h] might be considered as the greatest works of our immortal poet viz:—*Macbeth—King Lear—Hamlet*," and Percy Bysshe Shelley called it "the most perfect specimen of the dramatic art existing in the world."

If the play could be neither enjoyed nor ignored, only one course remained: to change it. *Lear* underwent more extensive adaptations and by more writers than any other play in the Shakespearean canon. The most famous adaptation of *Lear*—and the most infamous adaptation of any of Shakespeare's plays—appeared on stage in 1681, about seventy-five years after the original play's first performance. This version was the work of an aspiring Irish playwright, Nahum Tate, then twenty-nine years old. Tate's original works had limited success, so he turned his attention to other things. He wrote the libretto for one of the most successful English operas, Henry Purcell's *Dido and Aeneas*. He wrote dozens of hymns and produced a *New Version of the Psalms of David*. He eventually became England's poet laureate, the most distinguished literary post in the nation.

But his greatest success, and for later ages his greatest disgrace, came from stage adaptations of earlier works. He did a revised version of Shakespeare's *Coriolanus*, for instance, called *The Ingratitude of a Commonwealth*. He also reworked *Richard II*, hoping the story of a king trying to avert a civil war would be topical enough to attract attention in the 1680s. It was, unfortunately for him, a little too topical; plays about successful usurpers were not well received by nervous royals when there was fear of a revolution at home. A hasty rewrite did nothing to ease the king's discomfort, nor did a solemn declaration that "every Scene is full of Respect to Majesty and the dignity of Courts, not one alter'd Page but what breaths Loyalty." The play was canceled after just a few nights.

Tate became most famous to later generations for his treatment of *King Lear*. Shakespeare's original had never been very successful on the stage; after its initial run, it rarely appeared in the theatre. Apparently few people saw much in it. Tate, though, said in the dedication to his version that he found the play "a Heap of Jewels, unstrung and unpolisht; yet so dazling in their Disorder, that I soon perceiv'd I had seiz'd a Treasure." His job was to polish the jewels and to show that treasure to the rest of the world. He was convinced that the play needed work, even though he knew it would be an act of audacity to change it. In putting together his "Revival" of the play "with Alterations," he professed, "Nothing but . . . my Zeal for all the Remains of *Shakespear*, cou'd

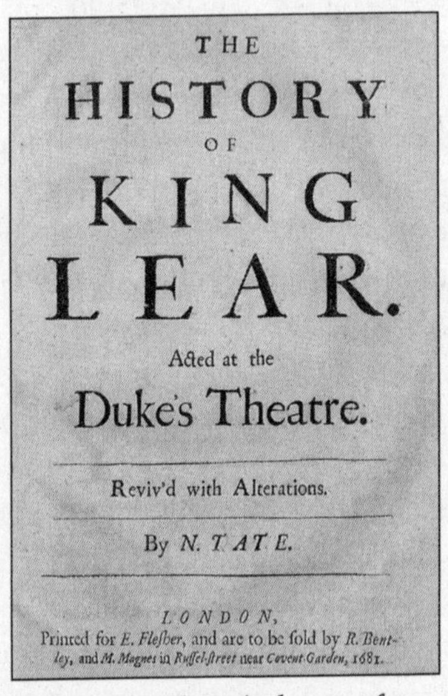

THE

HISTORY

OF

KING

LEAR.

Acted at the

Duke's Theatre.

Reviv'd with Alterations.

By *N. TATE.*

LONDON,

Printed for *E. Flesher*, and are to be sold by *R. Bentley*, and *M. Magnes* in *Russel-street* near *Covent-Garden*, 1681.

Nahum Tate's happy-ending King Lear *is the most famous—or notorious—of all the adaptations.*

have wrought me to so bold an Undertaking." But bold he was; in Tate's *Lear* whole scenes were moved, added, and deleted, and hardly a line went unaltered.

Some of the changes were small. Tate, like Davenant, clarified some of Shakespeare's language, which by 1681 had grown obsolete. He also cut some of the obscenities. Other changes were only a little more substantial, such as the removal of the king of France—not a particularly memorable figure in the original play, since he speaks just a few dozen lines. Other changes, though, were more extensive and more surprising. Consider, for instance, Tate's complete omission of the Fool: seventeenth- and eighteenth-century audiences found his low humor inappropriate and distracting, so out he went. Many of the most famous exchanges in the play are those between Lear and the Fool, but not one of them appears in Tate's adaptation.

Even that change was small compared to the treatment of Edgar and Cordelia. In Shakespeare's play the two are neatly parallel—each is the good child who, though devoted to his or her father, is mistaken for an enemy—but they also pose some dramaturgical problems. Edgar is framed by his brother and pretends to be insane to escape detection by his father; but why does he persist in his feigned madness even when his father is not around? Cordelia treats her father terribly when he asks how much she loves him; why can't she just play along and tell the old man what he wants to hear? Tate realized that by tinkering with the plot, he could satisfy viewers' concerns about all these matters. He was particularly proud of one change: "'Twas my good Fortune," he boasted, "to light on one Expedient to rectifie what was wanting [lacking] in the Regularity and Probability of the Tale." His solution? "To run through the whole a *Love* betwixt *Edgar* and *Cordelia*." Even though the two "never chang'd word with each other in the Original," they now share a secret love they must conceal from their disapproving fathers. "This," explained Tate, "renders *Cordelia*'s

Indifference and her Father's Passion in the first Scene probable. It likewise gives Countenance to *Edgar*'s Disguise."

This affair leads to new plot elements, as when Cordelia and her maid Arante (a character invented by Tate) are forced to travel across the countryside in disguise. On their way, they are molested by ruffians sent by Edgar's wicked brother Edmund. "Help, murder, help! Gods!" cries Cordelia. "Some kind Thunderbolt / To strike me Dead!" Edgar, who happens to be passing, hears the cries and springs to action:

> What Cry was That?—ha, Women seiz'd by Ruffians?
> Is this a Place and Time for Villany?
> Avaunt ye Bloud-hounds.

He fends off the attackers with his staff and becomes the women's "Guardian Angel"—all this in a long and action-packed scene, one of the most popular in the play, without a single line written by Shakespeare.

But even the Edgar–Cordelia affair, substantial as it may have been, wasn't Tate's biggest alteration. In his dedication he noted, "[My] method necessarily threw me on making the Tale conclude in a Success to the innocent distrest Persons"—in other words, the good characters had to be rewarded in the end. There's no denying that the conclusion to Shakespeare's play is devastating; one hope after another is dashed, as all the leading characters die in the final scene. But although modern viewers are often stunned by the catastrophe, few giggle at it. Tate, however, said he avoided the tragic conclusion for just that reason: "Otherwise I must have incumbred the Stage with dead Bodies, which Conduct makes many Tragedies conclude with unseasonable Jests." And so, to avoid the "jests," he decided *The Tragedy of King Lear* couldn't end as a tragedy.

Tate's last scene begins much like Shakespeare's: Lear and Cordelia, imprisoned, lament their fate."What Toils, thou wretched

King," Cordelia asks her sleeping father, "hast Thou endured / To make thee draw, in Chains, a Sleep so sound?" She spares a thought for her beloved: "And now, my Edgar, I remember Thee, / What Fate has seized Thee in this general Wreck / I know not." But despite the reappearance of the love interest, the mood is Shakespearean enough, including when the guards enter with ropes, preparing to hang Cordelia. Tate's Lear, like Shakespeare's, snatches a sword from one of the guards and strikes down two of them.

But what was in Shakespeare's *Lear* the last futile gesture of a defeated man—the final glimpse of hope before Cordelia is hanged and Lear dies of grief—is in Tate's *Lear* the turning point of the drama. The old man stands with his bloody sword, about to be taken away, when in rushes Edgar, who by now is making a habit of saving the day: "Death! Hell! Ye Vultures hold your impious Hands, / Or take a speedier Death than you would give!" In moments he has chased off the captors; Cordelia looks at her savior and cries, "My Edgar, Oh!" It's a scene more fitting for Nell in *Dudley Do-Right* than for a tragic heroine in *King Lear*.

From there things improve rapidly. "My dear Cordelia," explains Edgar, "Lucky was the Minute / Of our Approach." Lucky indeed: the chains come off, and Lear is restored to the throne with Cordelia at his side. "Old Lear," the king declares, "shall be / A king again," and "Cordelia then shall be a queen, mark that." Edgar, once rejected as unworthy of a king's daughter, is now welcomed with open arms, and Lear smiles on their love: "Thou serv'dst distressed Cordelia," says Lear; "take her Crowned." All the play's good characters return to receive their just reward: Lear's wronged but faithful servant Kent is welcomed, and even the blind Gloucester is given the opportunity to live the rest of his life with Lear and Kent, "retired to some cool Cell," where they can

gently pass our short reserves of Time
In calm Reflections on our Fortunes past,
Cheered with relation of the prosperous Reign
Of this celestial Pair.

Edgar, destined for the throne in a newly prosperous Britain, describes the joyous prospect:

Our drooping Country now erects her Head,
Peace spreads her balmy Wings, and Plenty Blooms.
Divine Cordelia, all the Gods can witness
How much thy Love to Empire I prefer!

He has the last word: "Truth and Virtue shall at last succeed." The change from tragic to comic conclusion comes so suddenly that modern readers hardly know what to make of it. Tate confessed he was "Rackt with no small Fears for so bold a Change"—he was, after all, completely rewriting the play—but he explained, "I found it well receiv'd by my Audience," and that was enough for him.

In fact his audience did receive it well. A few disapproved; as early as 1711, Joseph Addison complained that Tate had defaced a masterpiece: "*King Lear* is an admirable Tragedy . . . as *Shakespear* wrote it; but as it is reformed according to the chymerical [imaginary] Notion of poetical Justice, in my humble Opinion it has lost half its Beauty." But most viewers and many of the best critics condoned Tate's version. The critic Charles Gildon argued that "Mr *Tate* has very justly alter'd that particular, which must disgust the Reader and Audience to have Vertue and Piety meet so unjust a Reward," and Lewis Theobald agreed: "*Cordelia* and *Lear* ought to have surviv'd, as Mr. *Tate* has made them." Thomas Davies offered irrefutable empirical evidence about the play's reception: "Successive audiences, by their persevering approbation, have justified the happy ending of this tragedy." Or, as Johnson put it, "the publick has decided. *Cordelia*, from the time of *Tate*, has always retired with victory and felicity." They were right; people who went to see *The Tragedy of King Lear* anywhere in the English-speaking world between 1681 and 1823—almost a century and a half—saw that ending. For most of that time, almost everyone thought it was better than the original.

Beginning in the middle of the eighteenth century, though, as reverence for Shakespeare grew, people increasingly questioned the advisability of changing the play so radically. When David Garrick planned to stage *Lear*, someone urged him, "Why will you do so great an injury to Shakespeare, as to perform Tate's execrable version of him?—read and consider the two plays seriously, and then make the public and the memory of the authors some amends, by giving us Lear in the Original." Garrick rejected the advice, but the playwright George Colman the Elder took at least some of it in 1768. He justified his new version of *Lear* with the assertion that "it is generally agreed, that Tate's alteration is for the worse"—though there seems to be no such general agreement—and restored much of Shakespeare's plot and language to the first four acts of the play. Still, the Fool continued to be absent, and Tate's happy ending remained. The original *Lear* returned to the stage only in the nineteenth century, when Edmund Kean restored the tragic ending in 1823 and William Charles Macready hesitantly reintroduced the Fool in 1838. But survivals of Tate's version persisted even after 1838: Edwin Forrest's acting text of 1860 includes the scene in which Edgar rescues Arante and Cordelia from Edmund's villains.

From Shakespear One Play More

Another extensive, successful, and long-lasting adaptation was Colley Cibber's version of *Richard III*, which was first published in 1700 and became David Garrick's star vehicle forty-one years later.

Cibber was not only an actor and autobiographer but also a playwright with more than two dozen entertainments to his credit, including twelve comedies, seven tragedies, and four operas. Ten of his plays, though, were not entirely original but adaptations from other writers, including Corneille, Molière, and Dryden. His most important adaptations came from Shakespeare, and the most curious of these is *The Tragical History of King Richard III*. As the *Oxford Dictionary of National Biography* puts it, "Although technically an adaptation, it is so radically different from the Shakespeare play that it must surely be reckoned as an original play by Cibber."

Cibber's play gives us an unusual insight into how he set about adapting and improving Shakespeare's works, because the way he printed the text lets us see exactly what he did to the original script. "There was no great danger of the Readers mistaking any of my lines for *Shakespear*'s," wrote Cibber with mock modesty. But "to satisfie the curious, and unwilling to assume more praise than is really my due, I have caus'd those that are intirely *Shakespear's* to be Printed in the *Italick Character*; and those lines with this mark (') before 'em, are generally his thoughts, in the best dress I could afford 'em: What is not so mark'd, or in a different Character is intirely my own. I have done my best to imitate his Style, and manner of thinking." The accompanying photograph of a typical passage from act 5 shows just how much tinkering Cibber did. Of the thirty-nine lines of text on the page (not counting the stage directions), fully twenty-two—more than half—are entirely of Cibber's creation. Only the six lines in italics are Shakespeare's as he wrote them, and the remaining eleven, marked with an apostrophe, are merely "generally his thoughts." Why Cibber felt obliged to provide "the best dress" for Shakespeare's "thoughts"—implying that Shakespeare had somehow failed in his attempt to dress his own thoughts—he never explained. And those "thoughts" come not just from *Richard III*;

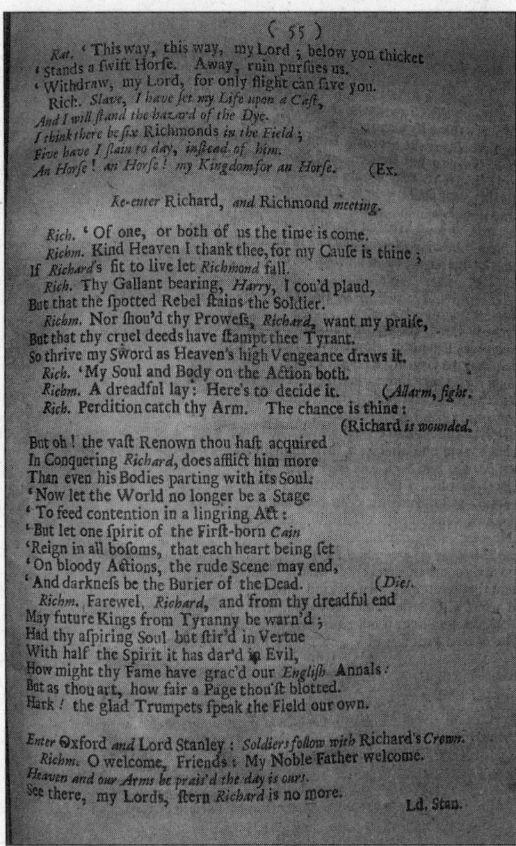

(55)

Rat. ‘ This way, this way, my Lord ; below you thicket
‘ Stands a ſwift Horſe. Away, ruin purſues us.
‘ Withdraw, my Lord, for only flight can ſave you.
Rich. *Slave, I have ſet my Life upon a Caſt,*
And I will ſtand the hazard of the Dye.
I think there be ſix Richmonds *in the Field ;*
Five have I ſlain to day, inſtead of him.
An Horſe ! an Horſe ! my Kingdom for an Horſe. (Ex.

Re-enter Richard, *and* Richmond *meeting.*

Rich. ‘ Of one, or both of us the time is come.
Richm. Kind Heaven I thank thee, for my Cauſe is thine ;
If *Richard*'s fit to live let *Richmond* fall.
Rich. Thy Gallant bearing, *Harry*, I cou'd plaud,
But that the ſpotted Rebel ſtains the Soldier.
Richm. Nor ſhou'd thy Prowefs, *Richard*, want my praiſe,
But that thy cruel deeds have ſtampt thee Tyrant.
So thrive my Sword as Heaven's high Vengeance draws it.
Rich. ‘My Soul and Body on the Action both.
Richm. A dreadful lay : Here's to decide it. (*Allarm, fight.*
Rich. Perdition catch thy Arm. The chance is thine :
(Richard *is wounded.*
But oh ! the vaſt Renown thou haſt acquired
In Conquering *Richard*, does afflict him more
Than even his Bodies parting with its Soul.
‘ Now let the World no longer be a Stage
‘ To feed contention in a lingring Act :
‘ But let one ſpirit of the Firſt-born *Cain*
‘ Reign in all boſoms, that each heart being ſet
‘ On bloody Actions, the rude Scene may end,
‘ And darkneſs be the Burier of the Dead. (*Dies.*
Richm. Farewel, *Richard*, and from thy dreadful end
May future Kings from Tyranny be warn'd ;
Had thy aſpiring Soul but ſtir'd in Vertue
With half the Spirit it has dar'd in Evil,
How might thy Fame have grac'd our *Engliſh* Annals :
But as thou art, how fair a Page thou'ſt blotted.
Hark ! the glad Trumpets ſpeak the Field our own.

Enter Oxford *and* Lord Stanley : *Soldiers follow with* Richard's *Crown.*
Richm. O welcome, Friends : My Noble Father welcome.
Heaven and our Arms be prais'd the day is ours.
See there, my Lords, ſtern *Richard* is no more.
Ld. Stan.

Colley Cibber marked the lines he added and changed in his adaptation of Richard III *(1700).*

some were lifted from *Richard II*, from both parts of *Henry IV*, from *Henry V*, and from all three parts of *Henry VI*, turning Cibber's *Richard III* into a kind of medley of eight of Shakespeare's ten history plays.

Cibber could denigrate Shakespeare's ability to express his thoughts; other adapters were willing to hit him even closer to home. Consider James Goodhall's version of *Richard II*, published in 1772. Although he found some "striking Beauties" in Shakespeare's original, he also worried that it is "defective in many Particulars, greatly incorrect, and abounding with indifferent Puns, put into more indifferent Verse." Maybe Shakespeare's verse was sometimes a little clumsy, and maybe he overdoes the puns. But most readers would still be inclined to think that Shakespeare at least knew how to write for the stage. Not so, said Goodhall. "The Play of RICHARD THE SECOND," he explained in his preface, "has so many necessary Alterations to be made, before it could possibly be even in the least Theatrical." Apparently, the great playwright didn't know how to write for the theatre. (In 1678 the playwright Thomas Shadwell made the same point: his version of *Timon of Athens* was "Made into a PLAY. By THO. SHADWELL.") In fact, said Goodhall, virtually all of Shakespeare's plays would benefit from his sort of rewriting. Surely Garrick was either exaggerating or wrong when he said "he was so fond of SHAKESPEAR, he could not think of receiving any Alteration." Goodhall knew better. And so in *King Richard II: A Tragedy, Alter'd from Shakespear, and the Stile Imitated*, he rewrote what he didn't like, added and deleted whole scenes, and used apostrophes to mark his own lines. As with Cibber's *Richard III*, little of Shakespeare is left; whole pages can go by without a single line from the original.

Goodhall did suggest that not every change of Shakespeare was for the better, and he singled out one adaptation for blame: "Not that I can approve of the Midsummer Night's Dream being turned into an Opera—a kind of Poetry very foreign to the Taste of SHAKESPEAR." He alluded here to *The Fairies: An Opera*, a work rumored to be by Garrick (though he denied it). It's hard to recognize Shakespeare's play in this opera, since so much had to be cut to make room for the music, and almost as much put in: "Where *Shakespear* has not supplied the Composer with Songs, he has taken them from *Milton*, [Edmund] *Waller*, *Dryden*, [William] *Hammond*, *&c*."

This strange mishmash of bits and pieces of other works (a dollop of Shakespeare, a dash of Milton, a sprinkle of Dryden) wasn't unusual in eighteenth-century handlings of Shakespeare. William Warburton's edition of the plays inserted poems by Christopher Marlowe and Sir Walter Ralegh into *The Merry Wives of Windsor*. One of the strangest adaptations was Charles Johnson's *Love in a Forest: A Comedy*, which appeared in 1723. The impression one gets is of Shakespeare's greatest comic hits all blended into one play. The plot mostly follows *As You Like It*, but the Pyramus and Thisbe episode from *A Midsummer Night's Dream* shows up in the wedding feast, and lines and plot elements from *Love's Labour's Lost*, *Much Ado About Nothing*, and *Twelfth Night* are inserted for good measure. The prologue describes how the author brought the dead to life:

> In Honour to his Name, and this learn'd Age,
> Once more your much lov'd SHAKESPEAR treads the Stage.

He asks forgiveness for his presumption, which is really nothing more than "Honest Zeal," and admits that he wants only "To tune the sacred Bard's immortal Lyre." The result will be

> The Scene from Time and Error to restore,
> And give the Stage, from SHAKESPEAR one Play more.

Unimitated, Unimitable Falstaff

Shakespeare was admired above all as a creator of great characters, and none was more beloved than the roguish Falstaff, who featured in many adaptations, sequels, and original works. If the legend is to be believed, Queen Elizabeth herself was so smitten with Jack Falstaff in the two parts of *Henry IV* that she asked Shakespeare to write a sequel, and the result was *The Merry Wives*

George Cruikshank, one of the most successful illustrators of the nineteenth century, published this etching of Falstaff in 1857.

of Windsor. Plenty of readers have since been seduced by Falstaff, at once charming and a scoundrel, the larger-than-life scalawag whose antics are in equal measure attractive and repellent. John Dryden called him "the best of Comical Characters," and even Samuel Johnson, always careful to balance "beauties" and "faults" in all of his discussions, lost his critical composure when he turned to "*Falstaff* unimitated, unimitable *Falstaff*." How, Johnson asked, "shall I describe thee? Thou compound of sense and vice; of sense which may be admired but not esteemed, of vice which may be despised, but hardly detested." Granted, "*Falstaff* is a character loaded with faults, and with those faults which naturally produce contempt. He is a thief, and a glutton, a coward, and a boaster, always ready to cheat the weak, and prey upon the poor; to terrify the timorous and insult the defenceless." But for all these flaws, Falstaff "makes himself necessary to the prince that despises him, by the most pleasing of all qualities, perpetual gaiety, by an unfailing power of exciting laughter." Later Ralph Waldo Emerson agreed, admitting that "A saint might lend an ear to the riotous fun of Falstaff; for it is not created to excite the animal appetites, but to vent the joy of a supernal intelligence." And Falstaff has plenty of twentieth- and twenty-first-century boosters. The critic Harold Bloom insists that, despite all the praise dished out by Johnson, Emerson, and others, Falstaff is still "the most undervalued personage in all of Western literature." No other character, he says, "seems to me so infinite in provoking thought and arousing emotion."

Falstaff was a favorite not only with monarchs and critics but with other writers—so compelling that several playwrights decided to revisit him, building their own sequels around Shakespeare's greatest comic creation. One of the earliest of the new Falstaff plays was *The Comical Gallant; or, The Amours of Sir John Falstaffe: A Comedy*, by Sir John Dennis, published in 1702. Alexander Pope, stung by Dennis's attacks on his translation of the *Iliad*, called him "a furious old Critic" who wrote "in a manner perfectly lunatic." Whatever the state of Dennis's mental faculties, he certainly had a high opinion of himself. When he took up *The Merry Wives of Windsor*, he confessed that he found Shakespeare's work "not so admirable, but that it might receive improvement"—improvement, of course, from himself. The problem was that the play, "as it has great Beauties, so it has strange Defects, which tho they past at first for the sake of Beauties, yet will come to be less endured as the Stage grows more Regular."

His preface laid out the many "Defects" in *The Merry Wives*. Shakespeare, it seemed, lacked Dennis's critical acumen. He didn't understand that "Humour is more properly the business of Comedy than Wit," or that "the design of Comedy is to amend the follies of Mankind, by exposing them"—all eighteenth-century critical commonplaces. Shakespeare also didn't know how to manage the private speeches: "the Soliloquies which [Falstaff] makes in the fourth Act . . . are not design'd for himself, but apparently address'd to the Audience, which is the greatest fault that can possibly be in the *Drama*." Having read the charges against Shakespeare's play, he explained his policy for fixing it: "I have alter'd every thing which I dislik'd, and retain'd every thing which I or my Friends approv'd of." At least he was admirably frank. Shakespeare's irregular verse is tidied up, and many passages are put into rhyme. Some of the extravagancies of the plot are eliminated. And some improbabilities are rendered plausible: the fat Falstaff is carried in a basket a full mile; with that in mind, Dennis added a character to the play, the Host of the Bull, who has the strength and the endurance to haul plump Jack the whole way.

Another writer who came under Falstaff's spell was William Kenrick. Kenrick was a minor writer of satires and essays, but his real passion was Shakespeare. (He was so dedicated to the Bard that he named his son William Shakespeare Kenrick.) He planned to edit a ten-volume edition of the plays but, when it came to nothing, he had to be content with criticizing the work of others. He published an attack on Johnson—*A Review of Doctor Johnson's New Edition of Shakespeare: In Which the Ignorance, or Inattention, of That Editor Is Exposed*—150 pages of mean-spirited assaults on Johnson's notes. A year later there appeared an anonymous *Defence of Mr Kenrick's Review of Dr. Johnson's Shakespeare*, another seventy-five pages of support supposedly written "by a friend." The author was actually Kenrick himself, who gallantly rushed to his own defense.

Kenrick observed "The Remarkable ill success of preceding imitators of Shakespeare," and he insisted that the Bard's greatest honor is "being truly *inimitable.*" This didn't stop him, though, from attempting an imitation of his own. Kenrick's most interesting bit of Shakespeareana, *Falstaff's Wedding: A Comedy, Being a Sequel to the Second Part of the Play of King Henry the Fourth, Written in Imitation of Shakspeare,* ran for only one night on the London stage but was popular enough in print to go through a half-dozen editions in the eighteenth century. The characters from 2 *Henry IV, Henry V,* and *The Merry Wives of Windsor* are brought back to life for another series of adventures. As the wicked Cambridge and Scroop plot against Henry V's life, a clergyman is trying to convince Falstaff to become a monk. Fat, jolly Falstaff will have none of it: "A monk; and to mortify the flesh! For heav'ns sake, good father, consider what a mortification indeed that must be to me, who have six times the quantity of any other man."

Kenrick was obviously taken with Falstaff's wild ways. He imagined him as a kind of tutor in vice to the prince, whose natural virtue makes him a slow study: "What a deal of pains it hath cost me," Falstaff laments, "to teach Hal to lie; and all thrown away upon him. He would never do it roundly. He had no genius that way." He has even introduced the newly crowned king to the pleasures of the flesh: "Had it not been for me," he boasts, "the milk-sop might have been crown'd before he had lost his maidenhead." In this version of the story Falstaff watches in discomfort as the new king begins to turn on his old drinking companion, and when the conspirators seek to involve him in their regicide, putting the knife in his hands, the audience begins to worry that he may have been won over to the dark side. But in the last scene Falstaff, now respectably married, saves the day: he agrees to take part in the plot on Hal's life but, at the last moment, betrays the traitors by revealing everything to the king. "Your majesty will doubtless pardon me," he says, "that I fail in so material a part of my commission, as that of lodging [the dagger] deep in your left breast." In the "compound of sense and vice," good triumphs over evil, and Falstaff retains his "perpetual gaiety."

No Quizzing

Not all of the adaptations were quite so reverent. In the nineteenth century parodies of Shakespeare's plays were becoming increasingly popular on the stage. The earliest and most famous of these was John Poole's *Hamlet Travestie*, published in 1810. The whole of *Hamlet* is turned into comic doggerel, as here, when Hamlet first meets Horatio:

HAMLET: My lads, I'm glad to see you. I implore
You'll tell me what brought you to Elsinore.
(*To* Horatio.)

HORATIO: To see dad's funeral I popp'd my head in.

HAMLET: No quizzing—'twas to see my mother's wedding.

The low diction (*My lads, dad*), the forced rhymes (*head in/wedding*), and the contemporary slang (such as *quizzing* for *fooling*) all seem to fight against the increasing reverence that was being given to the Bard. Not even "To be or not to be" escaped this comic tampering:

When a man becomes tired of his life,
The question is, "to be, or not to be?"
For before he dare finish the strife,
His reflections most serious ought to be.

When his troubles too numerous grow,
And he knows of no method to mend them,
Had he best bear them tamely, or no?
Or by stoutly opposing them end them?
Ri tol de rol, &c.

Poole also loaded up his printed text with long footnotes "after the manner of Dr Johnson . . . and the various Commentators," counting on his readers' familiarity with the increasingly learned editions that were coming off the press.

The nineteenth century abounded in these "burlesques" and "travesties": Charles Matthews turned the Venetian general into a London street sweeper in *Othello, the Moor of Fleet Street*; Andrew Halliday interrupted the balcony scene with a dog's incessant barking in *Romeo and Juliet Travestie*; even Gilbert and Sullivan got in on the act with *Rosencrantz & Guildenstern: A Tragic Episode, in Three Tabloids*. The earliest surviving literary manuscript by Charles Dickens is an unpublished burlesque called *O'Thello*. At midcentury these versions were so popular that six new Shakespearean parodies appeared in the London theatres in 1853 alone.

The crowds who flocked to these burlesques were not there to ridicule Shakespeare; they were actually engaging in a strange kind of adoration. The authors of these travesties sometimes took mean-spirited swipes at contemporary actors, but they rarely had anything bad to say about Shakespeare himself. The very existence of parodies like *Hamlet Travestie* shows that Shakespeare had transcended mere mortal standards of excellence, and any criticism of him must clearly be a joke. The point wasn't to desecrate a sanctified text, but to prove that it was above criticism. Parodying his works was like drawing a mustache on the *Mona Lisa*; it's a comment not on the work of art itself but on the reverence that surrounds it.

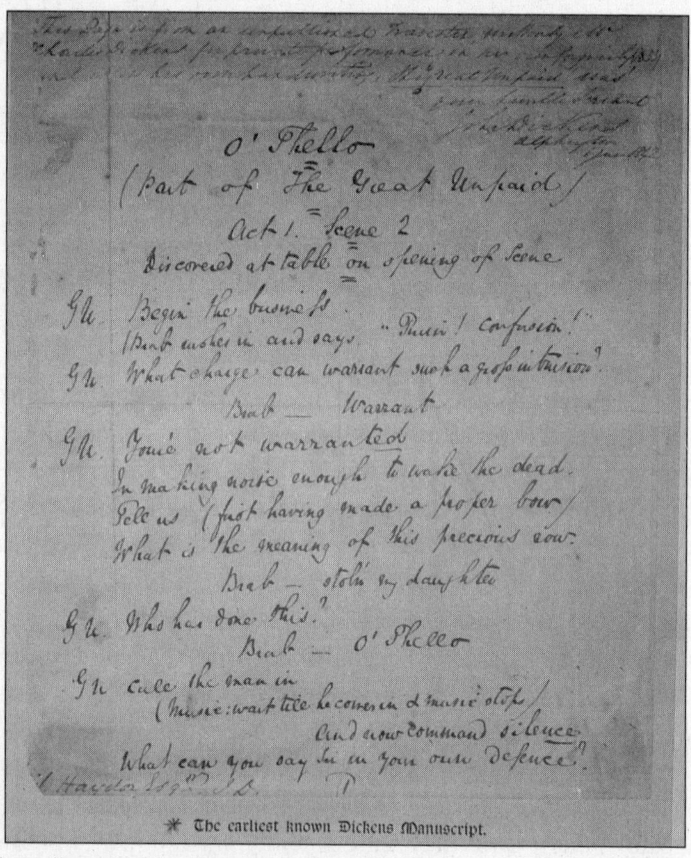

O'Thello
(Part of The Great Unpaid)
Act 1. Scene 2
Discovered at table on opening of Scene
G.U. Begin the business.
(Brab. enters in and says "Ruin! Confusion!"
G.U. What charge can warrant such a gross intrusion?
Brab — Warrant
G.U. You're not warranted
In making noise enough to wake the dead.
Tell us (first having made a proper bow)
What is the meaning of this precious row.
Brab — stolen my daughter
G.U. Who has done this?
Brab — O'Thello
G.U. Call the man in
(Music: wait till he comes in & music stops)
And now command silence
What can you say Sir in your own defence?

✱ The earliest known Dickens Manuscript.

The earliest surviving literary manuscript by Charles Dickens is the opening of a Shakespearean travesty called O'Thello.

Everlasting Disgrace

So for nearly two centuries, people who saw Shakespeare in the theatre actually saw something very different from what he wrote. And some of these alterations were surprisingly hardy. Tate's happy-ending *Lear* held the stage until 1823; Garrick's *Romeo and Juliet* was still being played in 1884; and some of Colley Cibber's additions to *Richard III*—"Off with his head! So much for Buckingham"—showed up in Laurence Olivier's film version of 1956. Perhaps, without these adaptations, Shakespeare would never have become the giant he is today. *Lear* and *Macbeth*, after all, were not very successful until they were rewritten.

From a twenty-first-century vantage point, it looks like horrible vanity and presumption to rewrite literary classics to suit eighteenth-century tastes. This distaste had already arisen in the nineteenth century, when most of the substantial rewritings had come to an end. Critics began to look back on the revisions with loathing. Of the revised *Lear*, for instance, the essayist Charles Lamb complained in 1817 that "Tate has put his hook into the nostrils of this Leviathan, for Garrick and his followers, the showmen of the scene, to draw the mighty beast about more easily." Most twentieth-century commentators were equally disgusted. Frederick Kilbourne's account of Tate's *Lear*, published in 1906, is typical—"bungling," "lame," "everlasting disgrace"—and in 1920 George C. D. Odell said Tate was "the most universally execrated of the daring souls who violated the precious shrine of the plays." But for Odell, Tate wasn't the worst of the lot; he called William Davenant "the very most culpable of Shakespearian alterers," and Davenant and Dryden's version of *The Tempest* "the worst perversion of Shakespeare in the two-century history of such atrocities," a "capital offence." If someone were to read this language without context—*everlasting disgrace, perversion, atrocities*, along with words like *abomination* and *blasphemy*—it might seem to describe war criminals or child molesters. It would be hard to guess that the only "capital offence" they committed was revising plays. All of these critics took it for granted that Davenant, Tate, and the rest were doing something self-evidently horrible.

Things began to change only in the 1950s, when George C. Branam found in the adaptations "a kind of laboratory manual of the diction, dramatic theory, and dramatic practice of the age in which they were written," and vowed not "to exclaim at the presumption and bad taste of a vitiated age, but to seek comprehension." The finger wagging and tongue clucking persist among many readers even today, but some are trying to be more open-minded and attentive to what these curiosities can teach us. The critic Jean Marsden, for instance, calls these versions "more than an embarrassing group of obscure plays symbolizing the Enlightenment's poetic bad taste," and notes that "they are also a manifestation of that period's perception of Shakespeare."

These plays certainly answered a need. Critics often say the adapted versions "drove the originals from the stage" or "banished Shakespeare's works for decades," as if audiences clamoring for unaltered texts were thwarted by these wicked adapters. That's simply not the case. However misguided they may seem, for nearly two hundred years many people really preferred the adapted versions to the originals. It wasn't a matter of not knowing what they were missing; at home they could read Shakespeare's plays as he wrote them, and if that's how they wanted to see the plays on stage, the theatres would have obliged. But they voted for the adapted versions in the only way that matters—by paying to attend productions of "improved" Shakespeare and leaving the originals in the library. Contemporary responses reveal that many of the most popular and successful scenes in these plays were not written by Shakespeare.

This answer may not seem a very good one, but there's every reason to think that it was a sincere one. The improvers of the eighteenth century may even have been more sincere than the directors of our own age, for the moderns make changes perhaps just as radical, setting *Richard III* in the fascist 1930s or putting bicycles in *A Midsummer Night's Dream*. It may be just as vain and presumptuous to think that Shakespeare would have approved of modern tastes. The difference is that his words have become our culture's holy Scripture, and no one is allowed to tinker with them, however much directors can change his settings and tone. Roman soldiers can carry guns on modern stages, as long as they call them swords, but heaven help the person who dares to alter the words. The screenwriter Sam Taylor has become the answer to a trivia question for tampering with a sacred text: in the 1929 movie production of *The Taming of the Shrew*, the screen credits read, "By William Shakespeare, with additional dialogue by Sam Taylor." In the twentieth century that could only look insanely cheeky, but eighteenth-century writers wouldn't have found it the least bit absurd. In fact they convinced themselves that Shakespeare would have wanted it that way. Here's the big paradox: for eighteenth-century critics and audiences, Shakespeare was most himself when most improved.

CHAPTER 5

Co-opting Shakespeare

MOST OF THE COMPLAINTS THAT led people to "improve" Shakespeare were artistic. Some critics disliked his ignorance of the unities, some his violation of poetic justice, some his wanton mixture of comic and tragic elements. His messy plots, his anachronisms, his low language—all interfered with people's enjoyment of the plays and led playwrights, editors, and theatre managers to try to clean them up.

Not all the revisions, though, were purely aesthetic. As Shakespeare became the great English genius, people increasingly used him to advance their own agendas, getting celebrity endorsements from beyond the grave. A choice quotation could lend Shakespeare's authority to a policy, a political party, an educational program, even a war. In revolutionary ages Shakespeare became a revolutionary; in conservative ages Shakespeare became a conservative—whatever was needed to preserve his position as the national poet. And if he didn't say quite the right thing, his works could always be rewritten to suit the purpose.

I Am Richard 2d

We know little about Shakespeare's own political beliefs, since his few clear allusions to contemporary politics are open to conflicting interpretations. But his plays have been used—some might say abused—for political purposes from the very beginning. A famous case is *Richard II*, which Shakespeare wrote early in his career, probably around 1595. The first published version appeared in 1597 and was followed by five more quartos before the First Folio was printed in 1623.

The differences among these published versions are more interesting than in many of the other plays. In particular, the fourth quarto exists in two slightly different states. The title page of one informs readers that the play now appears "With new additions of the Parliament Sceane, and the deposing of King Richard, As it hath been lately acted by the Kinges Maiesties seruantes, at the Globe." This "Parliament Sceane," a section of about 150 lines often called the "abdication episode," also appears in the fifth quarto, and again in the First Folio of 1623.

Differences between quartos and the folios aren't unusual, and they've been explained in many ways. The early quartos might have been "bad" texts, put together by pirate publishers who botched the job—but in this case the first quarto looks pretty sound. Or they might represent an early version of the play, suggesting the "missing" scene wasn't written until later, either by Shakespeare or by someone else. But many experts today believe the differences between the versions of *Richard II* arise from other motivations: the earlier editions, they speculate, were censored for political reasons, and the censored passage was restored only after it was safe to put it back.

The "abdication episode" shows Richard II resigning his throne to Henry Bolingbroke, whose army has attacked England. Richard is forced to hand over his crown to Bolingbroke, soon to be crowned Henry IV. York demands "The resignation of thy state and crown / To Henry Bolingbroke," prompting the devastated Richard to hand over the marks of his authority to his rival: "Here, cousin," says the heartbroken king, "seize the crown . . .

I give this heavy weight from off my head." That's all historical enough—the real Richard II was deposed by the real Henry Bolingbroke in 1399—but two hundred years later the events had acquired dangerous new overtones. Many people saw Richard in Queen Elizabeth—another weak monarch, one without an heir, one given to heavy taxation, one who relied too much on favorites—and some were agitating for her ouster. Whether or not Shakespeare intended to draw the connections between the old king and the current queen, plenty of people saw them, including the queen herself. According to one early account Elizabeth said, "I am Richard 2d. Know ye not that?" Showing the abdication of an old monarch was therefore risky business, because it made people think about the abdication of their own monarch.

Elizabethans read the play with this in mind. In 1601 an armed rebellion was brewing in England, and Shakespeare's play was at the center of it. Supporters of Robert Devereux, the second Earl of Essex, hoped to force the queen from the throne. Essex had once been among the queen's favorites, but, especially after he failed to put down an Irish rebellion in 1599, he fell from royal favor. The queen forbade him to return to England; he ignored her wishes. On his return he rushed into her chamber, where he found her undressed. Elizabeth's patience had run out, and she committed him to prison in York House. After eleven months Essex was released, but he was a ruined man.

Essex and his followers, stung by his treatment at the hands of the queen, began agitating to usurp Elizabeth and to install her cousin, James VI of Scotland, on the English throne. In February 1601 they met to plan a rebellion. To steel their own resolve and to convince the public of the righteousness of their cause, they paid Shakespeare's company to put on a production of *Richard II* at the Globe. They must have thought the parallels between Richard and Elizabeth would be obvious to the audience. The day after the performance Essex led three hundred armed men into the city, hoping to gain supporters as they went. But friendly forces failed to materialize, and the rebellion was a failure. Essex was captured, tried for treason, and beheaded at the Tower of London. Many of his supporters were arrested, and it seems some of the actors in *Richard II* were also investigated for dangerous political sentiments. They must have been able to talk themselves out of trouble, since it seems none were punished. But they were certainly taught a lesson, if they didn't know it already, about the way their plays could get tangled in the most serious politics of the day.

When Good Kings Bleed

So even plays about the distant past could have political resonances in the modern world. It makes sense that the most dangerous scene in the play, showing the monarch giving up his throne, would be suppressed for as long as it seemed too close to reality. It reemerged only in the fourth quarto of 1608, when Elizabeth was safely dead and her cousin James had legitimately followed her to the throne.

Other plays found new political meanings in changing times. It was James's grandson, Charles II, who authorized his supporter, William Davenant, to open a theatre in 1660. The grateful Davenant decided to return the favor by making Shakespeare's *Macbeth* into royalist propaganda. Shortly after the Restoration he revised it as *Macbeth, a Tragædy*, which was popular for many years. Davenant gave much of his attention to the witches, for whom he wrote several new speeches and songs. He also spruced up some of the original speeches, such as the chant around the cauldron:

> Black Spirits, and white,
> Red Spirits, and gray;
> Mingle, mingle, mingle,

> You that mingle may.
> *Tiffin, Tiffin*, Keep it stiff in,
> Fire drake *Puckey*, make it luckey:
> Lyer *Robin*, you must bob in.
> A round, a round, about, about,
> All ill come running in, all good keep out.
> Here's the Blood of a Bat!
> O put in that, put in that.
> Here's Lizard's brain,
> Put in a grain . . .

These scenes were audience favorites, though few people probably had any idea just how much of the text was Shakespeare's and how much Davenant's. But Davenant had changed the play to suit

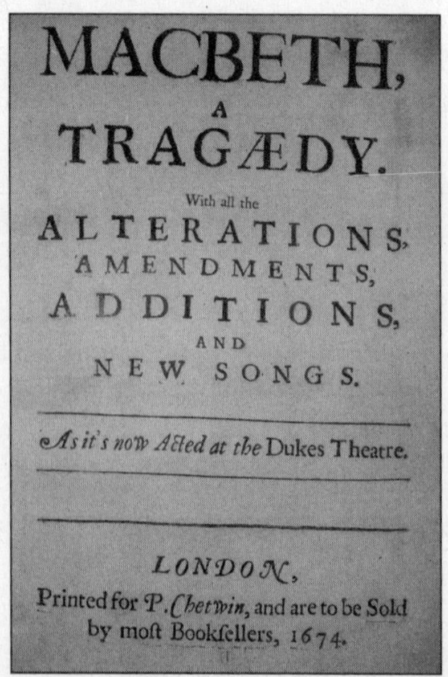

MACBETH,
A
TRAGÆDY.
With all the
ALTERATIONS,
AMENDMENTS,
ADDITIONS,
AND
NEW SONGS.

As it's now Acted at the Dukes Theatre.

LONDON,
Printed for *P. Chetwin*, and are to be Sold
by most Booksellers, 1674.

After the Restoration, William Davenant worked to turn Macbeth *into royalist propaganda.*

the times, and in the process he turned the Bard into a supporter of the current king.

Depicting a weak monarch could cause trouble, so it's not difficult to imagine how a play about the murder of a king might resonate in Restoration London, when the son of a murdered king was on the throne. The parallels were uncanny. Duncan was a Scottish king who was cruelly murdered by an ambitious rebel, who then ruled the country as a tyrant. Finally, the usurper met his just end, as Malcolm, the rightful heir to the throne, took his place at the head of the country and promised peace and prosperity. Charles I was also a Scottish king—he was from the House of Stuart—and he was also cruelly murdered by a band of ambitious rebels. Oliver Cromwell, the leader of the rebellion, then ruled the country as a tyrant (or so said the royalists). But once again the proper order asserted itself, as Charles II, the rightful heir to the throne, took his place at the head of the country. In his version of *Macbeth*, then, Davenant was promising his audience another reign of peace and prosperity. The audience may also have remembered that the Stuart monarchs claimed descent from Banquo himself, and that Shakespeare probably wrote the play to flatter Charles II's grandfather James I.

In this allegorical reading of the play, the sinister witches play the role of Charles's parliamentarian enemies. They are well suited to the part even in Shakespeare's original, but Davenant decided to make things clearer still. The language he gave his witches often came straight out of propaganda about parliamentarian wickedness: "We shou'd rejoyce," they sing, "when good Kings bleed." Macbeth is not just an eleventh-century rebel and usurper; he also stands for all the seventeenth-century rebels and usurpers who instigated the Civil Wars and killed the monarch. Malcolm's final speech leaves little doubt of the play's politics: "Drag his body hence," he says of Macbeth,

The witches in Macbeth *sound like wicked parliamentarians in this song from Davenant's adaptation, "We should rejoice when good Kings bleed."*

> and let it Hang upon
> A Pinnacle in *Dunsinane*, to shew
> To future Ages what to those is due,
> Who others Right, by Lawless Power pursue.

In the 1660s and '70s, no one could have missed the meaning of those who pursue others' right by lawless power: Macbeth had become a parliamentarian, and he deserved his tragic end. Shakespeare is pressed into service as a supporter of the monarchy and the status quo, even though he died long before Charles II was born.

Others drew the same moral from Shakespeare's story. More than a hundred years later, another writer saw in *Macbeth* a defense of kingship. In the 1790s the British felt threatened by the French Revolution across the Channel, as radical agitators like

Tom Paine were calling for an end to the monarchy in England. A conservative political pamphleteer named Thomas Ford imitated Shakespeare to attack these supporters of the French Revolution: in *Confusion's Master-Piece; or, Paine's Labour's Lost*, he rewrote some famous scenes from *Macbeth*. Once again, the witches are the rebels who threaten British monarchs, as this parody of the "double, double, toil and trouble" scene reveals:

1ST CITIZEN: Round about the country go,
Sow sedition, make it grow;
In each market-place a *tree*
Plant to wild *DEMOCRACY*;
Next eclipse, at murky hour,
Offerings bring, libation pour.

ALL: Double, double, strife and trouble;
Faction, blaze! and, treason, bubble!

Shakespeare's play was again being turned into a modern political allegory, and again Shakespeare was shown to be on the side of the righteous.

He Dar'd to Give Offence

As Shakespeare's stature grew, he came to embody everything Britain admired about itself. (The critic Michael Dobson catches this notion in the title of his book on the subject, *The Making of the National Poet*.) Shakespeare stood for Britishness itself. Many of the adaptations of his plays therefore stressed Britain's superiority to the rest of the world, especially the French.

Thomas Betterton's version of *2 Henry IV*, for example, was published around 1720, with a prologue by a minor author named

George Sewell, who used Shakespeare to assert a patriotic British identity. Remember that critics in France tended to be cold to Shakespeare's plays. French neoclassical taste favored order, structure, decorum, not the wild and woolly plots and blunt language so common in Shakespeare. French plays were either tragedies or comedies, not the strange mixture of the two that Shakespeare often used. Worst of all, the French critics were convinced, Shakespeare knew nothing of Aristotle's rules of the drama. This is what prompted Voltaire to insist that Shakespeare "had not so much as a single Spark of good Taste, or knew one Rule of the Drama." But if the French hated Shakespeare's irregularity so much, thought the British—well, then, it must have *something* going for it. Britain and France were at war through much of the eighteenth century, and literary squabbles became a proxy for political squabbles. It's no coincidence that one early work of Shakespeare criticism, John Dennis's *Essay on the Genius and Writings of Shakespear*, was dedicated "To the Right Honourable GEORGE GRANVILLE, Esq; Secretary at War." Any attack on French positions, whether critical or military, advanced British interests. Thus the British began to rally around Shakespeare, accepting, even celebrating, what had once been condemned as his faults. As the critic Joseph Warton put it in 1756, "CORRECTNESS is a vague term, frequently used without meaning and precision. It is perpetually the nauseous cant of the French critics."

John Dryden's *Essay of Dramatick Poesie* was written "to vindicate the honour of our English Writers, from the censure of those who unjustly prefer the French before them," but Sewell went further still. The English, he wrote in his prologue to 2 *Henry IV*, aren't servile and rule-bound like the hated French, and their greatest poet wasn't afraid to mix serious scenes with light ones: "*Shakespear* who gave our *English* Stage its Birth, / Here makes a medley Scene of War, and Mirth." After all, Shakespeare's seeming faults really just declared the English love of freedom:

> If sometimes, devious from old Rules he strays,
> And treads a-wry from *Aristotle*'s ways,
> Tis but to show—he dar'd to give offence,
> And laugh'd at slavish Ties—in any Sence.

Shakespeare broke Aristotle's rules, yes, but he did it only to prove the superiority of English liberty. Shakespeare was becoming the great British poet and playwright, the avatar of everything that was admirable about the British and lacking in the French across the Channel.

Other aspects of what it meant to be British were embodied in another popular and influential Shakespearean rewriting, *The Tempest; or, The Enchanted Island*, by William Davenant and John Dryden. Later critics have been baffled by its success; in 1957, for instance, the critic F. E. Halliday expressed only confusion and disgust at this reworked version of "Shakespeare's loveliest play." He found it "one of the most unpleasant of the adaptations," complaining that "all innocence is lost, and the delicate fantasy debased to a salacious musical comedy. The poetry is sacrificed to pantomime spectacle." But the Davenant–Dryden *Tempest* was hugely popular, not only in the original form but also in an operatic adaptation by Thomas Shadwell, for which the great composer Henry Purcell wrote a score. These revised versions were far more successful than the original had ever been. Samuel Pepys, for instance, saw the original Davenant–Dryden version at least eight times.

Such popularity perplexed critics like Halliday, but more recent readers have begun to understand the tremendous appeal of this *Tempest*. The first thing to remember is that Shakespeare's play is another tale of an unjustly deposed ruler who manages to regain his throne, a situation bound to resonate with supporters of the king during the Restoration. Those elements are there in the original, but Davenant and Dryden played them up even more in their adaptation. Dryden's verse prologue makes the play's political function clear with a metaphor of a tree brought back from what looked like death:

> As when a Tree's cut down the secret root
> Lives under ground, and thence new Branches shoot;
> So, from old *Shakespear*'s honour'd dust, this day
> Springs up and buds a new reviving Play.

He goes on to invoke Shakespeare, who, "Monarch-like," gave "his subjects law," and notes that his "pow'r is sacred as a King's." This begins to make sense in the context of the Restoration, when both the monarchy and the theatre had been cut down, but new branches were once again shooting from both.

The story of a restored ruler doesn't explain all the changes, though, because Dryden and Davenant introduced a new comic subplot about the love relations of the characters on the island. This involved some significant meddling with the original. In Shakespeare's story the magician Prospero and his daughter Miranda have lived alone on the island since her infancy. When Miranda sees Ferdinand, a shipwrecked sailor—the first man she's ever seen other than her father—she falls immediately in love. Davenant and Dryden thought this idea had promise, but that Shakespeare didn't go far enough. So they went to work improving the old play. For starters, they gave Miranda a sister, Dorinda. They also decided to make the plot more symmetrical by giving us a man, Hippolito, who grew up on the *other* side of the island, and who had never seen a woman. Hippolito finally meets Dorinda, and they fall in love. But the naïve Hippolito hasn't learned society's rules. In another scene, Hippolito has now spotted Miranda, the sister of his beloved, and decides he wants her too. He announces the "blessed news" to Dorinda: "I have heard there are more Women in the World," he declares breathlessly,

"As fair as you are too." Dorinda, unimpressed, asks, "Is this your news? you see it moves not me." Hippolito, though, excitedly declares he will "have 'em all." Dorinda doesn't relish the thought of being reduced to part of a harem, but Hippolito can't imagine why she's upset. He's surprised when he finds out Dorinda resents his love for Miranda:

> HIPPOLITO: Do not you love her?
> Then why should not I do so?
>
> DORINDA: She is my Sister, and therefore I must love her:
> But you cannot love both of us.
>
> HIPPOLITO: I warrant you I can:
> Oh that you had more Sisters!

These witty exchanges are entertaining and work brilliantly on the stage. But they're also performing a kind of political function, though a less obvious one: they're all about the proper relations between men and women, and in the end they promote a patriarchal vision of the family hierarchy. This will be no surprise to those who know royalist politics, for the king's supporters often likened the king's position at the head of the state to the father's role at the head of the family; one of the most influential works of royalist political theory was Robert Filmer's *Patriarcha*. Michael Dobson notes that the play's "initial success . . . can certainly be accounted for in part by its successful and ambiguous dramatization of Restoration political conflicts," but he reminds us that it also "owes its lasting appeal to its representation not only of patriarchal monarchy but of the patriarchal family." Halliday, writing in the 1950s, was not attuned to the various kinds of political meanings lurking in the Davenant–Dryden play, and to him it looked like ill-considered meddling with a masterpiece. Against the background of Restoration politics, though, the revised play's success makes much more sense and almost seems inevitable.

Our Harry Fought All Day and Slept All Night

Not all rewritings of Shakespeare's plays were so kind to the ruler on the throne. When Colley Cibber reworked *Richard III* in 1700—one of the most enduring adaptations of any Shakespeare play—he discovered the theatrical censors would not allow him to perform the first act. "All the reason I could get for its being refus'd," he explained, "was, that *Henry* the Sixth being a Character Unfortunate and Pitied, wou'd put the Audience in mind of the late *King James*." Supporting the exiled James instead of the current monarch, William III of the rival house of Orange, was a dangerous matter.

Cibber's problem with *Richard III* was probably accidental; he apparently had no intention of making the king uncomfortable. Others, though, used Shakespeare to prod the country's rulers. In 1723 Aaron Hill rewrote Shakespeare's *Henry V* as *King Henry the Fifth; or, The Conquest of France, by the English: A Tragedy*. Calling his version of Shakespeare "a *New Fabrick*, yet . . . built on *His* Foundation," Hill turned *Henry V* into fiercely jingoistic anti-French propaganda. "Mark, in their *Dauphin*, to our *King* oppos'd," he advised his audience, "The diff'rent genius of the *Realms* disclos'd." On one side,

> the *French Levity*—vain,—boastful,—loud:
> Dancing, in *Death,*—gay, wanton, fierce, and proud.

Not so across the Channel:

> *Here*, with a *silent Fire*, a *temper'd* Heat!
> Calmly resolv'd, our *English* Bosoms beat.

After a spirit called "The Genius of *England* rises, and sings," the French themselves announce what a miserable nation they are: Bourbon declares, "O! Shame, beyond Example! Let us stab our selves!" as the Dauphin chimes in, "Shame, and Eternal Shame! Nothing, but Shame!"

The French-bashing is obvious enough, but Hill also takes the current British monarch to task. One of the most curious of his changes to Shakespeare's text is the complete omission of Henry's wooing of the French princess Catherine. These scenes provide some of the most charming moments in the original play; they show the tender, romantic side of the warlike king and leaven the serious business of war with the humor of the two characters butchering each other's language. "Is it possible," asks Catherine, "dat I sould love de *ennemi* of France?" "No," replies Harry, "it is not possible you should love the enemy of France, Kate . . . When France is mine, and I am yours, then yours is France, and you are mine." But this witty speech has placed too many demands on the Frenchwoman's meager English: "I cannot tell vat is dat." "No, Kate?" asks the king. "I will tell thee in French." And then he strives to construct a grammatical sentence in his beloved's language: "*Je quand suis le possesseur de France, et quand vous avez le possession de moi*—let me see, what then? Saint Denis be my speed!—*donc vôtre est France, et vous êtes mienne*. It is as easy for me, Kate, to conquer the kingdom as to speak so much more French . . . But Kate, dost thou understand this much English? Canst thou love me?" Catherine, still confused, replies, "I cannot tell." "Can any of your neighbours tell, Kate?" demands the exasperated monarch. "I'll ask them." There's not a trace of this in Hill's version. That's because Hill's mind wasn't on Henry V in 1415; it was on his own king, George I, in 1723. George had a reputation for being too fond of his mistresses, and Hill was convinced that it was making him neglect important national business.

It would of course be imprudent—treasonous, even—to criticize the king directly. The usual way of safely attacking royal policy was to blame the king's ministers for giving him bad advice; this provided some cover for criticism of, say, tax policies or the conduct of a war. But it was impossible to blame the cabinet for the king's personal failings: how are royal advisers supposed to be accountable for the monarch's love life? There's no tactful way to tell anyone that he's sleeping around too much, and when that person is the king of England, the problem is infinitely compounded. Hill therefore used Shakespeare's play to criticize the king indirectly. He put a recognized English hero of yore on the modern stage and turned him into a model of modern virtue: no mistresses for Harry. The audience was invited to draw the comparison between the two.

It's a strange choice of a play for this sort of critique. Henry V was a great English hero, admired for his military prowess, but when he was a young man he was the wild Prince Hal. The young prince of the two parts of Shakespeare's *Henry IV* seems to enjoy all the boozing and womanizing that Hill wanted to chastise in his monarch. And so Hill simply edited out Hal's youthful indiscretions. Falstaff—whose sad end is mentioned at the beginning of Shakespeare's *Henry V*—disappears from Hill's entirely, so as to give us no reminder of Henry's rowdy past.

In Hill's version it's the French who waste their time with women. As the Dauphin says to his beloved, "Come to my Arms, thou more than manly Spirit! / Dress'd in a Woman's Softness! why, Thou Charmer! / Thou Angel of a Traitor!" Notice that the Frenchman is impressed by a "more than manly" lover; French men, according to a leading eighteenth-century British prejudice, were supposed to suffer from a confused sexuality. It's therefore only natural that they should be defeated by an English king who cares about macho matters like killing his enemies, rather than "woman's softness." Worse still, later English kings lost their

French possessions because their minds drifted back to thoughts of love. Henry's son and heir, Henry VI, was too devoted to his wife; he became a cuckold, and France was lost—hence the "tragedy" of the play's title. As the epilogue, delivered by the actress who played Catherine of France, explains:

> We've shown Ye, Sirs! how *France*, of Old, was *got*:
> And, now, I'll tell ye, why we *kept* it *not*—
> This *Hero*'s Son and Heir,—no warring Ranger!
> Lov'd *Grace*, obey'd his *Wife*, and *hated Danger*.

Obeying his wife—how pathetic, and how unlike his heroic father:

> *Our Harry* fought, all Day, and *slept*, all *Night*:
> Nor dreamt of gentler Joys, than those of *Fight*.

No Foreign Force This Country Shall Subdue

It's easiest to see the range of possibilities in interpreting Shakespeare by setting several versions of the same play beside one another. Shakespeare's *King John* is not one of his more popular plays today, but its fortunes have been higher in other eras. The Victorians, for example, adored it and turned it into the very first cinematic version of Shakespeare in 1899. It also appeared in two different guises in the eighteenth century, which show us how the plays could be reworked to suit their political context. The play presents two perennial enemies of the English: the French, in the person of King Philip, and the Roman Catholic Church, in the person of the pope's legate, Cardinal Pandulph. Although both France and the Catholic Church were favorite targets of English jingoism, their relative enmity has shifted back and forth over time, and that plays out in different ways in two adaptations.

Colley Cibber reworked *King John* in 1745, an important year in British history: it was the time of the last major Jacobite uprising, part of the complicated fallout from the Civil Wars of the seventeenth century. Charles II was restored to the throne in 1660; in 1685, after his death, the crown passed to his brother, James II (formerly the Duke of York, the patron of Davenant's company). But James was a Roman Catholic, and once again the tension between a Protestant Parliament and a Catholic monarch threatened to plunge the country into chaos. Civil war loomed, but this time no shots were fired: in the "Glorious Revolution" of 1688–89, James II was forced to flee from England, and the Protestant William of Orange was brought in from Holland to rule with Queen Mary. James's supporters—known as Jacobites, from the Latin *Jacobus* (James)—tried several times to invade the country and retake the throne. The biggest threat came in 1745, when Charles Edward Stuart, a descendant of James II better known as Bonnie Prince Charlie, led an invasion of England in the hopes of restoring the Stuart line.

Cibber's *King John*, written just as this battle was taking place, has the Jacobite threat in mind; the dastardly papal legate reminded loyal Protestant audiences of the Catholic invasion force. For Cibber, the enemy was the Roman Catholic Church, which was propping up the Pretender and his armies. His version of *King John* therefore turns the papal nuncio into the villain of the piece. He's no hero in Shakespeare's original, but neither is he particularly wicked. Cibber noted this and paused in his introductory note to express his surprise that "our *Shakespear* should have taken no more Fire" at "his insolent *Holiness*." Cibber took fire enough for both of them. Just in case there was any doubt about who deserved the English hatred, Cibber retitled the play: no longer *The Life and Death of King John*, as it was called in the First Folio, it became *Papal Tyranny in the Reign of King John: A Tragedy*.

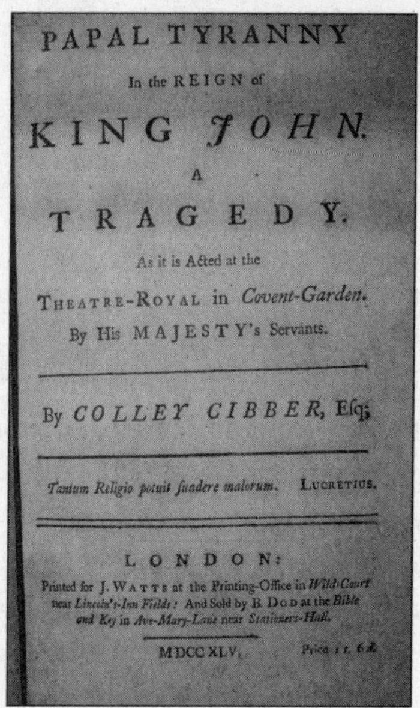
PAPAL TYRANNY

In the REIGN of

KING *JOHN*.

A

TRAGEDY.

As it is Acted at the

THEATRE-ROYAL in *Covent-Garden*.

By His MAJESTY's Servants.

By *COLLEY CIBBER*, Esq;

Tantum Religio potuit suadere malorum. LUCRETIUS.

LONDON:

Printed for J. WATTS at the Printing-Office in *Wild-Court* near *Lincoln's-Inn Fields*: And Sold by B. DOD at the *Bible and Key* in *Ave-Mary-Lane* near *Stationers-Hall*.

MDCCXLV. Price 1 s. 6 d.

Colley Cibber rewrote King John *during a Jacobite invasion (1745) and turned the pope's representatives into supervillains.*

Fast-forward from 1745 to 1800: the world looks very different. The Jacobites are no longer a threat, but England is still not secure. The French Revolution is in full swing, and patriotic Britons are becoming increasingly nationalistic. And although Protestant Great Britain is still none too fond of the Roman Catholic Church, there is a more pressing challenge to its peace and security: revolutionary France, with its atheism and its rejection of the monarchy and aristocracy, threatens everything patriotic Britons hold dear. The pope himself is being threatened by Napoleon—and the enemy of Britain's enemy has become a kind of friend, even if not a close one.

This was the world in which Richard Valpy produced his own version of *King John*. As a young man, Valpy had published an undistinguished collection of poetry, *Poetical Blossoms*, which included such formulaic lines as these:

> Oh! how painful not to love!
> Love will ever painful prove:
> But the most distracting pain
> Is to love, and love in vain.

The world can be thankful the poetic muse didn't bother Valpy after that. Valpy also considered a career on the stage but made no progress. Having failed as a poet and as an actor, though, he decided to devote his energy to scholarship, where he showed real promise. After finishing his degree at Oxford and becoming ordained as a minister, he became headmaster of Reading School, and it was there that he discovered his métier. When he took it over in 1781, Reading School was a small academy of only twenty-three students. Through his tremendous energy, Valpy increased the enrollment to 120 pupils within a decade and began attracting the children of some of the most distinguished families of the area. He was a popular and successful teacher, for several of his students later published fond remembrances of him and the school he ran. (His school was also just across a meadow from the Abbey School, where ten-year-old Jane Austen was a student in 1785–86. She probably socialized with Valpy's students and may even have seen some of the performances they put on.)

Valpy was always what might be called an establishment figure—a member of the Society for Promoting Christian Knowledge, for instance, and of the Society of Antiquaries of London. After the outbreak of the French Revolution, though, his conservatism intensified, and he became a fierce reactionary, attacking anything that smacked of foreign innovation. One of his sermons of 1791, published as *The Progress of Morality, Religion, and Laws*, noted that France was once the happiest nation in Europe—"But shocking," he says, "is the reverse in the present day. Of late a race of men has arisen in that country, who . . . bore with impatience every species of authority, and prepared an opposition to their civil and religious establishment." He had few kind words for the French revolutionaries, who were "Destructive of morals and public security," and "who build their laws on any foundation, but that of Religion." In spouting their mumbo jumbo about social equality, "they have cut asunder the sacred ties of the marriage state. With the plea of securing the rights of self defence, they have bared the knife of the assassin, and legalized wilful murder." And this even before the Terror had begun. The principles that the Revolution held dear—*liberté, égalité, fraternité*—were for Valpy preposterous. "Never was a principle so perverted in it's application," he wrote, "as that of Equality." And the kind of politics that emerges from equality is equally hateful: "In a Democracy, the mob proscribes with a blind fury the innocent and guilty . . . Experience proves that all democratical systems are dangerous and fatal . . . The sovereignty of the people tends to anarchy, and the destruction of personal liberty."

Consider now what Valpy did with *King John*. The contrast with Cibber's version of fifty-five years earlier is explicit. Valpy thought about producing Cibber's play instead of writing his own, but he "found two great obstacles to his wishes." He noted, first, that "CIBBER's object, during the rebellion in 1745, was to paint the character of the Pope's legate in the blackest colors, and to darken the principles of the Romish Church with circumstances of horror." That may have made sense fifty years earlier, but "in the present times, when the situation of the Pope had become a subject of commiseration to the Christian world, the aim of the Editor was to soften the features of Papal Tyranny, as far as historical evidence would permit him." And so the one Cibber had called "his insolent *Holiness*" became much less insolent. Valpy then added, almost as an afterthought, that he "also wished to preserve all the fine passages of SHAKESPEARE: CIBBER had scarcely retained a line of the great original." Nowhere did he consider that Shakespeare's play, not modified by anyone, would

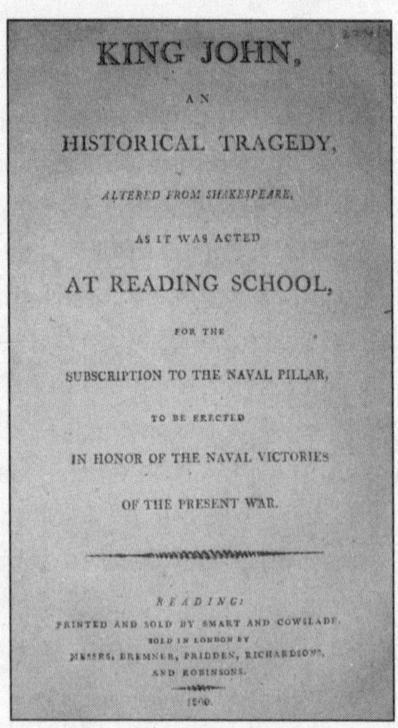

KING JOHN,

AN

HISTORICAL TRAGEDY,

ALTERED FROM SHAKESPEARE,

AS IT WAS ACTED

AT READING SCHOOL,

FOR THE

SUBSCRIPTION TO THE NAVAL PILLAR,

TO BE ERECTED

IN HONOR OF THE NAVAL VICTORIES

OF THE PRESENT WAR.

READING:

PRINTED AND SOLD BY SMART AND COWSLADE.

SOLD IN LONDON BY

MESSRS. BREMNER, PRIDDEN, RICHARDSONS,

AND ROBINSONS.

1800.

Richard Valpy presented King John *during the Napoleonic wars (1800) and made the French the enemy.*

be a suitable choice; the need for rewriting was taken for granted. He was particularly offended by the prospect that "the indecencies of the First Act should be tolerated by a *British* audience, in this age of moral refinement, in the reign of a PRINCE, who displays an exemplary detestation of every thing, that is not chaste in sentiment, and pure in expression."

Valpy's play makes the pope and the papal nuncio far more sympathetic, and it is the French who become the villains. "The proud Gaul" (Frenchman) is now the target of English hatred, because the French were the real-world enemy in the 1790s. Valpy's version was performed at Reading, where the admissions fees went to help erect a monument "in Honor of the Naval Victories of the Present War." And if the patriotic mission of the play wasn't obvious from that, it is impossible to miss it in the prologue, spoken by Valpy himself:

Then be this truth of ev'ry ENGLISH breast
In adamantine characters impress'd:
"That ENGLAND never did, and never shall"
Bow to a victor foe's inglorious thrall.

The end of the play repeats some of the same jingoistic sentiments of the prologue, as Falconbridge addresses the audience:

O never let dissension mar our peace!
For England never did, and never shall,
Lie at the proud foot of a conqueror . . .
No foreign force this country shall subdue,
While King and Subjects to themselves are true!

Looking Before and After

By the nineteenth century, it was difficult to find any high-profile public debate in which Shakespeare's name was not invoked by both sides. Should Roman Catholics have the right to vote? Should Jews become naturalized citizens? Should Ireland be granted independence? What's the proper function of education for women? Partisans on all sides of every issue were ready with their illustrations from Shakespeare.

Consider one of the most vexed arguments of the early nineteenth century, that over slavery. When Britain was debating abolition in the 1830s, both sides were keen to claim Shakespeare's authority. One member of the House of Commons argued that slavery was beneficial to the Africans—what, after all, could a freed slave hope for that he didn't have already? "Certainly, he is to enjoy the high privileges of serving on juries and in the militia," he argued sarcastically, "but I doubt his inclination to set a just value upon these civilized distinctions." And if the newly emancipated slaves "should make acquaintance with Shakspeare, I suspect it will be with them as it has been with many others who have been forced into distinction." He even imagines "their favourite quotation":

> ———'Tis better to be lowly born
> And range with humble livers in content,
> Then to be perk'd up—in a jury-box,
> And march as a militia-man.

These lines about the evils of rising above one's station are from Shakespeare's *Henry VIII*, tweaked to suit the occasion, with the jury box and the militia inserted where Shakespeare had "perk'd up in a glist'ring grief, / And wear a golden sorrow."

But abolitionists could invoke the Bard just as easily. In a work called *The History of the Rise, Progress, and Accomplishment of the Abolition of the African Slave-Trade*, published shortly after the previous speech, Thomas Clarkson argued that slavery debased humanity. "Nothing made a happy slave," he said, "but a degraded man. In proportion as the mind grows callous to its degradation, and all sense of manly pride is lost, the slave feels comfort. In fact, he is no longer a man." And once again readers are asked to imagine a slave conversant with Shakespeare's works, this time one who can quote (or slightly misquote) *Hamlet*:

> If he were to define a man, he would say with Shakspeare,
>
> > "Man is a being holding large discourse,
> > Looking before and after."
>
> But a slave was incapable of looking before and after. He had no motive to do it. He was a mere passive instrument in the hands of others.

Many antislavery activists remembered Shakespeare's greatest black character. John Jamieson's *Sorrows of Slavery* (1789) was one of the first abolitionist poems to invoke Othello:

A real tragedy, unmatch'd in song,
While Afric forces on your sight averse . . .
And many a Desdemona, who not needs
A Shakespeare to describe her woes unjust.

An anonymous author who wrote under the name "Othello" published *Strictures on the Slave Trade, and Their Manner of Treatment in the West-India Islands.* Most powerfully, the actress and antislavery campaigner Fanny Kemble imagined Othello as an American slave and Shakespeare as an abolitionist, offended, just as she was, by racial epithets. "Did I ever tell you," she wrote to a friend, "of my dining in Boston . . . and sitting by Mr. John Quincy Adams, who, talking to me about Desdemona, assured me . . . that he considered all her misfortunes as a very just judgment upon her for having married a 'nigger'?" Her mind immediately turned to ways that Shakespeare's play, now more than 150 years old, could be made perfectly topical: "if some ingenious American actor of the present day . . . could contrive to slip in that opprobrious title, with a true South Carolinian antiabolitionist expression, it might be made quite a point for Iago." And so she imagined the way the newly revitalized lines would resonate in antebellum America: " 'I hate the nigger,' given in proper Charleston or Savannah fashion, I am sure would tell far better than 'I hate the Moor.' Only think . . . what a very new order of interest the whole tragedy might receive."

Sometimes Shakespeare prompted not only disputes but actual riots. The most famous came in New York in spring 1849, when the English actor William Charles Macready played Macbeth at the Astor Place Opera House. Macready was born into a theatrical family, but his parents, hoping he would find a more respectable career, sent him to the prestigious Rugby School. Their strategy was unsuccessful; he and his friends sneaked away to watch plays in nearby Leicester. At the age of fifteen he left Rugby and entered the family business, taking on the parts of Romeo, Hamlet, Richard II,

William Charles Macready took his production of Macbeth *to New York's Astor Place Opera House in 1849, leading to riots in the streets.*

and Hotspur. Soon he was appearing on stage with some of the greatest figures of the age: Sarah Siddons, John Philip Kemble, Dorothy Jordan, and others. Not everyone knew what to make of the young man. The essayist Leigh Hunt called him "one of the plainest and most awkwardly made men that ever trod the stage," and his short, chubby build left many unsure whether he was suited to romantic or heroic parts. But others who saw his early performances, including Edmund Kean, saw something special in him, and over time he became famous as "the Eminent Tragedian." Macready became especially famous for his Macbeth, his favorite among all his dozens of parts. And so, when he traveled to New York in the 1840s, he was glad to play the Scottish usurper at the Astor Place Opera House.

The American actor Edwin Forrest played Macbeth *at the same time as the English actor William Charles Macready.*

The choice of venue was telling. As the critics Michael J. Davey and Duncan Wu explain, "The Astor was the preferred theatre of New York's elite and symbolized for New York's working class everything the Revolution had been fought to purge from American soil: effeminacy, snobbery, aristocracy, decadence, and anti-Yankeeism." Increasingly nationalistic Americans watched in disgust as Shakespeare the popular entertainer was being transformed into Shakespeare the God of High Culture. They didn't like it and were determined to reclaim the Bard as the working man's friend.

While the would-be aristocrat Macready played Macbeth to the bluebloods at the Astor, a more plebeian-friendly American actor, Edwin Forrest, was playing the same role at the Broadway Theater.

There seems to have been some ill will between the two actors even before this rivalry. A late nineteenth-century history of New York noted that Macready treated Forrest poorly when he visited England, so "the New York native American populace . . . determined to punish him for his ungenerous treatment of the American actor." And punish him they did. On 7 May, mobs of Forrest's supporters showed up at the Astor and interrupted Macready's performance with catcalls: "Down with the English hog," they cried, and "Remember how Edwin Forrest was used in London." Before the last act they threw pennies, eggs, fruit, and eventually even furniture at him. Shortly after he was hit by a bottle of foul-smelling liquid, he left the stage and threatened to leave America altogether.

Herman Melville and Washington Irving were among the American literati who signed an open letter published in the New York papers, entreating Macready not to leave the city. He consented, though he should have followed his first instinct. When Macready advertised his next performance at the Astor on 10 May, the Bowery district filled with flyers urging all working men to protest at the "English ARISTOCRATIC Opera House." Two hundred police officers were on hand to provide security, but they were overwhelmed by mobs of ten or fifteen thousand. Several protesters were arrested and other rowdies were driven out of the theatre, but things were even worse on the streets. Soon the whole area around Astor Place was consumed by riot. Some of the more violent members of the crowd began throwing paving stones at the police, who called in two regiments of the National Guard to keep the sides apart. The shout went up: "The military—the military are coming!" The troops fired into the air to break up the mob, but without success; when the crowd charged the militia, the commanders gave the order to "fire low." Counts of the casualties vary: between 17 and 31 dead, and between 30 and 150 wounded.

A contemporary pamphlet described the mayhem, and it's clear that the affair left a deep scar on America's psyche. It was "one of those horrors of civilization, which for a time make the great heart of humanity stop in its beatings . . . It was an evening of dread—and it became a night of horror, which on the morrow, when the awful tragedy became more widely known, settled down upon the city like a funeral pall." A placard produced a day or two after the riot announced:

> AMERICANS!
> AROUSE! THE GREAT CRISIS
> HAS COME!
> Decide now whether English
> ARISTOCRATS!!!
> AND
> FOREIGN RULE!
> shall triumph in this,
> AMERICA'S METROPOLIS,
> or whether her own
> SONS,
> whose fathers once compelled the base-born miscreants to succumb, shall meanly lick the hand that strikes, and allow themselves to be deprived of the liberty of opinion—so dear to every true American heart.

The Astor Place riot was about much more than a performance style; it was really about American identity. The two actors presented two visions of Shakespeare, one British and aristocratic, the other American and proletarian. American nationalists were determined to reclaim the great cultural icon as one of their own. He may have been English, but for these working-class Americans he was above all a democratic playwright, not a supporter of aristocracy.

Neither Straightforwardly Good nor Consciously Evil

The political appropriation of Shakespeare hasn't gone away. Similar uses of Shakespeare's works can be seen today, and though some critics complain that this is an abuse of classic works of literature, it's been going on since the very beginning. It's safe to assume it will go on for a very long time.

When the young Kenneth Branagh released a film of *Henry V* late in 1989, there were comparisons aplenty with Laurence Olivier's film of the same play from 1944. Both were big-budget productions by talented, classically trained actors. And yet, in many ways, the productions could not have been more different. Olivier's film appeared as both Britain and America were at war with the Axis powers. When people in the 1940s watched *Henry V*, they wanted to see a heroic English king leading his people to victory in Europe against overwhelming odds. With this in mind, the British government helped to fund the production. As the critic Terence Hawkes says, it "was conceived in great part as a propaganda exercise preparatory to the D-Day landings in Normandy, aimed at persuading its audience that a determined and united British force could defeat a ruthless enemy in pitched battle on the fields of northern France." As a result, Olivier's Henry was even more virtuous than Shakespeare's. Consider Henry's speech in Shakespeare's play as the king stands at the gates of Harfleur:

> I will not leave the half-achievèd Harfleur
> Till in her ashes she lie burièd.
> The gates of mercy shall be all shut up,
> And the fleshed soldier, rough and hard of heart,
> In liberty of bloody hand shall range
> With conscience wide as hell, mowing like grass

Your fresh fair virgins and your flow'ring infants . . .
What is't to me, when you yourselves are cause,
If your pure maidens fall into the hand
Of hot and forcing violation?

Focusing on English atrocities is unpleasant in a real war, so Olivier removed the scene. The Allies in 1944 did not want to think about their own troops resorting to rape and infanticide. And Shakespeare's play ends with a glimpse of the future in which the Chorus reveals that the whole expedition ultimately amounted to nothing:

Henry the Sixth, in infant bands crowned king
    Of France and England, did this king succeed,
Whose state so many had the managing
    That they lost France and made his England bleed.

Not Olivier's. No one in 1944 wanted to be reminded that war could be pointless.

Branagh, working forty-five years later, lived in a very different era. In the final phases of the cold war, the enemy no longer seemed quite so threatening, and in the aftermath of Vietnam and the Falklands, war no longer seemed quite so heroic. Branagh's vision of Henry's war is therefore much less romantic, his hero less virtuous, his vision of the whole enterprise more cynical. In the introduction to the published screenplay, he described his conception of the play, in which he "tried to realise the qualities of introspection, fear, doubt and anger which I believed the text indicated." Instead of a dignified leader, he saw "an especially young Henry with more than a little of the Hamlet in him." This is what led him to "the idea of abandoning large theatre projection and allowing close-ups and low-level dialogue to draw the audience deep into the human side of this distant medieval world." The close-ups turn the viewers' attention on Henry as a man—a conflicted man, not the spotless hero of Olivier's interpretation. As Branagh wrote in his memoir, the king "is a complicated, doubting, dangerous young professional, neither straightforwardly good nor consciously evil." Thus the audience sees him with tears on his face. The cinematography makes many of these points visually: Olivier's battle scenes are grand and heroic, while Branagh's are gritty and dark. Branagh traded Olivier's bright colors, shiny armor, and pomp for darkness, mud, and confusion. As the critic John Sutherland puts it, "My Lai, not El Alamein, was what came to mind watching the 1989 film." Branagh also restored several scenes that Olivier had eliminated, most notably the threat before Harfleur, which Branagh describes as "a speech which underlines the crueller aspects of an increasingly desperate English military campaign."

Reviewers got the political message, for good or ill. Conservative papers tended to attack Branagh's peacenik version of the play; the right-wing *Daily Express*, for instance, complained about the milksop king "who weeps openly on the battlefield in front of his demoralised troops." But the left-leaning *Guardian* praised "the humanity of the young King . . . He's clearly a pompous and merciless bastard towards his old drinking companions, an ambitious and unforgiving predator towards those who seek to undo him politically, but a man also capable of magnanimity, inspired leadership and the saving grace of youthful self-doubt." And *Henry V* continues to show up in political guise today. Nicholas Hytner's modern-dress production of the play at the National Theatre in 2003, a few months after the American and British invasion of Iraq, prompted the *Observer* to comment, "if there is any topical resonance in Shakespeare's play, it comes from the story of a national leader going to war on highly dubious grounds and who, in the play's best scene on the night before the battle, is put on the spot by one of his common soldiers: 'The king hath a heavy reckoning to make if his cause be not good.' "

Shakespeare, Our Contemporary

Even farther afield, Shakespeare has been used for political ends. In 1956, for instance, Jan Kott presented *Hamlet* in Kraków, Poland, shortly after the Soviet Communist Party's twentieth congress. Even though the text was a fairly straightforward translation, slightly abridged but otherwise unchanged, it was played on the stage in such a way as to leave no doubt that it was a work of protest literature, an assault on Soviet-era repression. When Hamlet said, "Denmark's a prison," the audience burst into spontaneous applause. Kott described the event in *Shakespeare, Our Contemporary*, a groundbreaking book on modern political readings of older literature. Another Polish production, this one of *Macbeth* in Warsaw, made unmistakable allusions to Stalin when Lady Macbeth held up her bloody hands. But Shakespeare could also be used by the other side, as the Soviet Union itself encouraged productions of his plays. In the year the Berlin Wall was completed, the Soviet critic R. M. Samarin argued that Shakespeare saw humankind in Communist terms, as "an active participant in the life of society and not a pitiable creature of God." Even though he died three centuries before the Russian Revolution, the playwright was a born socialist: "Shakespeare's man realizes not only his bond with society but also his responsibility for the state of society." The Soviets, Samarin explained, "cherish his desire to understand the historical essence of his time and to reveal it in his relationship with the past and the future . . . Of all the classical foreign authors in the Soviet repertoire Shakespeare is still the most popular dramatist."

So which side did the real Shakespeare support? What would the man from Stratford think about all the positions that have been attributed to him? What if it were possible to rouse him from the sleep of death—ignoring the warning on his tombstone, "curst bee hee that moves my bones"—and ask him? Would he have sided with the royalists or the parliamentarians? What would he have made of the French Revolution? Would he have favored slavery or abolition? What would he think about women's education, or communism, or the welfare state, or colonialism, or the invasion of Iraq? The fact is that no one knows, even though plenty of people have offered their speculations as fact. Many of these questions would have made no sense to Shakespeare, whose worldview probably had no categories for things like human rights or secular humanism. And many of our age's cherished beliefs—the value of democratic government, equal rights for women—were widely condemned at the end of the sixteenth century and the beginning of the seventeenth. If Shakespeare's opinions were anything like those of most of his contemporaries, he would have found many of our principles abhorrent.

But many people can't bring themselves to believe that his opinions were anything like those of most of his contemporaries. It's important that they be allowed to imagine him somehow transcending his age and agreeing with them. Convinced that Shakespeare is one of us, we play games of dueling quotations, with everyone trying to prove that the world's greatest literary genius is on their side. This remarkable adaptability led Samuel Taylor Coleridge to call him "myriad-minded," and it has led many others to talk about his "universal" mind. Just as in war both armies claim that God is on their side, so in reading or watching Shakespeare everyone wants to believe the Bard is on their side.

CHAPTER 6

Domesticating Shakespeare

BY 1800 SHAKESPEARE WAS SECURE in his position at the head of the English literary pantheon. To admit to disliking him was to admit to having no taste. What were once seen as "flaws" now came to be tolerated, even celebrated. Yes, he violated the dramatic unities—but mindless adherence to the rules was beneath the great English genius. Yes, he got many historical and geographic details wrong—but only pedants cared about such things. Yes, his poetic meter was sometimes irregular—but the Bard was too brilliant to count syllables on his fingers. His sprawling plots, his anachronisms, his puns—all these things became signs not of his weakness but of his strength.

One kind of vice, though, was harder to transform into a virtue, and that was his bawdry. Swearing abounds: oaths like *zounds* (from "God's wounds"), *'sblood* (God's blood), and *byr'lady* (by our Lady, that is, Mary) are found in almost every play. Worse still, his work is bristling with scatological humor, cross-dressing, obscenity, and sex—plenty of sex. Maybe that sort of thing was acceptable to the drunken rowdies in Shakespeare's original audience, but it certainly wouldn't do in a refined modern age. Something had to be done.

Foul-Mouthed Horndog

Look, for instance, at Hamlet's jokes with his old friends Rosencrantz and Guildenstern about being in the private parts of Lady Luck:

> GUILDENSTERN: On Fortune's cap we are not the very button.
>
> HAMLET: Nor the soles of her shoe?
>
> ROSENCRANTZ: Neither, my lord.
>
> HAMLET: Then you live about her waist, or in the middle of her favour?
>
> GUILDENSTERN: Faith, her privates we.
>
> HAMLET: In the secret parts of Fortune? O, most true, she is a strumpet.

Or consider the way Iago rudely informs Brabanzio that his daughter, Desdemona, has eloped with the Moor Othello:

> Even now, now, very now, an old black ram
> Is tupping your white ewe. Arise, arise!
> Awake the snorting citizens with the bell,
> Or else the devil will make a grandsire of you . . .
> Your daughter and the Moor are now making the beast with two backs.

And it's hard to find a comedy in which adultery doesn't feature somewhere. As Samuel Johnson wrote in his edition of Shakespeare, "There is no image which our authour appears so fond of as that of a cuckold's horns. Scarcely a light character is introduced that does not endeavour to produce merriment by some allusion to horned husbands."

The *Weekly World News*—in what may be the truest words ever printed in that down-market tabloid famous for headlines like MUMMY'S CURSE SANK THE TITANIC and AIDS IS KILLING THE WORLD'S VAMPIRES—reports in a short piece on Shakespeare that "researchers say the bawdy bard was a foul-mouthed horndog obsessed with sex and bodily functions, whose plays were packed with obscenity and racy themes!" "Foul-mouthed horndog" may not be the way most researchers would choose to put it, but the sentiment is accurate enough.

Shakespeare wasn't alone among his contemporaries in enjoying coarse humor. The profanity of the early drama was one of the things that irritated the Puritans and led them to close the theatres. Taking the Lord's name in vain was common; dirty puns were a perennial favorite; there were endless references to cross-dressing and adultery. And some plays went beyond the merely suggestive. In *Edward II*, Christopher Marlowe shows the brutal manner of the king's death: he screams in agony as a red-hot poker is thrust into his rectum. ("I fear me," says one of his murderers, "that this cry will raise the town.") John Webster, whose career was taking off as Shakespeare's was winding down, had a remarkable taste for the distasteful, especially in his tragedies *The White Devil* and *The Duchess of Malfi*. In the latter are depictions of incestuous desire, lustful cardinals, threatened rape, dancing madmen, revenge, and murder. Family-friendly it was not.

It's no surprise, then, that when the Puritans took over the Parliament, they were determined to keep such nastiness off the public stage. But when they lost power with the Restoration of 1660 and the theatres were reopened, naughty humor again came into vogue. Now the incest and the gore were largely gone—Webster and his ilk were nearly forgotten—but this made the theatre only slightly more acceptable to the sterner moralists of the day. Many of the best original plays of the late seventeenth century, after all, are sex comedies, filled with jokes about cuckolding and casual sex. In William Wycherley's play of 1675, *The Country Wife*, for instance, the young rake Horner pretends a treatment for venereal disease has rendered him impotent so that he can make his way, unsuspected, into the company of married women. And if some of the sexual references in the Restoration seem tame to modern eyes, the more libertine excesses of the age can be offensive even today. John Wilmot, the second Earl of Rochester, could be downright filthy, with poems about dildos, sodomy, venereal disease, and premature ejaculation described in the frankest language imaginable. Many of them are too obscene to appear in modern anthologies for students.

Although the Puritans lost political power in the Restoration, they never entirely went away, and they were no happier with this new drama than they had been with Shakespeare three quarters of a century earlier. Their complaints continued. As Jeremy Collier objected in *A Short View of the Immorality and Profaneness of the English Stage* (1698)—at nearly three hundred closely printed pages, the view wasn't really so short—"One Instance of Impropriety in *Manners* both Poetical and Moral, is their making Women, and Women of Quality talk Smuttily." And the way immoral characters tended to go unpunished bothered him: "To treat *Honour*, and *Infamy* alike, is an *injury* to *Virtue*, and a sort of *Levelling* in *Morality*." For Collier, violations of poetic justice are serious business: "I have no *Ceremony* for *Debauchery*. For to *Compliment Vice*, is but one *Remove* from *worshipping* the *Devil*."

Few readers went as far as Collier, and most probably saw some difference between letting adultery go unpunished in a play and actual Satan worship. But Collier was far from alone. In the same year, George Ridpath reminded his readers "That the wise Roman Senate approv'd the Divorce which Sempronius Sophus gave to his Wife for no other Reason, but that she resorted to the

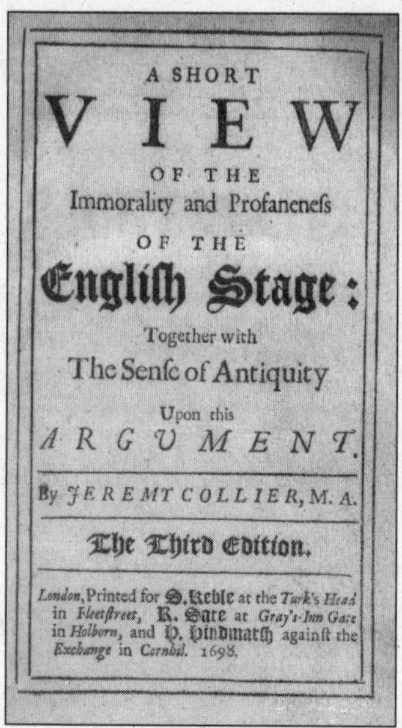

A SHORT

VIEW

OF THE

Immorality and Profaneneſs

OF THE

English Stage:

Together with

The Senſe of Antiquity

Upon this

ARGUMENT.

By *JEREMY COLLIER*, M. A.

The Third Edition.

London, Printed for S. Keble at the *Turk's Head* in *Fleetſtreet*, R. Sare at *Gray's-Inn Gate* in *Holborn*, and H. Hindmarsh againſt the *Exchange* in *Cornhil.* 1698.

At the end of the seventeenth century, Jeremy Collier objected to the indecency of stage plays in A Short View of the Immorality and Profaneness of the English Stage.

Cirques and Playhouses without his Consent; the very sight of which might make her an Adultress." Noting that the theatre's "*influence upon the Morals of the Audience must needs be dangerous,*" he hoped that "our *English Senators* will be as careful of the *Chastity* of the English Ladies, as the Antient Roman Senators were of theirs," and ban drama altogether. Even common people were becoming less interested in the debauchery of the contemporary theatre. It didn't help that royal patronage of the drama declined—Charles II adored and encouraged the theatre from 1660 into the 1680s, but when William and Mary took over in 1689, they wanted little to do with it—and middle-class moralizing increasingly took the place of witty libertinism. The age took pride in its refinement and politeness. A few actors were even indicted for speaking blasphemous lines. And so, as the seventeenth century turned into the eighteenth, the vogue for dirty jokes went into decline. In the mischievous formulation of the critic Gary Taylor, "plays went where the playgoers wanted to go, from sexually erect to morally upright." Of course there were always those who appreciated earthy humor, and the shift from bawdy to "sentimental" comedies shouldn't be overstated. But around 1700 there was an unmistakable move away from promiscuity on the stage. And this meant not only the decline of the kind of sexual frankness that was found in much Restoration comedy, but also a new attitude toward the racier passages in Shakespeare's works.

Expressions Improper to Be Pronounced

Although the most significant attempts to make Shakespeare safe for innocent eyes took place in the nineteenth century, there had been tentative steps in that direction long before. An unauthorized reprint of the poems from 1640 notoriously changed the pronouns in some of the sonnets; where the originals suggested a love between two men, the new version removed all hints of homoeroticism. In Sonnet 101, for instance, Shakespeare wrote, "Excuse not silence so, for't lies in thee / To make him much outlive a gilded tomb": in the version of 1640, *him* becomes *her*. And in Sonnet 108, the address to the "sweet boy" is traded for the safer "sweet-love." Similar things happened in the plays. An English college in Valladolid, Spain, owned a copy of the Second Folio; in the 1640s an English Jesuit working for the Spanish Inquisition used ink to blot many offensive passages and even razored the whole of *Measure for Measure* out of the college's copy. Other forms of censorship were less physical but just as clear in their intentions, and over time more and more objectionable passages were dropped from the adaptations of the plays.

Consider George Colman the Elder, a popular playwright who adapted *King Lear* in 1768. Even though he took pride in undoing Nahum Tate's more radical changes and boasted of his respect for the original text, he still omitted the more indecent passages. The opening scene of *Lear*, for instance, includes a number of ribald puns. When Kent asks Gloucester whether Edmund is his son, Gloucester replies cryptically: "His breeding, sir, hath been at my charge. I have so often blushed to acknowledge him that now I am brazed to't." Kent, confused, says, "I cannot conceive you"—that is, "understand you." Gloucester picks up on the word *conceive*: "Sir, this young fellow's mother could, whereupon she grew round-wombed and had indeed, sir, a son for her cradle ere she had a husband for her bed." And in act 4, Lear raves obscenely, imagining himself dispensing royal pardons: "I pardon that man's life. What was thy cause? / Adultery? Thou shalt not die. Die for adultery!" After all, "the wren goes to 't, and the small gilded fly / Does lecher in my sight. Let copulation thrive!" Remember, "Gloucester's bastard son / Was kinder to his father than my daughters / Got 'tween the lawful sheets." Even though Colman insisted he was more Shakespearean than his predecessor in revising Lear—"I have now endeavoured to purge the tragedy of Lear of the alloy of Tate"—he didn't hesitate to use the scissors when confronted with salacious scenes like these. In his edition, they disappear without a trace. Gloucester's mother never "grew round-wombed," and copulation has no chance to thrive. This kind of raciness, Colman thought, might have appealed to the unrefined groundlings of Shakespeare's day, but polite moderns could comfortably do without.

Similar squeamishness can be found in many of the eighteenth century's "improvements," but the most famous attempt to tame Shakespeare came early in the nineteenth century. As Noel Perrin argues in his history of attempts to clean up offensive literature, "Books had been expurgated during most of the eighteenth century, . . . but it had been the obscure action of a minority. Now the majority got involved." And the central figure in the transition was someone whose name was largely unknown until well into the twentieth century, Henrietta Maria Bowdler.

The Bowdler household was marked by deep moral seriousness. In 1843 one of Henrietta Maria's brothers recollected the family's early exposure to Shakespeare's works, as their father read to them aloud: "In the perfection of reading," he said, "few men were equal to my father; and such was his good taste, his delicacy, and his prompt discretion, that his family listened with delight . . . without knowing that those matchless tragedies contained words and expressions improper to be pronounced." Remembering this habit of her beloved papa, Henrietta Maria, known to her family as Harriet, decided to perform the same service for the reading public at large. Her four-volume set, *The Family Shakespeare*, appeared in 1807. It contained twenty of the thirty-six recognized plays, not adapted in the way Tate's *Lear* or Valpy's *King John* was adapted, but still not quite as Shakespeare wrote them. "It must . . . be acknowledged, by his warmest admirers," Bowdler wrote, "that some defects are to be found in the writings of our immortal bard . . . Many words and expressions occur which are of so indecent a nature as to render it highly desirable that they should be erased." And erase she did. Bowdler systematically removed all the passages unsuitable to refined sensibilities, and about 10 percent of each play was tossed into the waste bin.

No editor's name appeared on *The Family Shakespeare*, probably because the expurgation was the work of a lady. Miss Bowdler was already a successful author, but she kept her name off her title page and published her work anonymously. It would have been shocking for an unmarried woman even to recognize which scenes were improper, let alone to spend time looking for them. Two years later, though, the world learned the name of the editor of *The Family Shakespeare*: not Harriet, but her brother Thomas. Their secret remained safe for a long time. For more than a century and a half, when the world thought of Bowdler, it thought only of Thomas.

Thomas Bowdler had worked as a medical doctor, but his discomfort at the sight of blood drove him from the profession. Still, he was a successful society figure. He was one of the best chess players in England, and he also moved in literary circles; he knew Elizabeth Montagu, for instance, one of the most distinguished female intellectuals in England and the author of *An Essay on the Writings and Genius of Shakespear*. He was also active in many charities and benevolent associations, working to improve conditions in hospitals and prisons. In this respect he was a creature of his day; moral improvement was in the air. Thomas was a member of the Proclamation Society, inspired by George III's proclamation of 1787, *For the Encouragement of Piety and Virtue and for Preventing and Punishing of Vice, Profaneness and Immorality*. It tried to enforce laws against gambling on Sunday, excessive drinking, and blasphemy and swearing. After his sister had made her pass through Shakespeare's plays, he took the task on himself, trying to eliminate as much vice, profaneness, and immorality as he could.

Supreme Modesty!

We sometimes refer to this sort of prudishness as "Victorian" but, while *The Family Shakespeare* remained popular through the Victorian era, it first appeared a dozen years before Queen Victoria was born, and both Bowdlers were dead before she took the throne in 1837. It's actually a product of the Romantic period leading into the Regency, an era known for its melodramatic tortured souls and for the rakish young bucks depicted in the cartoons of George Cruikshank and Thomas Rowlandson, not for moral squeamishness. But the late eighteenth century saw increasing concern with domesticity, as "female delicacy" became ever more important.

Women in the 1790s could buy many stout volumes like *The Lady's Preceptor; or, A Series of Instructive and Pleasing Exercises in Reading, for the Particular Use of Females*, where they would find exhortations like this: "Supreme modesty! Supreme pleasure of love! How many charms does a woman lose, when she loses thee!" And this was serious business, for the survival of the nation depended on female chastity, modesty, and delicacy. In 1790 the educational theorist John Adams worried about the "many evils attending the loss of virtue in women," warning that "a general contamination of their morals" would amount to "one of the greatest misfortunes that can befal a state, as in time it destroys almost every public virtue of the men." History leaves no doubt: "all wise legislators have strictly enforced upon the sex a particular purity of manners."

Fortunately, Shakespeare was a great instructor in this domestic morality. In *The Morality of Shakespeare's Drama Illustrated* (1775), Elizabeth Griffith extracted lessons from all the plays, for the playwright teaches us about "those moral duties which are the truest source of mortal bliss—domestic ties, offices, and obligations." *A Midsummer Night's Dream*, for instance, shows us "the duty of children to their parents"; *As You Like It* gives "a very proper hint . . . to women, not to deviate from the prescribed rules and decorums of their sex"; and in *Twelfth Night* "There are some good rules and reflections . . . upon that principal and interesting event of life, our marriage." Even the raunchy *Measure for Measure* "gives an admirable lesson on the nature of *contrition* . . . and, at the same time, expresses a just but severe sentence against a woman's failure in the point of chastity."

Too often, though, Shakespeare's practice didn't live up to his theory, and his works had to be handled with care. All books, in fact, had to be handled with care, especially by the fair sex.

Women were supposed to be especially subject to being unduly influenced by their reading, and novels were especially dangerous. In 1800 Samuel Whyte spelled out "a method of teaching young ladies to read well," warning them to steer clear of anything that might be injurious to morality. "In this way, ladies! you would be in your proper sphere," he wrote. "Nature made you of a softer clay, of a more delicate mould than ours . . . Let the part of man be, to guide the more vigorous understanding. Man, is formed for public, as well as for private life; woman, for private life only."

This spirit had been expressed in literary expurgation before. Around 1780 there appeared an anonymous book called *The Delicate Jester; or, Wit and Humour Divested of Ribaldry*, a seventy-page joke book "put together with such particular Care as not to offend the Ears of Chastity, or infringe on the Rules of Morality, Decency and good Manners." The book, boasted the editor, was "worthy the Sanction of sober Families, who cannot be too watchful over the private Amusements of their Children." Other works came out with a similar attention to protecting decency and good manners, but the project began on a new scale when *The Family Shakespeare* appeared.

Correct for Family-Reading

The first edition of *The Family Shakespeare* was the work of Henrietta Maria Bowdler alone, but later the brother-and-sister team worked together, expanding the set to include all the plays. Thomas took primary responsibility for the sixteen plays omitted from the first edition, and he made revisions to Harriet's work on the others. The new version of 1818 was *The Family Shakspeare* (marked by a change in the spelling of the Bard's name), and, after a slow start, it became one of the most successful Shakespearean publications of the nineteenth century.

Shakespeare, W.

THE

FAMILY SHAKSPEARE,

In Ten Volumes;

IN WHICH
NOTHING IS ADDED TO THE ORIGINAL TEXT;
BUT THOSE WORDS AND EXPRESSIONS
ARE OMITTED WHICH CANNOT WITH PROPRIETY
BE READ ALOUD IN A FAMILY.

BY

THOMAS BOWDLER, Esq. F.R.S. & S.A.

Only Thomas Bowdler's name appeared on the second edition of The Family Shakspeare, *even though much of the work was done by his sister, Henrietta Maria.*

Sex was the Bowdlers' biggest problem. Here are some examples of the expurgators in action. In *Troilus and Cressida*, the repugnant Thersites speaks of "the Neapolitan bone-ache" (syphilis); in *Measure for Measure*, Lucio suggests someone might be executed for "the rebellion of a codpiece" (the codpiece covered the male genitals); in *Henry V*, Pistol boasts that his "cock is up" (supposedly a reference to the hammer on his gun) "and flashing fire will follow"—there is no room for such smut in *The Family Shakspeare*, so out it goes. Not every change, though, could be made quite so easily. It wasn't always enough to cut words or even a few lines; some whole scenes needed significant trimming. Colman removed a few passages about adultery from *King Lear* in 1768; of course they were also excised from the Bowdlers' text fifty years later. Even worse are the lines that follow "Let copulation thrive," Lear's remarkable outburst of disgust at female sexuality:

> Down from the waist
> They're Centaurs, though women all above.
> But to the girdle do the gods inherit;
> Beneath is all the fiend's. There's hell, there's darkness,
> There's the sulphurous pit, burning, scalding, stench,
> consumption. Fie, fie, fie; pah, pah!

Colman had allowed that to stand, but there's no trace of it in Bowdler. Another bawdy passage in *The Taming of the Shrew* also disappears, one of the first exchanges between Katherine and Petruccio:

> PETRUCCIO: Come, come, you wasp, i'faith you are too angry.
>
> KATHERINE: If I be waspish, best beware my sting.
>
> PETRUCCIO: My remedy is then to pluck it out.
>
> KATHERINE: Ay, if the fool could find it where it lies.
>
> PETRUCCIO: Who knows not where a wasp does wear his sting?
> In his tail.
>
> KATHERINE: In his tongue.
>
> PETRUCCIO: Whose tongue?
>
> KATHERINE: Yours, if you talk of tales, and so farewell.
>
> PETRUCCIO: What, with my tongue in your tail?

Tongues in tails?—not in *The Family Shakspeare*. The whole passage is gone.

Some cuts are even more extensive than that. The opening of *Romeo and Juliet*, where two servants of the Capulets make a series of bawdy jokes, is characteristic of Shakespeare's racy style. "I will take the wall of any man or maid of Montague's," boasts Sampson, referring to the practice that allowed women and social superiors to walk on the pavements close to the walls, avoiding the dirt in the streets. "That shows thee a weak slave," replies his friend Gregory, invoking an old proverb: "the weakest goes to the wall." "'Tis true," answers Sampson, relishing the opportunity for a dirty joke, "and therefore women, being the weaker vessels, are ever thrust to the wall; therefore I will push Montague's men from the wall, and thrust his maids to the wall." Even when Gregory reminds him that "The quarrel is between our masters, and us their men," Sampson boasts, "I will show myself a tyrant: when I have fought with the men I will be civil with the maids—I will cut off their heads." Gregory asks for a clarification: "The heads of the maids?" "Ay, the heads of the maids," says Sampson, adding, with a sneer, "or their maidenheads, take it in what sense thou wilt." Gregory, now getting into the spirit of the naughty repartee, remarks that "They must take it in sense that feel it." "Me they shall feel," boasts Sampson, "while I am able to stand, and 'tis known I am a pretty piece of flesh." But as their enemies draw near, Gregory exchanges a sex metaphor for a military one: "Draw thy tool," he says, prompting Sampson to continue the obscene joke: "My naked weapon is out."

The jokes about taking maidens' virginity; the priapic puns about being "able to stand"; the leering reference to how the women will "feel it"; the use of *tool* as a euphemism for *penis*, which dates at least back to 1553—all of it probably acted in Shakespeare's day with the requisite pelvic thrusts and crotch grabbing—these were the sorts of thing no nineteenth-century father could read to a daughter; no husband could watch such a scene in the presence of his wife without blushing to the tips of his ears. When Harriet published her first version of the expurgated plays, she simply omitted *Romeo and Juliet*, but the expanded version contained the entire canon. So here is what the Bowdlers made of the entire passage:

SAMPSON: I will take the wall of any man or maid of Montague's.

GREGORY: That shows thee a weak slave, for the weakest goes to the wall.
The quarrel is between our masters, and us their men.

SAMPSON: 'Tis all one. I will show myself a tyrant.

GREGORY: Draw thy sword, here comes of the house of Montagues.

SAMPSON: My naked weapon is out.

The speech is less than half its original length, and all the humor—thrusting maids to the wall, taking their maidenheads, able to stand, a pretty piece of flesh, draw thy tool—is gone. The only wonder is that Sampson's "naked weapon" survived the cutting process.

Sometimes the Bowdlers' cuts left Shakespeare's text little more than nonsense. Here, for example, is the passage in *Hamlet* right before the famous "mousetrap," as Hamlet jokes with Ophelia:

GERTRUDE: Come hither, my good Hamlet. Sit by me.

HAMLET: No, good-mother, here's mettle more attractive. [*He sits by* OPHELIA.]

POLONIUS: O ho, do you mark that?

HAMLET: Lady, shall I lie in your lap?

OPHELIA: No, my lord.

HAMLET: I mean my head upon your lap?

OPHELIA: Ay, my lord.

HAMLET: Do you think I meant country matters?

OPHELIA: I think nothing, my lord.

HAMLET: That's a fair thought to lie between maids' legs.

OPHELIA: What is, my lord?

HAMLET: No thing.

OPHELIA: You are merry, my lord.

Some of the dirty references, like lying between maids' legs, are obvious enough to modern sensibilities; others would have been clearer to Shakespeare's original audience. The actor playing Hamlet probably put a hard accent on the first syllable of the word *country*, for example, and it helps to know that in the seventeenth century *nothing* was a common term for the female genitals. It's no wonder that the Bowdlers were convinced they couldn't leave this text as it was.

Here's what they made of it:

GERTRUDE: Come hither, my good Hamlet, sit by me.

HAMLET: No, good mother, here's metal more attractive. [*Lying down at* OPHELIA'*s feet.*]

POLONIUS: O ho! do you mark that?

OPHELIA: You are merry, my lord.

The "improvements" to this passage make it nonsensical; nothing Hamlet says in this version would lead Ophelia to say "You are merry, my lord." He's also decently at her feet and nowhere near her lap.

The plot of *Othello* revolves around Desdemona's supposed infidelity with Cassio, and the motivation of the murder depends on Othello's jealousy at the thought that the two of them are having an affair. Iago, a master of psychological manipulation, fills Othello with graphic thoughts of his wife in bed with another man, and the audience can see his mind beginning to become unhinged with suspicion. Othello asks what Cassio has said about Desdemona:

> IAGO: Faith, that he did—I know not what he did.
>
> OTHELLO: What, what?
>
> IAGO: Lie—
>
> OTHELLO: With her?
>
> IAGO: With her, on her, what you will.
>
> OTHELLO: Lie with her? Lie on her? We say "lie on her"
> when they belie her. Lie with her? 'Swounds,
> that's fulsome! Handkerchief—confessions—
> handkerchief. To confess and be hanged for
> his labour. First to be hanged and then to
> confess! I tremble at it.

Not so in the Bowdlers' version:

> IAGO: 'Faith, that he did—I know not what he did.
>
> OTHELLO: What? what?—confessions,—handkerchief.—
> I tremble at it.

It wasn't only sex that bothered the Bowdlers; impiety was also a serious concern. Their edition includes an explanation about *Love's Labour's Lost*: "an allusion is made (very improperly) to one of the most serious and awful passages in the New Testament"—this is where Holofernes dresses as Judas Maccabeus, the Old Testament warrior, and Dumain jokes about his being Judas Iscariot, the "kissing traitor" who betrayed Jesus. The betrayal of the Savior is no laughing matter, so the lines are nixed. In the same play, "The most Sacred Word in our language"—that is, *God*—"is omitted in several instances, in which it appeared as a mere expletive; and it is changed into the word Heaven, in a still greater number, where the occasion of using it did not appear sufficiently serious to justify its employment." The "mere expletive" isn't as juicy as one might expect—no "God damn it" or even an "Oh God," but merely the comparatively tame "God knows," "God help me," and even the blessing "God save you." Tame, perhaps, today, but not to the Bowdlers; their characters have to be helped and saved by "heaven" if they're to be helped or saved at all. Religion is a solemn matter and shouldn't be mixed with humor.

Bodily functions also have to go. In *Twelfth Night*, Malvolio hints at both the female genitalia and urination when he examines the handwriting in a letter supposedly from Olivia: "These be her very c's, her u's, and her t's, and thus makes she her great P's." But Olivia makes no "great P's" in the Bowdlers' text: "These be her very *P*'s her *U*'s and her *T*'s, and thus makes she her great *C*'s." And when the Clown in *Othello* makes fart jokes—talking about "wind instruments" as he puns on *tale* and *tail*—the whole passage is omitted from *The Family Shakspeare*. Ditto Iago's cynical comment about "clyster-pipes"—enemas—in *Othello*, another passage that the Bowdlers were content to omit.

Service to Shakespeare

There were arguments over the sanitized Shakespeare even while the book was current. In 1821 *Blackwood's Magazine* published a critique of the whole venture. Another magazine, the *British Critic*, leveled a more serious attack, and this one prompted a response from Thomas Bowdler. In *A Letter to the Editor of the British Critic*, a pamphlet of forty pages, Bowdler defended his enterprise in detail.

The *British Critic* reviewer insisted that, of all the poets he knew, Shakespeare was "precisely that one of whom you can least afford to lose one original *iota*, a single word, a very syllable." Bowdler, on the other hand, was shocked—shocked—that anyone would want to keep Shakespeare's scandalous passages intact. The reviewer said that there weren't many passages in the plays that were objectionable. If he really believed that, said Bowdler, he must "have been very imperfectly acquainted with Shakspeare." For Bowdler, Shakespeare "is of all poets, precisely that one in respect to whose writings, a cautious and delicate correction is the most necessary and the most applicable." The *British Critic* writer argued that Hamlet's joke about "country matters" is innocent, but Bowdler was convinced he couldn't be serious: "I call on him to lay his hand on his heart," wrote Bowdler, "and declare, whether he believes that Hamlet in that speech alludes to rural occupations, to the concerns of his native land, or to what is not to be named? The Reviewer must not—will not answer the question."

All this public attention, even the attacks, caused sales to take off. The cleaned-up versions of Shakespeare's plays were among the most popular texts of the nineteenth century, and critics generally approved; they actually thought the plays felt more "natural" without the bawdy bits. One reviewer wrote in 1821 that "it is better, every way, that what cannot be spoken, and ought not to have been written, should now cease to be printed." The poet Algernon

Charles Swinburne was all in favor: "More nauseous and foolish cant was never chattered than that which would deride the memory or depreciate the merits of Bowdler. No man ever did better service to Shakespeare." And in an essay in the *Edinburgh Review*, Lord Jeffrey explained that Bowdler had "only effaced those gross indecencies which every one must have felt as blemishes, and by the removal of which no imaginable excellence can be affected." This "every one" apparently included the playwright himself, who was "by far the purest of the dramatists of his own or the succeeding age,—and has resisted, in a great degree, the corrupting example of his contemporaries." Jeffrey compared Shakespeare to the playwrights of the late seventeenth century, in whom "the indecency belongs not to the jest, but to the character and action." In Shakespeare, on the other hand, the indecency can be lifted out easily, as if it had been grudgingly added to appease the groundlings: it is "easy to extirpate the offensive expressions of our great poet, without any injury to the context, or any visible scar or blank in the composition." Jeffrey concluded that "the work generally appears more natural and harmonious without them." Shakespeare, that is to say, is even more Shakespearean without the bawdry. For some readers even these expurgated editions didn't go far enough. Many Victorian copies of *The Family Shakspeare* survive with lines crossed out; readers found it necessary to make their own cuts.

Thomas Bowdler died in 1825 and his sister followed him to the grave five years later, but their legacy lived on. The verb *to bowdlerize* was coined in 1836, and bowdlerization became very popular in the nineteenth century, with at least fifty abridged editions of Shakespeare in print by 1900. Others did the same thing to other works. Francis Turner Palgrave, editor of *The Golden Treasury*, issued an edition of Shakespeare's *Sonnets* but found a few of the poems had "a warmth of coloring unsuited for the larger audience," so he removed them. And many other literary classics have been cleaned up. Those who know Jonathan Swift's *Gulliver's Travels* as a children's book will be surprised to hear that Gulliver is expelled from Lilliput for putting out a palace fire by urinating on it, or that the Yahoos, who lick one another's "posteriors," are cured of their diseases with "a mixture of their own Dung and Urine forcibly put down the Yahoo's Throat." Chaucer's raunchy humor has often been toned down, both in Middle English editions and in modern translations. Many Victorian editors silently changed lines like "This Nicholas anon leet fle a fart, / As greet as it had been a thonder-dent" and "A shiten shepherde and a clene sheep." Even in the late twentieth century, one edition renders Chaucer's "And prively he caughte hire by the queynte" as "And privily he grabbed her where he shouldn't"; another, slightly more risqué, settles for "And unperceived he caught her by the puss." But both are euphemisms: Chaucer's *queynte* is best rendered as a four-letter word that retains the *u*, the *n*, and the *t* of the Middle English.

It would seem that if one book should be treated like Scripture, it would be Scripture, but even the Bible hasn't escaped bowdlerization. Passages like Noah's drunkenness and nakedness (Genesis 9:20–22), Lot's seduction by his daughters (Genesis 19:31–36), Onan's "spilling his seed on the ground" (Genesis 38:9), and the erotic poetry of the Song of Songs—all of this was sometimes too much for some nineteenth-century readers. The King James Version refers to men who "eat their own dung, and drink their own piss" (2 Kings 18:27) and women who "committed whoredoms in their youth: there were their breasts pressed, and there they bruised the teats of their virginity" (Ezekiel 23:3). It may be the word of God, but apparently He sometimes forgot that ladies might be present. If Shakespeare could benefit from judicious trimming, so too could the Lord. There were several nineteenth-century attempts to polish the translations or to hide the racier bits among the genealogies and other slow-moving passages.

The heyday of bowdlerization was the mid- and late nineteenth century, the height of the Victorian era. By the 1880s, though, there was the beginning of a reaction against it. The American poet Walt Whitman, writing in 1888, had unkind words for the castrated books so popular with his contemporaries. "Damn the expurgated books!" he said. "I say damn 'em. The dirtiest book in all the world is an expurgated book." By the 1920s bowdlerization, once the rule, had become the exception. But it never entirely disappeared. As recently as June 2002 the New York State Board of Regents sanitized some of the stories it required high school students to read, cutting not only the nudity and profanity but even racially sensitive passages like Annie Dillard's reference to "Negro part of town" and Isaac Bashevis Singer's references to "Jews" and "Gentiles." Even words like *fat* have been replaced with *heavy* on the Regents Exam reading list, because the State Education Department's guidelines say that test materials shouldn't "degrade people on the basis of physical appearance." And today, two centuries after the Bowdlers, some school editions of Shakespeare are direct descendants of *The Family Shakspeare*, with some of the same passages removed.

Little Master Tommy and Pretty Miss Polly

Having made Shakespeare suitable for men and women, all that remained was children—a project that happened at the same time as the Bowdlers' edition and under similar conditions. Like *The Family Shakespeare*, *Tales from Shakespear* was first published in 1807; it was also mostly the work of a woman who published under the name of her brother. It was one of the first attempts to make the great English poet accessible to young readers, and it became one of the enduring classics of children's literature, still widely read two centuries after its first appearance. But it was also the work of one of the most troubled minds of early nineteenth-century London: a lunatic and a murderer.

Tales from Shakespear appeared in the midst of a major surge in children's publishing. Schoolbooks had been around for a long time, but not books written specifically for the pleasure of young people. In Shakespeare's day there were very few: conduct books like *A Lytell Booke of Good Manners for Chyldren*, translations of Aesop's fables, homegrown adventure stories like *A Lytell Geste of Robin Hode*, the annual sermons that marked the Massacre of the Innocents described in the book of Matthew, and so on. The Puritans published many moral tales in the seventeenth century, sober works with titles like *A Token for Children: Being an Exact Account of the Conversion, Holy and Exemplary Lives, and Joyful Deaths of Several Young Children*. But children's deaths, however joyful, don't strike modern readers as particularly appealing stuff.

Things began to change shortly after 1700. In 1729 the first English versions of "Little Red Riding-hood," "The Sleeping Beauty in the Wood," and "Cinderella, or the Little Glass Slipper" appeared. But a new era in children's publishing began in 1744, when John Newbery published *The Little Pretty Pocket Book*. Newbery explained that it was "intended for the instruction and amusement of little Master Tommy and pretty Miss Polly." It even came with a marketing tie-in: it was sold with a ball for boys and a pincushion for girls. Newbery's venture into the world of children's publishing led to an explosion of reading material for young people. Over the next few decades Newbery's publishing house developed a line of children's books, commissioning some of the early classics, including *The History of Little Goody Two-Shoes*.

In Newbery's wake came the first great age of children's publishing in English. The timing was significant, for people were rethinking what it meant to be young, and childhood came to be valued, even romanticized. As John Rowe Townsend, a historian of children's publishing, puts it, "Before there could be children's books, there had to be children—children, that is, who were accepted as beings with their own particular needs and interests, not merely as miniature men and women." Many social historians argue that before the late eighteenth century, children were viewed as imperfect adults with empty minds, waiting to be filled with knowledge as they matured. But attitudes were changing. Jean-Jacques Rousseau's celebration of primitive simplicity—what came to be called the "noble savage"—led people to think of civilization as a corrupting influence, and his educational treatise *Emile* regretted that teachers "always seek for the *man* in the *child*, without reflecting what he is before he grows up to manhood." No longer were children imperfect adults; instead adults came to be seen as corrupted children. What was once condemned as ignorance was now celebrated as innocence.

As children became more prominent in the culture, publishers began to see them as a source of income, and many followed Newbery by specializing in children's literature. Recognizing the market potential, a husband-and-wife team came together in 1805 to open their own bookshop and to start their own line of children's books. Some of the works in the Juvenile Library were written by William Godwin, notorious in his own day as an anarchist political philosopher and the widower of the feminist Mary Wollstonecraft, but known today as the father of Mary Wollstonecraft Shelley. It was his second wife, Mary Jane Godwin, who ran the business. She thought children might benefit from exposure to the works of Shakespeare, and decided to commission a version of his works for young readers.

There had been a few earlier attempts to introduce young people to Shakespeare. A children's spelling book from 1778 included a selection of speeches from Shakespeare: " 'tis hoped they will be useful and agreeable to youth, as it will serve to give a Variety to their Taste, and to bring them acquainted with the higher and more poetical Style of their own Language." A collection of children's poems published in 1785 called *Mother Goose's Melody; or, Sonnets for the Cradle* also included a selection of poems by "that sweet songster and nurse of wit and humour, Master William Shakespeare." In 1800 *The British Nepos; or, Mirror of Youth*, a collection of

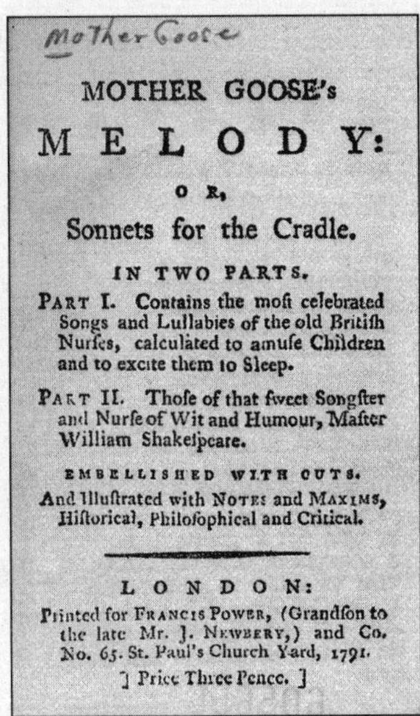

Mother Goose

MOTHER GOOSE's

MELODY:

OR,

Sonnets for the Cradle.

IN TWO PARTS.

PART I. Contains the moſt celebrated Songs and Lullabies of the old Britiſh Nurſes, calculated to amuſe Children and to excite them to Sleep.

PART II. Thoſe of that ſweet Songſter and Nurſe of Wit and Humour, Maſter William Shakeſpeare.

EMBELLISHED WITH CUTS.

And Illuſtrated with NOTES and MAXIMS, Hiſtorical, Philoſophical and Critical.

LONDON:

Printed for FRANCIS POWER, (Grandſon to the late Mr. J. NEWBERY,) and Co. No. 65. St. Paul's Church Yard, 1791.

[Price Three Pence.]

An eighteenth-century children's book, Mother Goose's Melody, *devotes a section to Shakespeare.*

short biographies for children, gave ten pages to the life of "William Shakspeare, the Prince of Dramatic Poets."

Mary Jane Godwin wanted to go further still. Rather than collecting a few speeches, or retelling the story of a single play, she wanted someone who could introduce children to many of Shakespeare's stories. The writer she approached to execute the task was Mary Lamb.

The Death of Her Own Mother

Mary Lamb was born in 1764, the year before Johnson's edition of Shakespeare appeared. Unlike her two brothers, who were sent to a distinguished charity school, she got little formal education. But she more than made up for it with her voracious reading habits and became a distinguished autodidact: she read a wide range of English authors in her youth, and in later years she would teach herself Latin, French, and Italian. But not only was Mary Lamb bright and motivated; she was also extremely troubled.

It's notoriously difficult to diagnose people centuries after their death, but modern experts who have examined her story say Mary Lamb probably suffered from bipolar disorder. She was therefore subject to dangerous mood swings in the Lamb household, especially after the family's fortunes took a turn for the worse. Mary's father, John, was a servant in the Inner Temple, working as a waiter in the Great Hall, where lawyers and law students dined. Samuel Salt, one of the highest-ranking figures in the Inner Temple, took a liking to him and employed both him and his wife, Elizabeth. John Lamb was not a gentleman, and the family was far from rich, but the work was steady and they were comfortable enough.

In the 1790s, though, they started to come down in the world. In 1792 Samuel Salt died, leaving the family's income insecure. They were forced to move out of the Temple into cheaper quarters. John also seems to have suffered a stroke around the same time; records show that he was "very infirm" and "had nearly lost the use of his left hand." At the same time, Elizabeth was also in bad health, probably suffering from arthritis. Mary Lamb must have felt the pressures of running the household. The family took on an "apprentice"—a nine-year-old girl, whose name is not recorded—to help with some of the household tasks, but early in her stay, when she still had much to learn, she must have been more of a burden than a help.

Things finally came to a head in September 1796 when, in a fit of insanity, Mary Lamb stabbed her mother through the heart, killing her instantly. The London newspapers included accounts of the killing taken from the official coroner's inquest. "While the family were preparing for dinner," reported the *Times*, "the young lady seized a case-knife laying on the table, and in a menacing manner pursued a little girl, her apprentice, round the room. On the calls of her infirm mother to forbear, she renounced her first object, and with loud shrieks approached her parent." A few days later her brother Charles wrote to his friend from school, the poet Samuel Taylor Coleridge: "My poor dear dearest sister in a fit of insanity has been the death of her own mother. I was at hand only [in] time enough to snatch the knife out of her grasp."

An inquest concluded she was legally insane, and therefore she was not condemned to hang, but escaping the noose still often meant being sent to London's largest asylum for the insane, the Hospital of St. Mary Bethlehem, better known by the shortened version of its name: Bedlam. Contemporary descriptions show the place was dreary, a grim sort of tourist attraction, where fashionable Londoners paid visits to the poor lunatics in their dank cells. As Henry Mackenzie's novel *The Man of Feeling* points out, "Of those things called Sights in London, which every stranger is supposed desirous to see, Bedlam is one." That novel gives a description—probably not far from the truth—of one group's visit to the asylum, where they see "the dismal mansions of those who are in the most horrid state of incurable madness. The clanking of chains, the wildness of their cries, and the imprecations which some of them uttered, formed a scene inexpressibly shocking." Samuel Johnson and James Boswell paid a real-life visit in 1775 and found "the general contemplation of insanity was very affecting."

Mary Lamb, though, was doubly fortunate, for she avoided not only the gallows but also the notorious madhouse. The law specified that "violent lunatics" could be released into the care of their families if someone vowed to take responsibility, and Mary's brother Charles made such a promise. On several occasions, when her condition got out of control, she had to be removed to private madhouses. But for most of the next forty years the two of them lived together in what Charles called a state of "double singleness."

Courtesy, Benignity, Generosity, Humanity

It was during one of her healthier intervals that Mary Lamb was approached by Mary Jane Godwin, and she put her extensive learning to use. Working with her brother Charles, she turned twenty of Shakespeare's plays into short prose tales for children. (Mary did about two thirds of the labor, working on most of the comedies, as her brother did most of the tragedies.) The result was *Tales from Shakespear, Designed for the Use of Young Persons*, an attractive work that appeared in two small illustrated volumes at the end of 1806 (with 1807 on the title page). But, as with *The Family Shakspeare*, only Charles Lamb's name appeared on it. In this case, it was probably only partly a matter of female delicacy that

Mary and Charles Lamb turned Shakespeare's plays into short narratives for children. Some of the pictures may have been engraved by William Blake.

led to the concealed name; the Lambs were also eager to conceal the scandal surrounding Mary Lamb and the death of her mother.

Not much of Shakespeare's language survives in the *Tales*; these are stories, not plays, and the language has been both modernized and rendered suitable for young readers. But the plots survive more or less intact. The Lambs tried to give young readers "a few hints and little foretastes of the great pleasure which awaits them in their elder years." But it was no easy task. Susan Tyler Hitchcock, Mary Lamb's biographer, describes some of the challenges she faced: "To turn a play by Shakespeare into a story for a young reader, Mary had to find graceful ways to evoke foreign contexts, explain underlying moral values, turn action into narrative, and maintain diverse characters." Although she occasionally includes direct quotations from the plays—"O Romeo, Romeo! wherefore art thou Romeo?"—she usually uses the simpler once-upon-a-time language that's evident on the first page of the first tale, from *The Tempest*: "There was a certain island in the sea, the only inhabitants of which were an old man, whose name was Prospero, and his daughter Miranda, a very beautiful young lady. She came to this island so young, that she had no memory of having seen any other human face than her father's."

It's not just the language that is simplified, but the plots, too. In the Lambs' version of *Twelfth Night*, for example, the central action (Viola disguised as Cesario, Olivia falling in love with her) is preserved more or less intact, but the entire subplot (Malvolio, Toby Belch, Andrew Aguecheek, Maria, and Feste) is cut. The same happens to Trinculo in *The Tempest*, Jaques and Touchstone in *As You Like It*, the changeling child and the mechanicals in *A Midsummer Night's Dream*, and so on.

The *Tales* are also stripped of indecency and cleansed of passages unsuitable for children. In *Cymbeline*, Cloten's gruesome beheading is omitted, and a distinguishing physical trait—"On her left breast / A mole, cinque-spotted"—becomes "a mole . . . upon Imogen's neck." For the Lambs and their generation, childhood was a time of innocence, and innocence was to be protected. Children shouldn't be exposed to the harsh realities of adult life. In the Lambs' *Hamlet*, therefore, there is no hint that Ophelia may have been a suicide; she was merely the unfortunate victim of an accidental drowning: "There was a willow which grew slanting over a brook, and reflected its leaves on the stream. To this brook she came one day . . . and clambering up to hang her garland upon the boughs of the willow, a bough broke, and precipitated this fair young maid, garland, and all that she had gathered, into the water."

But the Lambs weren't too fastidious, and they thought that children could handle some more mature topics. The interracial love that so horrified Thomas Rymer a century earlier was taken in stride: Desdemona loves the black Othello because she "regarded the mind more than the features of men . . . Bating [excepting] that Othello was black, the noble Moor wanted [lacked] nothing which might recommend him to the affections of the greatest lady." And it's surprising that the Lambs should have taken on *Measure for Measure*, one of the most sexually charged plays in the canon. Even the Bowdlers found this one too much, the only Shakespearean play they were unable to tidy up by their normal means: "Feeling my own inability to render this play sufficiently correct for family-reading," wrote Thomas Bowdler, "I have thought it advisable to print it . . . from the published copy, as performed in the Theatre Royal, Covent Garden." But the Lambs included it, though they left out some of the details more suited to a mature audience. They describe "a law dooming any man to the punishment of death, who should live with a woman that was not his wife," and note that because the duke did not enforce it, "the holy institution of marriage became neglected."

There was a political aspect to the stories. On the one hand, they strike us as progressive, even feminist, in their attempts to

Although the Lambs toned down some of the racier passages in Tales from Shakespear, *they showed Othello's murder of Desdemona.*

make Shakespeare's plays available to girls: "For young ladies too it has been my intention chiefly to write," they explain, "because boys are generally permitted the use of their fathers' libraries at a much earlier age than girls are." But there was also a more conservative program at work. As the critic Susan Wolfson writes, the *Tales* "reveal some of the feminist sensitivities of the post-Revolutionary, post-Wollstonecraft era in which they were published," but they are also "marked by conservative ideology" and "display contrary psychological tendencies and ambivalent social attitudes." This isn't unusual. Children's literature has often had a conservative function, indoctrinating young people with the moral and political values of the culture at large. And in 1807, when Britain was at war with Napoleonic France, the *Tales* worked to produce loyal British subjects in a turbulent age. They are supposed to be "enrichers of the fancy, strengtheners of virtue, a withdrawing from all selfish and mercenary thoughts, a lesson of all sweet and honourable thoughts and actions, to teach you courtesy, benignity, generosity, humanity." The *Tales* often reinforce the kind of domestic ideology that appeared in the Bowdlers' *Family Shakspeare*.

Tales from Shakespear proved a success from the very beginning. The *Critical Review* declared that "unless perhaps we except Robinson Crusoe, they claim the very first place, and stand unique, without rival or competitor." The Godwins printed a second edition in 1809, and the book has never been out of print. The *Cambridge History of English and American Literature*, an eighteen-volume work that appeared early in the twentieth century, had high praise for the *Tales*: "It is not too much to say that the collection forms one of the most conspicuous landmarks in the history of the romantic movement. It is the first book which, appealing to a general audience and to a rising generation, made Shakespeare a familiar and popular author." And the Lambs' legacy is still alive and well. There are now dozens of children's versions of Shakespeare's works, ranging from editions of the plays with notes for beginners to complete retellings for grade-school children. In 2001 Carol Rawlings Miller offered "classroom-tested, kid-pleasing scenes and activities!" from Shakespeare for ages ten and up, and Lois Burdett wrote *Hamlet for Kids* in 2000 (with a foreword by Kenneth Branagh), an attempt to bring a rhyming version of the Bard to the seven- to nine-year-old set:

> "I am thy father's spirit doomed to walk the night.
> At dawn, I render up myself and disappear from sight."
> The mournful voice resounded from above,
> "If thou didst ever thy dear father love,

> Revenge his foul and most unnatural murder!" he cried.
> "Murder?" Hamlet trembled, and looked horrified.

And so, two hundred years after the Bowdlers and the Lambs worked to make Shakespeare fit for all readers, the project is still going on. Shakespeare's cultural cachet is so great that everyone wants to bask in his glory. At the same time, he can be dangerous, and his genius has to be tamed. That's one of the risks with adopting a foul-mouthed horndog as a patron saint of the English language: he must be handled with great care.

CHAPTER 7

Forging Shakespeare

ONE OF THE RECURRING FRUSTRATIONS for Shakespeare's many adorers is how few traces of his life have been preserved. The printed plays and poems survive, of course, but no drafts in Shakespeare's handwriting. There are no autograph letters from Shakespeare. He must have been a passionate reader, but no books he owned have come down to posterity. His will survives, containing a few words in his own handwriting, but those hoping to find in it insights into his soul have been sadly disappointed. It's a businesslike document, famous only for the quirky bequest "I gyve unto my wief my second best bed." The only other manuscripts in Shakespeare's hand are a few signatures and maybe portions of the play *Sir Thomas More*—though the latter was unknown in the eighteenth century and remains questionable now.

For most people, this lack of Shakespearean relics was a cause for regret. For a few enterprising souls, though, it was an opportunity, a chance to supply the reading public with what it wanted.

Love's Labour's Won

Even while Shakespeare was alive, a few unscrupulous writers and publishers tried to profit from his reputation. A number of plays appeared with his initials on them: *Locrine* (1595), *The True Chronicle Historie of the Whole Life and Death of Thomas Lord Cromwell* (1602), and *The Puritan* (1607) were all published by "W.S." Maybe this was innocent confusion—there may have been several playwrights with those initials at the time—but when *The London Prodigall* appeared in 1605, it clearly bore the name William Shakespeare on the title page, even though he had nothing to do with it. After a string of successes Shakespeare had become a brand name, and publishers were eager to use it to their advantage; associating a play by a no-name author with one of the most successful names on the London stage was just smart marketing. And the practice continued after Shakespeare was dead and unable to object. *The Birth of Merlin*, published in 1662, was attributed to Shakespeare on the title page, and the Third Folio of 1664 included the "seven Playes, never before Printed in Folio"—*Pericles, The London Prodigall, Thomas Lord Cromwell, Sir John Oldcastle, The Puritan Widow, A Yorkshire Tragedy*, and *Locrine*—of which only the first is now believed to be authentic.

In addition to plays written by others that someone tried to pass off as Shakespeare's, there are a number of ghosts in the Shakespeare canon, plays that he may or may not have written. As early as 1598, Francis Meres listed the works by the young but promising playwright in a volume called *Palladis Tamia*. "As *Plautus* and *Seneca* are accounted the best for Comedy and Tragedy among the *Latines*," wrote Meres, "so *Shakespeare* among y[e] English is the most excellent in both kinds of the stage." As evidence of Shakespeare's brilliance in both forms, he lists some of his comedies ("his *Gentlemen of Verona*, his *Errors*, his *Loue labors lost*, his *Loue labours wonne*, his *Midsummers night dreame*, & his *Merchant of Venice*") and then some of his tragedies ("his *Richard the 2. Richard the 3. Henry the 4. King John, Titus Andronicus* and his *Romeo* and *Iuliet*"). Most of these are familiar titles in the Shakespeare canon: *Two Gentlemen of Verona, The Comedy of Errors, Love's*

Labour's Lost, *A Midsummer Night's Dream*, *The Merchant of Venice*, *Richard II*, *Richard III*, the two parts of *Henry IV*, *King John*, *Titus Andronicus*, and *Romeo and Juliet* are now in every collection of his works. But *Love's Labour's Won*? No play with that name survives.

There are a few possibilities. One is that Meres simply had bad information, and that there never was a play by that name by Shakespeare or by anyone else. But a surviving fragment of a bookseller's list from 1603 does mention *loves labor won* alongside plays like *marchant of vennis* and *taming of a shrew*, so it seems likely that a play by that title was not only acted but printed. Another possibility is that *Love's Labour's Won* is an alternative title to a work that already exists. Several of Shakespeare's plays went under two titles, like *Twelfth Night, or What You Will* and *Henry VIII, or All Is True*. Some have suggested that *Love's Labour's Won* may be a subtitle to *Much Ado About Nothing*.

The most tantalizing possibility of all, though, is that *Love's Labour's Won* is a lost play, perhaps a sequel to *Love's Labour's Lost* still waiting to be found. It's not entirely out of the question. By one estimate, as many as 3,000 plays were written between 1558 and 1642, of which only about 650—fewer than one in four—survive in any copy today. It's possible, maybe even probable, that plays by Shakespeare are among the missing. Many works were never printed, and when the last handwritten copy was lost, the play was gone forever. Even many printed books have vanished completely. The first edition of *Titus Andronicus* was believed to be lost for more than three hundred years, until a single copy turned up in 1904. Of the first edition of *1 Henry IV*, not even a single complete copy survives, only a few pages, and there's good evidence that the first printing of *Love's Labour's Lost* hasn't survived at all—what critics call the first edition is probably (at least) the second. So its ostensible partner, *Love's Labour's Won*, may yet be discovered in a neglected library or in someone's attic. It may even be hiding inside another book. Paper was expensive in

Shakespeare's day, and when books didn't sell well, they were often recycled as scrap paper. Most were destroyed pretty quickly, used for lighting fires, for lining pie tins, even as toilet paper. (Thus John Dryden's wicked lines in *Mac Flecknoe* on the fate of second-rate authors: "From dusty shops neglected authors come, / Martyrs of Pies, and Reliques of the Bum.") But sometimes waste-paper was used to make new bindings for books, and every few years a previously unknown work turns up when an old binding is opened up for restoration. In 1892 a piece of scrap paper in a binding turned out to be the oldest known piece of printing in the Western world, printed by Johannes Gutenberg himself. It's just possible that *Love's Labour's Won* awaits a similar discovery.

Lost to the World for Above a Century

Another Shakespearean ghost has a particularly interesting history. In 1653, nearly forty years after Shakespeare's death, the Stationers' Register—the government's list of who claimed the rights to which plays, the rough equivalent of a modern copyright registry—listed a work called "*The History of Cardenio*, by Mr Fletcher and Shakespeare." No play by that name survives, but Cardenio is a character in Cervantes's *Don Quixote*, which was first published in English in 1612. It's conceivable that Shakespeare came out of retirement and teamed up with John Fletcher to write a play based on an episode in *Quixote*. There are even hints that make it likely: in 1613 the King's Men, Shakespeare's company, were paid for presenting *Cardenno* at court, and again for playing *Cardenna* a few months later.

In the 1720s a prominent scholar made the startling claim that he had recovered Shakespeare's lost *Cardenio*. The announcement came from Lewis Theobald, the surly editor who took Alexander Pope to task for his shoddy editorial practices. In December 1727 he presented a play at Drury Lane, and a published edition appeared early in the new year: *Double Falshood; or, The Distrest Lovers: A Play . . . Written Originally by W. Shakespeare; and Now Revised and Adapted to the Stage by Mr. Theobald*. "I bear so dear an Affection to the Writings and Memory of SHAKESPEARE," he wrote, that "it is my good Fortune to retrieve this Remnant of his Pen from Obscurity." Theobald knew he'd have to face skeptics: "It has been alledg'd as incredible," he wrote, "that such a Curiosity should be stifled and lost to the World for above a Century." But Theobald claimed to have discovered several old manuscripts, one "of above Sixty Years Standing," and he was "credibly inform'd" it "was early in the Possession of the celebrated Mr. *Betterton*." He even had reasons to believe that Shakespeare himself had given it "as a Present of Value, to a Natural [illegitimate] Daughter of his, for whose Sake he wrote it, in the Time of his Retirement from the Stage." His version was an adaptation of the play that appeared in the three manuscripts.

Where are these manuscripts? No one else has ever seen them. If they ever existed, they're now assumed to have been lost in a fire at Covent Garden in 1808. Already in Theobald's day there were accusations of forgery; one malicious poet imagined Theobald declaring, "I something will be thought: / I'll write—then—boldly swear 'twas Shakespear wrote." And experts today are unsure how to interpret *Double Falshood*. Did Theobald have genuine old manuscripts at all? Did he honestly believe the play to be Shakespearean? Did he destroy evidence to cover his tracks? Did he just make the whole thing up? Most people who have considered the evidence closely believe that he was actually working from an older play, though it's unclear whether it was genuinely Shakespearean; he may have allowed his excitement to overrule his judgment, his optimism to overrule his skepticism. But why such a meticulous critic was so cavalier with his evidence, publishing it only in an altered form and allowing it to disappear after he had finished with it, remains a mystery. "Why," asks the critic Jonathan Bate, "did he never publish a reasoned refutation of the accusation of forgery? Did he keep the manuscript close to his chest because it was a fabrication or out of a desire to keep a precious piece of Shakespeare to himself?" After nearly three hundred years, there's still no good answer.

Unexhaustible Plenty

Imitation is said to be the sincerest form of flattery. It may be a tribute to Shakespeare's genius that some people felt compelled to imitate him, even to write the plays he never got around to writing. "*Shakespeare*," wrote Samuel Johnson, "opens a mine which contains gold and diamonds in unexhaustible plenty." Most readers agreed; but some were beginning to think that, with only thirty-six recognized plays, Shakespeare's "unexhaustible" canon was starting to become exhausted. They longed for more, and the forgers were ready to provide it for them.

The critic Arthur Freeman argues convincingly that a minor writer named William Chetwood was the author of a short Shakespearean forgery that ran in a London magazine in 1748. The critic and editor George Steevens also puckishly slipped a few forgeries, fakes, and frauds into his publications in the 1770s, hoping to embarrass other scholars who accepted them as genuine. But the most brazen of all the hoaxers was a young man named William Henry Ireland. Theobald may have tinkered with the story behind an old manuscript, and Steevens had a mischievous sense of humor, but they didn't begin to compare with the eighteenth century's most audacious forger.

Ireland's father, Samuel, an engraver, made a specialty of lavishly illustrated "picturesque" travel books. In 1790, for instance, he issued *A Picturesque Tour Through Holland*, which he followed up the next year with *Picturesque Views on the River Thames*, and then in 1793 with *Picturesque Views of the River Medway*. Samuel's real passion, though, wasn't for picturesque views, but for Shakespeare. William said many years later that his father "entertained an unbounded enthusiasm for the writings of Shakspeare: four days, at least, out of the seven, the beauties of our divine dramatist became the theme of conversation after dinner." In the evenings, he would read aloud to his family from the plays and even have them do group readings, with each family member taking a part. "With him," wrote William, "Shakspeare was no mortal, but a divinity."

Samuel's feelings toward his own William, though, were far less positive: he was convinced William was a sorry excuse for a son, bad at school, bad at work—and William certainly felt his father's disapproval. Still, when Samuel traveled to Stratford-upon-Avon in October 1792 to do sketches for another collection of engravings, *Picturesque Views on the Upper, or Warwickshire Avon*, seventeen-year-old William tagged along to act as an assistant. And while they were in Shakespeare's native town, they chased leads about his life, hopeful that relics might still be found. As William remembered it, "no inquiries were spared, either at Stratford or in the neighbourhood, respecting the mighty poet." Manuscripts in particular were Samuel Ireland's obsession, and he asked everywhere about stashes of Shakespeare's personal papers that may have escaped detection.

A tip led them to Clopton House, the home of a Mr. Williams, about a mile outside Stratford. A comic scene in Ireland's book-length autobiography, *Confessions of William-Henry Ireland*, describes Samuel's horror at hearing that Williams had just burned a pile of worthless old papers—and, now that he thought about it, some of them may have had Shakespeare's name on them. "By G—d," said Williams, "I wish you had arrived a little sooner! Why, it isn't a fortnight since I destroyed several baskets-full of

Samuel Ireland etched this view of New Place and the Stratford Grammar School in Picturesque Views on the Upper, or Warwickshire Avon.

letters and papers." (This section in Ireland's *Confessions* is headed "IF TRUE, WHAT A CONFLAGRATION!") Williams was almost certainly twitting the earnest amateur antiquarian, but the humorless Samuel seems to have missed the joke and was horrified at what he heard. His son, however, took the hint and remembered his father's longing for Shakespearean manuscripts.

The story took its most interesting turn a few years later, when nineteen-year-old William approached his father with a startling story. "On Saturday y^{e} 22^{d} Nov^{r}," Ireland père scribbled in his diary in 1794, "my Son was invited to dine at the house of our mutual friend Mr M.____ where amongst other Company he met with a Gent^{n} from   , of very considerable property." This gentleman, it turned out, owned a chest of old documents, some of them hundreds of years old, passed down in his family from generation to generation. He had been meaning to sort through them but never found the time, so if William was willing to look through them, he'd be most grateful. In fact, he'd even allow William to take away anything he found there, with only two conditions: he had to be given the chance to make a copy of anything important, and he would not allow his identity to be known to the world. He signed his letters only "Mr. H."

Young Ireland began passing his time at H's house, sorting through dusty old documents. And a few weeks later he told his father some exciting news: he had discovered a legal document, a deed between Michael Fraser and William Shakespeare, bearing Shakespeare's signature. "It was about eight o'clock," Ireland wrote, "that I presented the deed in question . . . I had placed the deed within my bosom; when, after informing Mr. Ireland that I had a very great curiosity to show him, I drew it forth and presented it, saying—'There, sir! what do you think of that!' " Samuel recorded the event in his diary: "On Tuesday ye 16th Decr 1794 he brought me ye beforementioned deed signed by Wm Shakspeare & Mich^{l} Fraser & putting it into my hands beg'd my opinion as to its originality, which after attentively examining & pronouncing it to be my opinion it was so, he very kindly offer'd it to me for my acceptance." A document like this hadn't turned up in many years. Samuel was delighted; he had adored Shakespeare for as long as he could remember, and now he held in his hands a document the Bard himself had signed.

As young Ireland tells the story, this was the first time in his life he received any affection from his usually disapproving father. "It is impossible for me to express the pleasure you have given me by the presentation of this deed," said Samuel. "There are the keys of my book-case; go and take from it whatever you please." Not many days later came even more exciting news: "The Gent^{n}," Samuel wrote in his diary, "has every reason to believe he says that among those papers is a finished play by Shakspeare, the Subject taken from Hollingshed Chronicle called Vortigern & Rowena."

A finished play by Shakespeare! Early in the new year came confirmation: "This day my Son informed me in Confidence, that y^e $Gent^n$ had shewn him the manuscript play before mentioned & with it the Tragedy of King Lear . . . These 2 plays are all in y^e hand writing of Shakspeare." With each new discovery Samuel Ireland showered his son with more love. And so the hoard of Shakespearean manuscripts grew. William turned up legal documents; letters to and from Queen Elizabeth; a love letter to "Anna Hatherrewaye"; the original handwritten draft of *King Lear*; then the lost masterpieces *Vortigern* and *Henry II*. Samuel arranged for the publication of the papers in a deluxe edition, with facsimiles of the author's handwriting, and he invited the curious to visit his house to inspect the manuscripts with their own eyes: "Any Gentleman," he wrote, "may view the MS. at No. 8, Norfolk Street, on Mondays, Wednesdays, and Fridays, between the hours of Twelve and Three."

Shakspeare's, & Shakspeare's Only

Those visitors were most excited by *Vortigern*, the most important of all the Shakespearean "discoveries." The idea of a Shakespearean play on the topic was plausible enough. The story of Vortigern, a legendary fifth-century British warlord, appeared in Geoffrey of Monmouth's *History of the Kings of Britain*, where Shakespeare had found the stories for his *King Lear* and *Cymbeline*. Ireland's play recounts the complicated story of Vortigern's plot to kill King Constantius and the consequences that follow. To modern readers it seems to be little more than a pastiche of Shakespeare's surviving plays, and it's not difficult to spot the ideas, images, and language lifted out of other works. The ambitious man's murder of a king, for instance, comes straight out of *Macbeth*. When in the first scene Constantius tells Vortigern,

> As frozen age we find doth fast approach, . . .
> We here to thee half of our pow'r resign,

it's hard to miss Lear's division of the kingdoms. *King Lear* similarly provides the "Fool, whimsically attired," who also has a bit of Touchstone from *As You Like It*. When Vortigern declares, "O what an inconsistent thing is man!" he seems to be echoing Hamlet's "What a piece of work is man"; when he hires two murderers to kill Constantius at a banquet, he recalls *Macbeth* and *Richard III*. Vortigern's wife, Edmunda, begins to lose her mind, prompting her maids to speculate that her "reason wanders"; again, Lear's dementia and the conversation between the gentlewoman and the doctor in *Macbeth* provided the model. Vortigern's incestuous lust for his own daughter, Flavia—"Is it not strange, a flinty heart like mine, / Should stagger thus at thinking of a daughter?"—comes from *Pericles*; Flavia's cross-dressed flight to the forest suggests *As You Like It*; and so on. Instead of tipping off readers that Ireland's play was a fake, though, all these echoes of familiar passages served only to convince many of them that *Vortigern* was genuine. Surely young Ireland's vanity was gratified when he heard people insisting that *Vortigern* was unmistakably the work of the Bard. One believer wrote to a friend during the height of *Vortigern*-mania that the play "must be Shakspeare's, & Shakspeare's *only*. It either comes from his pen, or from Heaven."

This was the verdict Samuel hoped to hear. He began to make arrangements to have *Vortigern* produced on the stage. After negotiating with both of London's patent theatres, he settled on Drury Lane, then under the management of an old acquaintance, Richard Brinsley Sheridan. This experienced playwright was not convinced the play was genuine, and he knew that the overlong work would have to be trimmed substantially if it were to be a success on stage. But he thought it was worth the risk, and he and Samuel began discussing the practical matters of putting on a play. The negotiations did not go smoothly. Samuel complained at how slowly the Drury Lane management took to reply to his concerns, and then complained again when the promised scenery was not ready. He sent Sheridan an angry note, insisting, "y^{r} Conduct & that of some persons ab^{t} ye theatre has done an irreparable injury to the interests of my Son as well as to ye publication of ye papers in general." But, despite all the frustration, the rehearsals went forward, and London was excited about the forthcoming performance. It was to be the first Shakespeare premiere in nearly two hundred years.

A Manne More Trewe Thanne Willy Shakspeare

It was not just the big items, the lost plays, that attracted attention. The smaller pieces were in some ways even more appealing. While *Vortigern* was in rehearsal, Samuel Ireland collected most of the papers in a deluxe edition and published it on Christmas Eve, 1795: *Miscellaneous Papers and Legal Instruments under the Hand and Seal of William Shakspeare: Including the Tragedy of King Lear and a Small Fragment of Hamlet, from the Original MSS. in the Possession of Samuel Ireland, of Norfolk Street*. In a preface Samuel insisted that a train of experts had "unanimously testified in favour of their authenticity." His conclusion: *"these Papers can be no other than the production of Shakspeare himself."*

As the title suggests, the *Miscellaneous Papers* volume included a great many small pieces: a declaration of faith proving Shakespeare was not a Catholic; a letter from Queen Elizabeth to "Master William Shakspeare atte the Globe bye Thames," praising his "prettye Verses" and complimenting him for "theyre greate excellence"; a receipt from Shakespeare to the Earl of Leicester for fifty pounds; a "Note of Hand" promising to pay Shakespeare's "good and Worthye Freynd John Hemynge the sume of five Pounds and five shillings English Monye," along with a receipt from Heminges for that amount; and a letter addressed to "Anna

Hatherrewaye." The love letter from a youthful Shakespeare to his future wife generated much excitement. "As thou haste alwaye founde mee toe mye Worde moste trewe," he wrote, "thou shalt see I have stryctlye kepte mye promyse." The letter was accompanied by a cutting of Shakespeare's hair—"thys mye poore Locke"—which he begged his beloved to accept. "O Anna," he declared, "do I love doe I cheryshe thee inne mye hearte." With the letter came love verses to Anne Hathaway:

Is there inne heavenne aught more rare
Thanne thou sweete Nymphe of Avon fayre
Is there onne Earthe a Manne more trewe
Thanne Willy Shakspeare is toe you

The forgery revealed a tender and intimate side to Shakespeare's private character, which appealed to the age's ideal of the sensitive and romantic genius.

One of the most bizarre items in the collection was a letter from William Shakespeare to his "goode freynde Masterre William Henrye Irelande"—a long-forgotten ancestor and namesake of our William Henry Ireland, who happened to be friendly with the playwright. As the supposed Shakespeare told the story, he, Ireland, and some friends took a "boate neare untowe myne house," but their friends were "muche toe merrye throughe Lyquorre," and the drunkards managed to overturn the boat. "Alle butte myeselfe," said Shakespeare, "savedd themselves bye swimmyng." But when "oune of the Companye dydd answerre thatte I was drownynge," Ireland immediately "Jumpedd inn afterre mee," and "withe muche paynes he draggedd mee forthe I beynge then nearelye deade and soe he dydd save mye life." In gratitude for this remarkable act of bravery, Shakespeare continued, "[I gave to Ireland] mye writtenn Playe of Henrye fowrthe Henrye fyfthe Kyng John Kynge Leare," as well as "mye written Playe neverr yett impryntedd whych I have

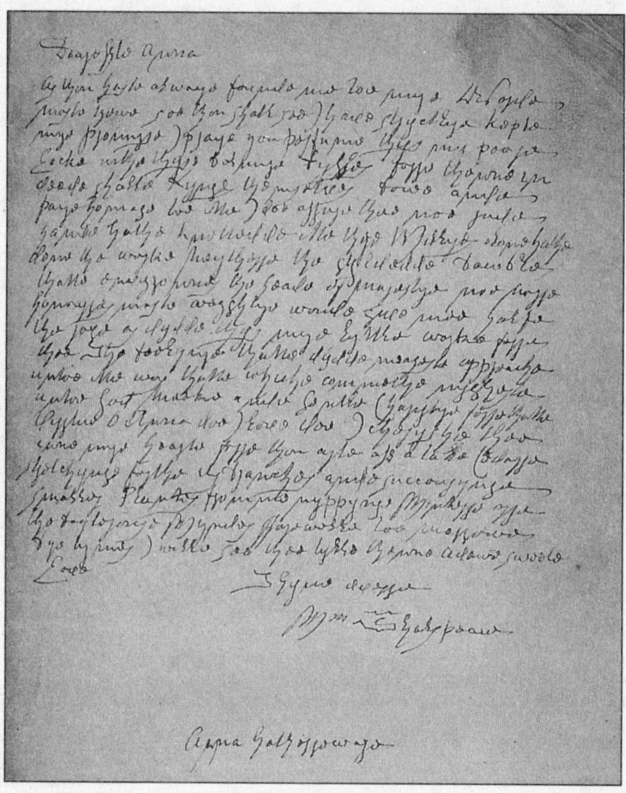

William Henry Ireland's forgery of a love letter from a young Shakespeare to "Anna Hatherrewaye" shows his fantasy version of Shakespeare's handwriting and spelling.

named Kynge henrye thyrde." Ireland and his heirs were to enjoy "alle the profytts" from these plays. This document served a practical purpose: Ireland worried that "if a descendant of *Shakspear*'s could be found, he might claim the papers." After all, his story about an unnamed gentleman giving them to him might not stand up in court if someone asserted the legal rights to the discoveries. And so, Ireland admitted, "I determined on proving that a friendship had subsisted between our *Bard* and some person of the name of *Ireland*;

for that purpose I wrote the deed of gift, and formed the story of his saving *Shakspear* from *'drowning.'*" But it also allowed Ireland to cast his namesake as the hero who saved Shakespeare's life.

Unpolluted by Any Modern Sophistication

The Shakespeare papers convinced the right people. Sheridan may have had his doubts, but he was willing to take the risk of producing the play at Drury Lane. Others were more confident. The poet laureate, Henry James Pye, signed a document avowing his belief. Sir Isaac Heard, who sported a series of impressive titles—Garter Principal King-of-Arms; Gentleman Usher of the Scarlet Rod for Knights of the Bath—joined him. James Boswell, Samuel Johnson's biographer, supposedly fell on his knees before the papers, declaring, "I now kiss the invaluable relics of our bard: and thanks to God that I have lived to see them!" (He was dead not many weeks later.)

Not everyone, though, was won over, and literary London split into factions, the faithful and the skeptics. Some doubters questioned the absurd "ye-olde" spelling and were bothered by the abundant anachronisms. Others were convinced that *Vortigern* simply wasn't good enough to be Shakespeare's. Most of the serious experts of the day were ranged among the doubters, including George Steevens (himself a sometime forger), Joseph Ritson, and Richard Farmer. But the most important skeptic by far was Edmond Malone, the greatest of the Shakespearean critics in the generation after Johnson—Ireland called him the "generalissimo of the non-believers." Two days before *Vortigern* opened at Drury Lane, Malone published a four-hundred-page demolition of the Shakespeare papers, giving hundreds of reasons why the works could not be authentic. The book, *An Inquiry into the Authenticity of Certain Miscellaneous Papers and Legal Instruments, Published Dec. 24, M DCC XCV. and Attributed to Shakspeare*, was a masterpiece of

Edmond Malone, the leading Shakespeare critic at the end of the eighteenth century, was William Henry Ireland's fiercest critic.

scholarly invective. It opened by declaring how urgent was the task of separating Shakespeare's gold from Ireland's base metal, for Shakespeare stood for Englishness itself: "Every individual of this country, whose mind has been at all cultivated, feels a pride in being able to boast of our great dramatick poet, Shakspeare, as his countryman." Therefore, he argued, his works should be treated with "respect and veneration." His goal was to protect Shakespeare's "valuable writings," and "to preserve them pure and unpolluted by any modern sophistication or foreign admixture whatsoever." The book laid out, in astonishing detail, how almost every assertion about the Shakespeare papers must be false. "The spelling," for instance, is "the orthography of no age whatsoever . . . The absurd manner in which almost every word is over-laden with both consonants and vowels will at once strike every reader." He couldn't resist a cheap shot: "I may perhaps be expected to say a word on the far-famed tragedy of KYNGE VORTIGERNE," he advised, "and all the KKYNGES and all the QQUEENES which have been announced from the same quarter."

Solemn Mockery

Still the play went on, opening at Drury Lane on Saturday, 2 April 1796. The cast included a number of superstars: John Philip Kemble played Vortigern, his brother Charles played Pascentius (Vortigern's son), and Dorothy Jordan played Flavia. (Sarah Siddons was supposed to play Edmunda, but she dropped out—supposedly for health reasons, but many believe she suspected the play was a fake and sought an excuse to dissociate herself from it.) Samuel Ire-

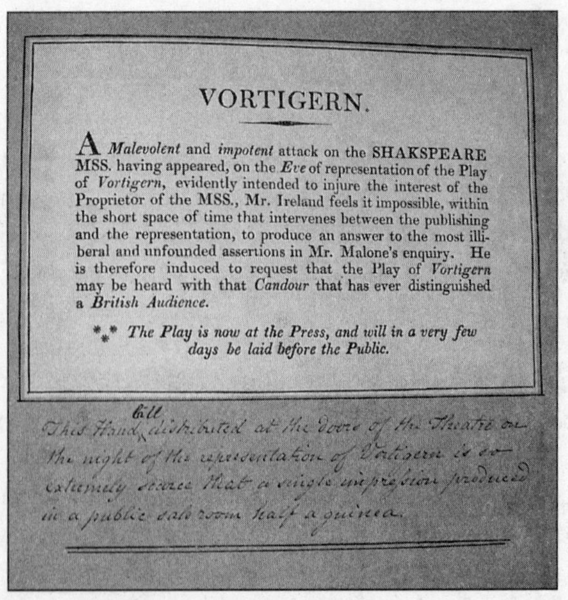

VORTIGERN.

A *Malevolent* and *impotent* attack on the SHAKSPEARE MSS. having appeared, on the *Eve* of representation of the Play of *Vortigern*, evidently intended to injure the interest of the Proprietor of the MSS., Mr. Ireland feels it impossible, within the short space of time that intervenes between the publishing and the representation, to produce an answer to the most illiberal and unfounded assertions in Mr. Malone's enquiry. He is therefore induced to request that the Play of *Vortigern* may be heard with that *Candour* that has ever distinguished a *British Audience*.

*** *The Play is now at the Press, and will in a very few days be laid before the Public.*

This Hand bill distributed at the doors of the Theatre on the night of the representation of Vortigern is so extremely scarce that a single impression produced in a public sale room half a guinea.

An angry Samuel Ireland distributed this handbill outside the theatre before the production of Vortigern *to counter Edmond Malone's criticism.*

land sat in a box at the center of the house; William, more nervous, recounted, "I did not enter the theatre till a very short period previous to the rising of the curtain; and the box being so very conspicuous, I soon retired from observation behind the scenes; where I continued the greater part of the time of representation, engaged in conversation with Mrs. Jordan."

Several accounts survive. All agree that the house was packed: a new Shakespeare play was big news. One London newspaper, the *Gazetteer*, declared, "The long-expected play of VORTIGERN produced all that overflow and press that might naturally be expected. The pit and galleries were completely filled, almost as soon as the doors were opened, and long before the curtain drew up, not a place was to be had in the boxes." The *Morning Herald* agreed: *Vortigern* "was attended by the most numerous and respectable audience we ever witnessed. All the avenues leading to the Theatre were crowded at an early hour, and thousands were forced to return, who could not, from the immense crowd, gain admittance into any part of the House." The artist Joseph Farington recorded in his diary, "Prologue spoken at 35 minutes past 6: Play over at 10."

After that, though, there's not much agreement. The report in the *Times* was obviously written by a skeptic, who said that "The *first Act*, in every line of it, spoke itself a palpable forgery—but it was heard with candour. The second and third grew more intolerable." The *Morning Post*, on the other hand, suggested that things weren't so bad: the first three acts, the reporter said, "were heard with the most profound attention, without the least mark of disapprobation, and occasionally with applause." *Ayre's Sunday London Gazette* suggested there were elements of truth in both stories: "The three first acts were received with a mixture of applause and contempt."

But things started to turn after the halfway point. The *Morning Post* reported that "early in the third act, the most vulgar colloquial phrases were introduced with the greatest pomp, the *Bathos* became too strong, and ridiculous nonsense produced—not hissing—but laughter, which, when once it seizes the house, is the most fatal symptom for any Tragedy." The account in *Ayre's*, however, put the turning point a little later: "at the beginning of the fourth [act], the laugh against the piece was completely established; and from that time, to the dropping of the curtain, it was successfully kept up." Farington wrote in his diary that "some ridiculous passages caused a laugh, which infected the House during the remainder of the performance, mixed with groans." John Philip Kemble then interrupted the performance and "requested the audience to hear the play out."

All the accounts agree that everything was lost at what should have been the high point of the play. John Philip Kemble, playing the lead, was never impressed with *Vortigern*, telling a friend years later, "Mr. Malone, in a few minutes conversation, convinced me they were spurious, and the fraud betrayed itself in the endless contradictions." Kemble even proposed an opening on the first of the month—April Fool's Day—but was overruled by Sheridan and Samuel Ireland. But if he couldn't sabotage the opening date, he could still sabotage the performance. He did it when Vortigern has received bad news from his barons and knows that his tragic end is approaching. "Time was, alas! I needed not this spur," he begins. "But here's a secret and a stinging thorn, / That wounds my troubled nerves. O! conscience! conscience!" This gloomy meditation turns to speculation on death:

O! sovereign death!
That hast for thy domain this world immense:
Church-yards and charnel-houses are thy haunts,
And hospitals thy sumptuous palaces;
And, when thou wouldst be merry, thou dost choose
The gaudy chamber of a dying King.

O! then thou dost ope wide thy boney jaws,
And, with rude laughter and fantastic tricks,
Thou clapp'st thy rattling fingers to thy sides.

But then came the line "And when this solemn mockery is o'er." Kemble decided to ham it up, hinting that the play itself was the "solemn mockery." As Ireland described it, "No sooner was the above line uttered in the most sepulchral tone of voice possible . . . than the most discordant howl echoed from the pit that ever assailed the organs of hearing." The audience burst into uproarious laughter, and the tragic dignity was lost beyond recovery. "From that moment," Ireland recalled, "so deafening became the uproar produced by conflicting applause and disapproval,

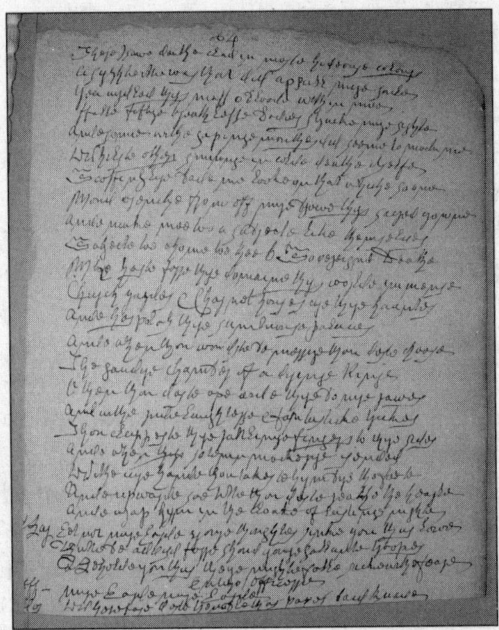

When John Philip Kemble recited this speech from Vortigern*—"And when this solemn mockery is o'er"—the audience broke out in hoots of laughter.*

that not one syllable more of the play was rendered intelligible." The cast limped to the end and, when one of the actors announced *Vortigern* would be presented again the following week, he was heckled until he relented: "When BARRYMORE came forward to announce the second representation of the Play for Monday night, there was the most violent contest we ever witnessed in a Theatre. It lasted for a quarter of an hour." The theatre dissolved into chaos: Farington recorded that Sir Charles Sturt "was in a Stage Box drunk, & exposed himself indecently." Samuel Ireland "for a little time leant his head on his arm, and then went out of the Box and behind the scenes." William, on the other hand, went home and "retired to bed, more easy in my mind than I had been for a great length of time, as the load was removed which had oppressed me." *Vortigern* would not be performed again until 1997.

The Shakespear Phantom

In the aftermath of the disastrous performance, the London press went into a literary feeding frenzy. Nearly all the newspapers published hostile reviews; only *Ayre's Sunday London Gazette* objected that many in the audience "came with every possible prejudice upon their minds, and from their taking an advantage of every trivial occurrence, and constant endeavours to give a ludicrous turn to every little incident, we are unable to enter into that critical examination of the merits of the piece as it was our intention to have done, had it been heard by an *impartial* audience."

But that sort of fairness couldn't be expected from the other papers. The *Morning Post* thought the audience was impartial enough: "Vortigern has been fairly heard by one of the most crowded, and we will add, candid audiences that ever filled a Theatre." The *Morning Chronicle* likewise offered the praise that "no audience ever was more patient, and long suffering," but they would not stand to see the national poet's reputation besmirched by the miserable forgeries: "The effrontery of producing such crudities, such bombast, such impotent and audacious plagiarisms, and challenging the whole kingdom to deny the farrago to be SHAKSPEARE's, exceeds credibility! . . . Need we add the abortion was treated as it deserved?" The *Observer* declared, "Throughout the Piece, we could not discover a single thought or expression which might denote the mighty master's mind: for the energetic dignity conspicuous in his writing, was substituted the most incoherent rhapsodies." The *Oracle* added insult to injury by opining that "The INCIDENTS were not merely dull but ludicrous—the LANGUAGE low, flat, and feeble; of no age, of no choice. One tremendous yell of indignation from the pit, burst simultaneously—it was the knell of fate, and consigned the offender to literary damnation." What just a few months ago "must be Shakspeare's, & Shakspeare's *only*" was now an obvious forgery; what had been praised as the sublime voice of the Bard was now an "abortion," "incoherent," "low, flat, and feeble."

After the failure of *Vortigern*, when it was no longer possible to sustain the hoax, William Henry Ireland realized his only option was to confess—and, in what might be the most pathetic part of the whole pathetic story, his father refused to believe him. Even after Malone's book was published, even after *Vortigern* produced such an uproar at Drury Lane, Samuel Ireland remained a believer—not because he thought his son was too honest to fool the world, but because he thought he was too stupid to pull it off. "Can you for a Moment think so meanly of me as to be the *Fool* to some person of Genius?" wrote William to his father. "No Sir," he insisted, "I wou'd scorn the thought." The works were original: "The Vortigern I wrote if I copied anyone it was the Bard himself . . . If there is Soul or Imagery it is *my own*." He even dared his father, "[Offer a reward] to any one that will come forward & swear he furnish'd me even with a single thought throughout the papers." No, wrote young Ireland: "If the writer of the papers I mean the Mind that breathes through them shows any spark of Genius and deserves honour *I Sir* YOUR *Son* am that person & if I live but for a little I will prove it." He ended with a solemn oath: "if I speak false may the Almighty Judge me accordingly." But even the asseverations failed to convince Samuel.

Bitter at his play's failure and his father's rejection, William fled London. When he returned a few months later he ran into his father, who recorded his son's "coolness and indifference." The subject of the Shakespeare papers inevitably came up, and William announced he was at work on a pamphlet "in wch he would avow himself the Author of the papers." Samuel was convinced he was doing it only for attention. Even when William produced a Shakespearean forgery on the spot, in the handwriting and spelling of all the others, Samuel refused to believe him. A few months later they passed on the street: "He addressed me in a very cool insulting manner," wrote Samuel, and "neither touched his hat, nor offer'd his hand . . . [I] told him I neither did, nor would believe him to be the author of the papers, till he gave specimens of his abilities equal to what I had in my possession," but his son "again & again asserted boldly, that he was the Author of the whole." Samuel, still convinced the papers were genuine, "then called for *proofs* without which," he maintained, "neither ye world, nor myself w^{d} Credit him—he said he cared not for ye world, & as for myself, he was sure I never would believe him ye Author." Samuel stormed off and never again saw his son. He died in 1800 and went to his grave a believer in the authenticity of the Shakespeare papers.

In a way it's unsurprising that Samuel should have refused to believe his son. William was a compulsive and pathological liar who lied not only about the forged Shakespeare papers but about almost everything else. He spent his entire adult life, for instance, lying about the year of his birth, subtracting two years from his true age, probably in the belief that a seventeen-year-old forger would be more precocious and less culpable than a nineteen-year-old forger. He also told his family an elaborate story about his impending marriage to a beautiful young woman: as Samuel recorded, "he let me into a great secret which was that he would very shortly be Married to a Miss Shaw . . . She was an only child, had an Independant Fortune of 7 thousand Pounds, & her Father was esteem'd very rich." William was ready with a detailed story about their meeting: "the Lady was struck with him at first sight at the Opera & tho they did not exchange a word she contriv'd in a few days to find him out & appoint him a meeting as if by accident." And his kindly benefactor, Mr. H, "highly approv'd of the business." But when Samuel Ireland went to pay his respects to the Shaw family, he discovered no family by that name on the street his son had mentioned. And so Samuel went back to confront William, who said that he must have misheard: not *Shaw*, he said, but *Shard*. Back Samuel went to the street, where he did indeed find a Shard family—but "they did not answer his description there not being any daughters in the Family." Ireland lied so often that everything that has been said about him is in doubt.

Even after the Shakespeare imposture, the lies kept coming. Ireland thought that once he announced the Shakespearean masterpieces had come from his pen, the world would realize it was dealing with a genius and eagerly await his next productions. Instead the world ignored him, and he passed his adult life resenting the literary establishment that refused to pay him his due. The forger lived another thirty-nine years after *Vortigern* was exposed, and in that time he turned out dozens of books in nearly as many forms. His historical and biographical works sometimes contained minor lies and forgeries, though nothing on the scale of the Shakespeare papers. He also wrote Gothic and sentimental novels, satirical poems, political tracts, histories of the theatre, and a dozen other genres beside, but sales were always disappointing, and he often found himself in debt. As he aged, he became a kind of legendary figure—the poet John Clare called him "Ireland the Shakespear Phantom"—and he knew his original autograph forgeries would be worth money. So he pasted the Shakespeare manuscripts into albums, added prefaces and captions, and sold them to a book collector. Then he pasted *more* "original" Shakespeare manuscripts into more albums and sold them to another book collector, and another, and another. Every copy was billed as the "original forgeries," an oddly postmodern notion, although they were being mass-produced to cash in on his youthful notoriety. Around two dozen "original" love letters to "Anna Hatherrewaye" survive today, and most of the great libraries in the Anglophone world have these "original" forgeries. Poor Ireland was reduced to forging himself. He died poor in 1835, a faker to the end, never having achieved the fame and fortune he was convinced he deserved.

His Propensity for Invention

The story of *Vortigern* is pleasingly dramatic, but Ireland's forgeries themselves were fairly clumsy. He managed to fool many people, but the real experts—people like Joseph Ritson and Edmond Malone—never took him seriously. All sorts of anachronisms tipped off the conscientious, such as a letter to Lord Leicester that could only have been written long after Leicester's death. Ireland's Shakespeare also observed, "Each titled dame deserts her rolls and tea," prompting Malone to scold him for "introducing our fragrant Chinese beverage" long before it was introduced to England. (Thomas Garway first offered the drink called "China Tcha, Tay or Tee" for sale in 1657, more than forty years after Shakespeare died.) Another giveaway was his bizarre fantasy version of sixteenth-century handwriting, which was almost as preposterous as his notion of old spelling. Ireland's usual rule was to change *i*'s to *y*'s (and vice versa), to double as many consonants as possible, to sprinkle silent *e*'s liberally, and to do away with all punctuation, producing passages like this from Queen Elizabeth's supposed letter to Shakespeare, "Wee shalle departe fromme Londonne toe Hamptowne forre the holydayes," or even "toe bee orre notte toe bee." The newspaper the *Telegraph* made fun of this by pretending to publish a letter from Shakespeare to "Missteerree BEENJAAMMIINNEE JOOHNNSSONN," inviting him to lunch "too eatte sommee muttonne choppes andd somme poottaattoooeesse." Ireland was destined to be found out simply because he didn't know much about Shakespeare or other Elizabethan literature.

If, however, a real scholar decided to go over to the dark side, it would be much more difficult to catch him. That scholar was John Payne Collier, who was born in 1789, a few years before Ireland began his Shakespearean project. As a young man Collier served as a reporter, editor, and reviewer for several newspapers and magazines, and then went on to study law. His real passion, though, was older English literature, and even when he was writing for magazines he contributed learned essays on Elizabethan literature and culture, including a series of nine articles "On the English Dramatic Writers who Preceded Shakespeare."

In the mid-1820s Collier worked on a new edition of Robert Dodsley's *Select Collection of Old Plays*, an important set of dramas from Shakespeare's era, and a few years later he was doing pioneering work on the history of popular culture, providing a history of Punch and Judy. The most important work of his early career, though, was *A History of English Dramatic Poetry and Annals of the Stage*, published in three fat volumes in 1831. Much of the *History* is impressive and scholarly, covering a tremendous amount of information on the early English theatre. The leading experts on Collier's career, Arthur Freeman and Janet Ing Freeman, argue that the *History* is the first "extended and coherent overview of the drama adjacent to Shakespeare," and that it gave much-needed attention to the works of Shakespeare's contemporaries. And yet, stirred in with the meticulous research, there were some fifteen or twenty oddities. Some of them quote from documents that have never turned up anywhere else: a "Ballade in praise of London Prentices, and what they did at the Cock-pitt Playhouse in Drury Lane" was said to come from an early manuscript, but no one has ever been able to track down the original. And a "private letter, written by a person of the name of Thomas Brande, which I discovered among some miscellaneous papers in the library of the Archbishop of Canterbury at Lambeth" has been quoted in many scholarly histories for its information about the early theatre, but no one has ever turned up the mysterious letter.

The generous interpretation is that modern Shakespeareans simply haven't yet discovered Collier's sources; as the Freemans admit, "It remains possible . . . that the Brande letter will someday turn up." Possible, yes, but not likely, because other passages in the same book are now known to be forgeries, and fakes tend to travel in packs. Some of the passages came from manuscripts in several library collections where Collier's own forgeries can still be found. Collier often quoted the diary of Shakespeare's contemporary Philip Henslowe, one of the most important sources for information about the Elizabethan theatre. At least three of the quotations, though, are suspicious. Collier quoted a passage about the payment the playwright Thomas Dekker received "for adycyons to *Fosstus* [i.e., Marlowe's *Doctor Faustus*] . . . and fyve shellinges more for *a prolog to Marloes Tamburlan*." The original handwritten draft of Henslowe's diary, now owned by Dulwich College in southeastern London, does in fact contain those lines—but they're in a different handwriting from Henslowe's. And since the passage didn't appear in published selections from the diary in the 1790s, it's hard to resist the suspicion that someone altered the manuscript early in the nineteenth century.

Had Collier written only the *History*, he might be remembered to posterity as a serious scholar whose work was only slightly marred by his uncritical acceptance of a few questionable documents. Collier's defenders argue, even now, that others committed the forgeries, and that Collier's only sin was credulity. The sheer amount of forgery that surrounds him, though, leaves little doubt that he was behind it from the beginning. The Freemans ask the obvious question: "Why would anyone risk his reputation for a pittance?" But risk it he did, and the Freemans add, "whatever the reason or reasons, once indulged, his propensity for invention never subsided."

In the early 1830s, though, no one suspected anything. Collier was a promising scholar who worked to catalog several noblemen's libraries. This work impressed people in high places, who invited him to join clubs that both studied and celebrated the culture of Shakespeare's age. Collier was a member of the Garrick Club, named for Shakespeare's most distinguished eighteenth-century interpreter, and he was elected to the Society of Antiquaries. He also attended several of Samuel Taylor Coleridge's famous lectures on Shakespeare, and his shorthand notes are the only record that survives from some of them. All the while he was a tireless critic and editor, turning out dozens of books and countless articles on little-known aspects of Elizabethan and Jacobean culture. In the 1830s came a series of short books on Shakespearean subjects: *New Facts Relating to the Life of Shakespeare*, *New Particulars Regarding the Works of Shakespeare*, and *Farther Particulars Regarding Shakespeare and His Works*. But once again, the tracts, while usually reliable, included a number of suspicious assertions. *New Facts*, for instance, was the first book to quote a certificate of 1589, showing that Shakespeare was a sharer in James Burbage's theatre company. This discovery, if genuine, would be hugely important, the only surviving shred of evidence about Shakespeare's life between 1585 and 1592. And yet a careful examination of the document reveals it to be a forgery, a product of the nineteenth rather than the sixteenth century. Collier also cataloged as old ballads things he had in fact written himself, and a number of letters and documents referring to Shakespeare, supposedly found in a nobleman's library, were also of his own invention.

The Old Corrector

Documents now recognized as forgeries, though, had not yet aroused skepticism in the 1830s and '40s, in part because the individual "discoveries" were small and undramatic. Collier continued publishing such discoveries, mixing genuine antiquarian research with his own fabrications, but he grew more daring in the early 1850s when he announced his discovery of the so-called Perkins Folio (which takes its name from an early owner). This copy of the Second Folio, published in 1632, included many comments and corrections written in a seventeenth-century hand. When Collier published the annotations in 1853—*Notes and Emendations to the Text of Shakespeare's Plays, from Early Manuscript Corrections in a Copy of the Folio, 1632, in the Possession of J. Payne Collier, Esq. F.S.A.*—he professed not to know the identity of this "old corrector," but he was confident that the annotations were made "not much later than the time when [the book] came from the press." More important, the changes this corrector made to the Second Folio seemed to be more than just uninformed guesses; the supposed corrections were "so admirable," a friend wrote, "that they can hardly be conjectural." The clear implication was that these changes were made by someone who knew Shakespeare's text better than Shakespeare's publishers, and that the Perkins Folio was therefore the most reliable source for establishing what Shakespeare really wrote. When Collier came to publish a complete edition of the plays in 1858, the Perkins emendations were the source of many of his readings.

As with his earlier supposed discoveries, the new information

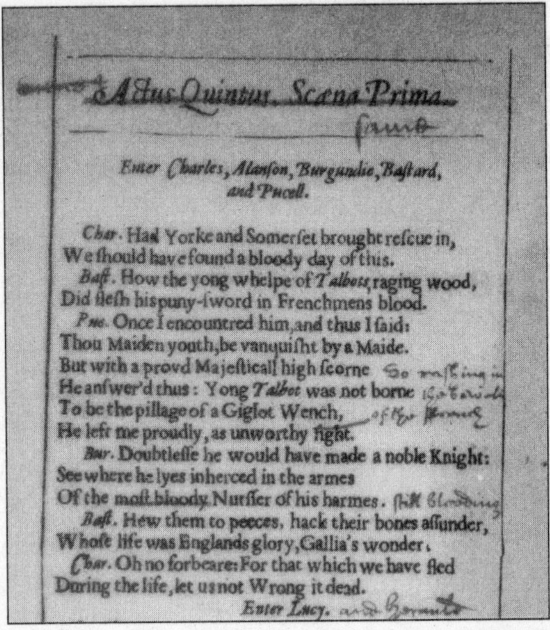

Actus Quintus. Scena Prima.

Enter Charles, Alanſon, Burgundie, Baſtard, and Pucell.

Char. Had Yorke and Somerſet brought reſcue in,
We ſhould have found a bloody day of this.
Baſt. How the yong whelpe of *Talbots*, raging wood,
Did fleſh his puny-ſword in Frenchmens blood.
Puc. Once I encountred him, and thus I ſaid:
Thou Maiden youth, be vanquiſht by a Maide.
But with a provd Majeſticall high ſcorne
He anſwer'd thus: Yong *Talbot* was not borne
To be the pillage of a Giglot Wench,
He left me proudly, as unworthy fight.
Bur. Doubtleſſe he would have made a noble Knight:
See where he lyes inherced in the armes
Of the moſt bloody Nurſer of his harmes.
Baſt. Hew them to peeces, hack their bones aſſunder,
Whoſe life was Englands glory, Gallia's wonder.
Char. Oh no forbeare: For that which we have fled
During the life, let us not Wrong it dead.
Enter Lucy.

John Payne Collier claimed to have discovered a marked-up copy of the Second Folio, bearing the annotations of "the old corrector." Reproduced from Notes and Emendations to the Text of Shakespeare's Plays.

was rarely shocking; to anyone other than an expert, it might even seem niggling. Some changes were as small as a single letter or punctuation mark, and even the most extensive passage is only thirteen lines long—a tiny fraction of Ireland's forgeries. In the Second Folio, for instance, one line in *1 Henry IV* reads, "My Selfe, and Sonne *Harry* will towards Wales"; the old corrector inserted the word *your* before *Sonne*. Where *Titus Andronicus* reads, "The fields are fragrant, and the Woods are greene," the corrector changed *greene* to *wide*. He also tidied some of the punctuation and introduced some new stage directions. Few of his changes were more extensive than that. Taken individually they seem trivial. And yet, with around twenty-seven hundred of these "corrections," the changes collectively amounted to a significantly new text. Real knowledge, after all, is built up out of thousands of little discoveries.

Some of the corrector's changes sound reasonable enough. Collier, for example, discussed a troublesome passage in *King Lear*, where the disgraced Cordelia begs her father to

make known
It is no vicious blot, murder or foulness,
No unchaste action, or dishonour'd step,
That hath depriv'd me of your grace and favour.

Collier was bothered by the word *murder*, noting that "Cordelia could never contemplate that any body would suspect her of 'murder.'" He therefore was glad that "the old corrector has given us the real language of Shakespeare," which showed that the typesetter had misread the handwritten copy: not *murder* (once commonly spelled *murther*) but *nor other*. The passage should have read

make known
It is no vicious blot, *nor other* foulness,
No unchaste action.

Had Collier proposed this change himself, it might well have been accepted as plausible, just as more than a century earlier Lewis Theobald convinced the world that Falstaff "babbled of green fields." But suggesting changes like this is risky, because editors are hesitant to accept emendations without sound reasons. As the Freemans write, "many of the Perkins emendations sound like the night-thoughts of an editor bound by his own good principles to repress them in his considered, conservative text, yet anxious somehow to air them, even claim priority for them, should they appeal." The authoritative corrector allowed him to present his own speculations as well-grounded facts.

After the announcement of the Perkins Folio, though, Collier's string of too-good-to-be-true discoveries finally began to prompt doubt, and others began checking his assertions carefully. Some of the leading Shakespeareans of the Victorian era joined the investigation, and many found troublesome inconsistencies—enough to make even Collier's friends suspicious, and to give his enemies an excuse to be brutal. In 1856, for example, Samuel Weller Singer complained of "the absurd and sweeping blunders" by the "pseudo antique corrector," and Howard Staunton hoped that the changes "will speedily find the oblivion they so well deserve." Dozens of reviews, articles, pamphlets, and books were published to dispute the Perkins revisions.

In 1859, hoping to settle the questions, a team of experts from the British Museum examined the Perkins Folio in great detail, even putting its pages under a microscope. One investigator was puzzled to discover "a great number of pencil marks in the margins of the Shakspere," noting, "in some cases, I think I can perceive traces of pencil *under* the ink." What's more, these pencil marks "have not even the pretence of antiquity in character or spelling, but are written in a bold hand of the present century." In other words, the ostensibly old handwriting was written over modern pencil marks. "I consider it positively established," wrote another scholar from the British Museum, "that the emendations, as they are called, of this folio copy of *Shakespeare* have been made within the present century." After several letters appeared in the *Times* laying out the charges against the Perkins Folio, critics swarmed to see the book: as the museum's keeper of manuscripts observed, "We do nothing else all day but shew the volume to persons deeply interested in the question."

After a few halfhearted attempts at self-defense, Collier maintained a determined silence about the Perkins Folio affair, never answering the challenges in public. He remained a prodigiously productive scholar over his long career: the Freemans' bibliography of his publications stretches to nearly 350 pages. But his reputation had been damaged irreparably. It was clear that someone had forged the annotations in the Perkins Folio. In 1859 it still seemed far-fetched to suggest that Collier might be the culprit; he did, after all, have an impressive record of publication. But even under the most generous interpretation, Collier must have been a sloppy scholar who foolishly and repeatedly fell prey to someone else's forgeries. And through the 1860s the evidence began to mount that Collier was not merely sloppy but dishonest. It was becoming more and more difficult to stand by him.

The most damning indictment was delivered by another Victorian critic, Clement Mansfield Ingleby. First came *The Shakespeare Fabrications; or, The MS. Notes of the Perkins Folio Shown to Be of Recent Origin*, a work of 144 pages, in 1859; two years later he published *A Complete View of the Shakspere Controversy, Concerning the Authenticity and Genuineness of Manuscript Matter Affecting the Works and Biography of Shakspere, Pub. by Mr. J. Payne Collier as the Fruits of His Researches*, stretching to more than 350 pages. Not all of Ingleby's criticisms hit the mark, and he missed many genuine problems with the Perkins Folio. And yet he made his case against Collier with such vehemence that the charges stuck. As the Freemans write, "what *Shakespeare Fabrications* lacked in persuasive presentation it made up for in bluster." He also mischievously included an appendix in *The Shakespeare Fabrications* "on the authorship of the Ireland forgeries," forever associating the distinguished Collier with the inept forger of a half century earlier.

In many respects the comparison was unfair. Collier was far more sophisticated than his teenage predecessor. Ireland was an outsider to the literary and scholarly community; Collier was not only an insider but worked at the very heart of the learned world. And Collier's forgeries were not nearly so bold as Ireland's—no long-lost plays, no love notes, no letters to his own forgotten ancestors. But it was for this very reason that Collier's forgeries were so successful. Ireland's forgeries were big and striking, but their nature immediately aroused suspicion. Collier's forgeries were less dramatic and less brazen than Ireland's, but for that very reason they were more insidious.

Collier lived a long life, dying at the age of ninety-four, and in that time he published dozens of works of groundbreaking investigations into Shakespeare and his world. And yet researchers still have trouble telling his genuine scholarship from his fabrication, and worry that every book and manuscript he handled may contain undetected forgeries. Ireland was a colorful character, but he had nothing genuine to teach the world about Shakespeare's life and career. Everything he wrote about it can be safely dismissed as bogus. Collier, though, mixed his deceptions with some genuinely important discoveries, so anyone reading his works can't simply ignore the lot. Some of the misinformation he introduced into his works in the 1830s continues to circulate in books and articles today. Lies, once they are accepted as true, take on a life of their own, one that lasts long after the original falsehoods have been exposed.

Ireland and Collier were not alone. It's telling that the keyword *forgery* shows up more than a hundred times in the catalog to the Folger Shakespeare Library: forged signatures, forged poems, books on how to distinguish genuine old handwriting from the imitations. Some of these frauds were more a product of wishful thinking than wickedness; in the absence of reliable evidence, many critics have passed off their guesswork as fact, which then gets passed from generation to generation as if it were true. The wheelwright and poet John Jordan, for example, appointed himself a guide to Stratford and made up stories to impress the tourists, some of which have entered the scholarly record. And a painting of Shakespeare, now known as the Flower Portrait after its onetime owner, Sir Desmond Flower, turned up in 1840. For decades people had longed for an authoritative portrait, and this seemed to be the answer to their prayers. The engraving by Martin Droeshout in the First Folio, the most famous image in all of English literary history, must have been copied from an earlier portrait—but no painting from the playwright's lifetime seems to survive. At last the Flower Portrait, dated 1609, seemed to fill the bill: it showed Shakespeare in the same pose as the folio's engraving. Only in 2005 did sophisticated forensic techniques—X-rays, ultraviolet light, and chemical analysis of the paint—prove that the painting dated not from the early seventeenth century but from the early nineteenth, some two hundred years after the playwright's death. The Flower Portrait, in other words, was not the source of the Droeshout engraving but a copy.

It's reasonable to assume that many of the "facts" about Shakespeare and his age were not discovered but invented. The major findings have been checked and rechecked so many times that they're probably reliable: the dates of Shakespeare's baptism and burial, the records of the theatre companies, and so on. But who can tell whether some of the research on, say, Elizabethan proverbs or ballads was fabricated? And only recently did experts discover that, just a few years after Shakespeare's death, a printer named Thomas Pavier issued a few quartos backdated to make them look like first editions: his version of *King Lear* says "1608" on the title page, but it's now been shown that it was really printed in 1619. No one will hazard a guess as to how many supposed "facts" will eventually be proven to be equally bogus. It should give us pause any time we think our knowledge about Shakespeare is on firm ground.

CHAPTER 8

Worshipping Shakespeare

According to legend—a legend that may have the rare distinction of being true—Shakespeare, on his retirement to Stratford-upon-Avon, planted a mulberry tree in the garden of his house, New Place.

For more than a hundred years after Shakespeare's death, New Place wasn't a museum or a tourist destination, just a private residence. It was one of the more spacious houses in town—Shakespeare had a good mind for business and accumulated a sizable fortune in his work in the theatre—but beyond that it was nothing special. And no one seems to have cared about its history; it was extensively remodeled in 1702, and there wasn't so much as a plaque to indicate its former owner. In the 1750s it was bought by the Reverend Francis Gastrell, vicar of Frodsham in Cheshire, as a summer home. He bought it not because it was Shakespeare's house but because it was comfortable, convenient, and available.

At first no one paid any special attention to the tree in Gastrell's garden. It had been standing for a very long time, more than a century, and had never attracted any notice before, certainly not from Londoners. Although Stratford-upon-Avon is just a two-hour train ride from central London, an eighteenth-century stagecoach would take the better part of two days to cover the hundred miles—even when the weather cooperated and the roads were in good condition. Stratford was a reasonably prosperous market town, but few Londoners had any reason to travel to Warwickshire. Neither did those who lived closer; Stratford is fifty miles from Oxford and only twenty miles from Birmingham, but residents of those cities almost never made the trip. By most accounts there was nothing to see.

There were a few early visitors to Shakespearean sites in Stratford, though most were simply passing through. In 1634, eighteen years after Shakespeare's death, a Lieutenant Hammond of the Military Company of Norwich stopped in the Church of the Holy Trinity and saw "A Neat Monument of the famous English poet, Mr. William Shakespeere, who was borne heere." Around 1708 Thomas Betterton was probably the first professional actor to make the trip to Stratford since Shakespeare's own company had visited nearly a century earlier. Daniel Defoe, famous as the author of *Robinson Crusoe*, stopped in Stratford during his tour of the country in the early 1720s, but his published *Tour Through the Whole Island of Great Britain* gives just a few sentences to the town's favorite son. And these few tourists were the exceptions; there wasn't yet any significant traffic. One guide to English towns published in 1724 noted that "The Town has two Churches, is well inhabited, has a good Market on *Thursdays*, and has a considerable Trade by Malt made here"—but not a word about Stratford's most famous native. Only in the 1740s and '50s did "traveller's companions" start listing Shakespeare's birthplace as an attraction for those few who visited.

And yet, as the two hundredth anniversary of Shakespeare's birth approached, a few devotees began making the long trip. Of course there were no tourist bureaus or information kiosks in the 1750s; there were no maps or guidebooks pointing out the Shakespearean high spots in the town. Some locals were happy to lend assistance to the small but growing trickle of London tourists checking out their town, and many doubtless took advantage of the credulous city folk. It seems some hucksters made a habit of pointing to any old building and making up stories to please the visitors, always taking a few shillings for their trouble. One local identified a house in Stratford as the home of Shakespeare's mother—an identification that stood until experts disproved it in 2000.

Gastrell, though, didn't like the attention his adopted town was getting, and he especially disliked the fact that his home was becoming a regular stop on these tours. Londoners were milling about his house, pointing and gawking. And when people remembered the old story that Shakespeare had planted a mulberry tree in his garden—and when they saw an old mulberry tree at New Place—they imagined that owning a piece of that tree would bring them a little closer to the Bard they adored. Gastrell watched with increasing frustration as fans of the playwright trespassed on his property and broke twigs from the tree. Finally, in 1756, Gastrell became so annoyed by the stream of pilgrims coming to look at his tree that, in a fit of pique, he simply chopped it down.

In that action, he became the blackest villain in the entire history of Shakespeare's afterlife. James Boswell, Samuel Johnson's biographer, referred to him as "the clergyman who . . . with Gothick barbarity cut down his mulberry-tree." Gastrell's "Gothick barbarity" would soon go even further. He was engaged in a tax dispute with the town council of Stratford. Gastrell maintained he wasn't a year-round resident, and therefore he shouldn't be a year-round taxpayer. Stratford maintained he was a year-round owner, and demanded the full payment. The bureaucratic battle went back and forth for a while, until finally Gastrell pulled the house down; if there's no house, there's no house to tax. Shakespeare's birthplace still stands today; Anne Hathaway's cottage is open to the public; the church in which Shakespeare was baptized and buried can be visited. But New Place, the house in which he spent his final years, the house in which he may well have written *The Tempest*, was reduced to kindling in a mean-spirited act of spite in 1759.

Shakespeare retired to New Place in Stratford-upon-Avon; Francis Gastrell tore the building down in the eighteenth century. From Edmond Malone's edition of The Plays of William Shakespeare.

The mulberry tree, however, while no longer standing, didn't disappear—nor did it stop growing. A clever local watchmaker and entrepreneur, Thomas Sharp, bought up most of the wood and began fashioning it into trinkets, selling them to devotees of the Sweet Swan of Avon. His ingenuity knew no bounds. The critic Christian Deelman's description of this miraculous tree gives some idea of how effective Sharp was in marketing Shakespeare's cultural cachet:

> The tree must surely have been of prodigious growth, for the list of objects which the ingenious carpenter made and sold is endless. At first, Sharp's products were fairly simple: little boxes, for snuff or for trinkets, tea-chests and small trunks. Then, as his imagination rose to the chal-

> lenge, more and more domestic items found themselves fashioned from mulberry wood. Records are to be found listing cups and goblets, punch-ladles, card-cases, cribbage boards, tobacco-stoppers, tooth-pick cases, writing standishes, ink-horns and pen-cases, knives and forks, nutmeg-graters, knitting sheaths, comb cases, and many more specifically local objects, such as carvings of Shakespeare's monument in the church.

Plenty of people bought these souvenirs over the next few decades. Local merchants all claimed to have the remains of the genuine tree, accusing their rivals of using wood from some other mulberry. Many of them grew rich.

To Flatter Mr. Garrick

The most famous owner of a piece of the tree, though, didn't have to pay for it. In 1769 David Garrick, the actor and impresario whose realistic acting style took London by storm, was at the height of his fame, the most celebrated actor in the English-speaking world. But in organizing a three-day lovefest in the town of Shakespeare's birth, the Jubilee, he would link his name with Shakespeare's in a way that even he had never done before. He would also begin a new era in Shakespeare worship: as Deelman writes, "The importance of the Jubilee in the history of Shakespeare's reputation can hardly be exaggerated. It marks the point at which Shakespeare stopped being regarded as an increasingly popular and admirable dramatist, and became a god."

The ostensible purpose of the Jubilee was to dedicate Stratford's new town hall. The old town hall was in bad shape by the middle of the eighteenth century, and funds for renovation were in short supply. The town council thought they might be able to cash in on Shakespeare's growing fame by approaching actors

David Garrick received gifts made of mulberry wood at the Jubilee of 1769. From a painting by Benjamin van der Gucht.

and seeking donations. Garrick was at the top of their list. The generous interpretation is that they approached him because he was the leading performer of the day, the man who did more than anyone else to bring Shakespeare's plays to the masses. The less generous interpretation is that he was an easy mark: rich, vain, and susceptible to flattery. They employed plenty of flattery, offering him the "freedom of the town"—an honor equivalent to the key to the city—if he would provide a statue to decorate the new town hall. Francis Wheler wrote a letter in November 1767 suggesting that "it would be an Ornament to our New Town Hall at Stratford if we cou'd get from Mr. Garrick some very handsom bust, statue, or picture of Shakespear." He realized, though, that it might be necessary "to flatter Mr. Garrick into some such Handsom present," and therefore advised the township "to propose to make Mr. Garrick an Honourary Burgess of Stratford & to present him therew[th] in a Box made of Shakespeare's Mulberry tree." The actor was intrigued by the idea. Not content with sending money from afar, though, he became intimately involved in planning a grand event. The bicentenary of Shakespeare's birth had gone unnoticed, but now, five years later, Garrick thought a public celebration was called for. It would be an opportunity to promote his beloved Shakespeare, as well as an opportunity to promote himself—an opportunity the successful showman rarely missed.

The most interesting thing was his decision to hold this Shakespearean celebration in Stratford. Garrick had visited the town once before: he toured it in 1742, near the beginning of his theatrical career. In making it the center of attention, Garrick and the Stratford town council were marking a major change in how Shakespeare was to be appreciated. London, after all, was the site of all of his professional triumphs, and where he chose to live most of his adult life. The Globe and Blackfriars had been in London; his audiences—both courtly and common—had been based there. His poems and plays were printed in London. His plays speak of the Thames and the Tower, but there's not a word about the Avon or the Church of the Holy Trinity.

And yet, by the middle of the eighteenth century, Shakespeare the universal genius was becoming more important than Shakespeare the craftsman and businessman. The books and the theatres could all be seen in London, but bardolaters increasingly wanted to go beyond the works, to get close to the *man*. Eighteenth-century readers were developing a new interest in the importance of childhood, and they wanted to see the places where the young genius was born, grew up, went to school, and fell in love. They wanted to touch the font where he was baptized and to visit the house of his darling Anne Hathaway. They wanted to stand over his remains and contemplate their own mortality.

And so the fledgling Shakespeare Industry began to shift its location from the metropolis to a small provincial market town.

Logistic problems abounded, because Stratford wasn't prepared for the huge influx of visitors during the Jubilee. Getting there was difficult for those who couldn't afford their own carriages, since the stagecoaches were slow and crowded. Boswell's experience was all too typical: he took a stagecoach late at night and, afraid that he might be stopped by robbers, hid his watch, his money, and his letters in various parts of the coach. In the small hours he transferred to another coach, and then to another, before he finally realized that he had left all his valuables in the original coach. He had to hire a horse to gallop back many miles to recover his lost possessions, arriving in Stratford very late and very tired.

A bigger problem for most visitors was accommodation; finding a suitable room on short notice was all but impossible. The few inns had filled quickly. Many locals rented out rooms in their houses, attics, and even henhouses, most for the outrageous sum of a guinea a night—this at a time when a tradesman might hope to earn about fifty guineas a year. Some charged extravagant fees on top of that, as many visitors were forced to pay the equivalent of fifty dollars for breakfast. But money was pouring in from London to the provinces, and Stratfordians were keen to get some of it. Commerce has never been far from the celebration of high culture. It seems every merchant was eager to profit from the event. On the first day of the Jubilee, for instance, one newspaper carried the following advertisement for a tooth powder under the heading FOR THE STRATFORD JUBILEE:

> To those who would appear really elegant there, or elsewhere, the Albion Dentifrice is recommended, as without a sweet Breath and clean Mouth (which no cloying Odours of perfumed Essence will give) there can be no communicative Satisfaction. This Dentifrice in a few Times using

> will evince its superior Efficacy and Elegance; it has no Taste, yet it will make the Teeth white and beautiful, the Saliva pure and balsamic, all which it does by concocting the acrimonious Juices of the salival Glands.

As the critic Michael Dobson writes, "What is most striking" about these things at the Jubilee "is not their kitsch strangeness but their unnerving familiarity."

All Shall Yield to the Mulberry Tree

Everything seemed in order for a fitting three-day tribute to England's greatest poet and playwright. Garrick gave the town council the statue, and they in return gave him the freedom of the town, a scroll housed in a box made from the mulberry tree. They also offered him a goblet carved from the same wood. A medal was struck to commemorate the occasion, reading "WE SHALL NOT LOOK UPON HIS LIKE AGAIN," and most visitors wore ribbons designed "in imitation of the rainbow, which uniting the colours of all parties, is likewise an emblem of the great variety of his genius." Garrick planned what Boswell called "a procession of allegorical beings," an elaborate outdoor parade of both professional actors and local dignitaries dressed as Shakespeare's characters.

But the organizers hadn't counted on the weather, and the rain was disastrous. The parade was canceled: Boswell fretted that the downpour risked "destroying the valuable dresses, and endangering the still more valuable health of the fair performers, who might have been rendered incapable of appearing in public for a whole season, perhaps for life." Worse still, on the second day of the Jubilee, the River Avon overflowed its banks and nearly washed away the pavilion in which the most important events were held. Planned fireworks came to nothing as the rain soaked the fuses and dampened the gunpowder.

Mother Nature was unkind to the outdoor celebrations, but indoors the Jubilee went on. The highlight was Garrick's "Ode," a long celebratory poem devoted to Shakespeare's genius. This selection gives a good taste of the whole:

> O! from his muse of fire!
> Could but one spark be caught,
> Then might these humble strains aspire
> To tell the wonders he has wrought;
> To tell how, sitting on his throne,
> Unaided and alone,
> In dreadful state,
> The subject passions round him wait;
> Who, though unchain'd, and raging there,
> He checks, enflames, or turns their made career,
> With that superior skill
> Which winds the fiery steed at will:
> He gives the awful word,
> And they all foaming, trembling, own him for their
> lord.

As Garrick read the poem, the orchestra played dramatic music in the background. It was a hit, one Garrick would repeat in London to great acclaim. His first biographer, Thomas Davies, called it "that part of the general exhibition which most excited the regard and gained the applause of the candid and judicious part of the company." Boswell was even more effusive in his praise: "The performance of the dedication ode was noble and affecting: it was like an exhibition in Athens or Rome. The whole audience were fixed in the most earnest attention, and I do believe, that if any one had attempted to disturb the performance, he would have been in danger of his life." As Garrick read the

Rising waters from the River Avon flooded the pavilion where most of the Jubilee events were held. From Samuel Ireland's Picturesque Views on the Upper, or Warwickshire Avon.

poem, said Boswell, "he seemed in extacy, and gave us the idea of a mortal transformed into a demi-god, as we read in the Pagan mythology." Boswell found the whole affair "an elegant and truly classical celebration of the memory of Shakespeare, that illustrious poet, whom all ages will admire as the world has hitherto done."

And then there were the songs. Garrick was one of several poets who wrote lyrics praising Shakespeare, and two of Britain's most fashionable composers, Charles Dibdin and Thomas Arne, set them to music. (Arne is best remembered today as the composer of the opera *Alfred*, from which the chorus "Rule Britannia" is taken.) "Warwickshire Lads" and "Sweet Willy-O" were hits at the Jubilee and soon became popular across England. And of course the mulberry tree earned a song, in which it is impossible to miss the religious language:

Behold this fair goblet, 'twas carved from the tree,
Which, O my sweet SHAKESPEARE, was planted by thee;
As a relick I kiss it, and bow at the shrine,
What comes from thy hand must be ever divine!

And then the whole chorus joins in:

All shall yield to the Mulberry-tree,
Bend to thee,
Blest Mulberry,
Matchless was he
Who planted thee,
And thou like him immortal be!

A popular song from the Jubilee proclaimed "The Pride of all Nature was sweet Willy Ho." From Charles Dibdin, Shakespear's Garland; or, The Warwickshire Jubilee.

(Boswell noted, "The chorus is very fine.") The other verses—eight in all—are equally over the top. Shakespeare's mulberry tree dominates the "trees of the forest, so rampant and high"; it beats out the "royal" oak, "*Britain*'s great boast"—all because "The Genius of SHAKESPEARE out-shines the bright day, / More rapture than wine to the heart can convey." The song ends with a call for everyone in the audience to join in the ritual, at once poetic, religious, and nationalistic:

> Then each take a relick of this hallow'd tree,
> From folly and fashion a charm let it be;
> Fill fill to the planter, the cup to the brim,
> To honour the country, do honour to him.

And then all join, once more, in the chorus: "All shall yield to the Mulberry-tree."

Part of an Englishman's Constitution

In one respect the Jubilee was unprecedented. Never before had a writer—any writer—been the object of such veneration, and never before had a poet or playwright been honored with tour guides, souvenir trinkets, and songs. In another respect, though, the pattern is strangely familiar: the mulberry tree had become a modern equivalent of the True Cross and, to the Stratford pilgrims, Shakespeare was the secular equivalent of Christ. The faithful were determined to get their hands on a piece of history, and the less faithful were willing to provide as many pieces as the market would bear. Shakespeare's tree had been chopped up and turned into relics, hawked the way unscrupulous friars had sold saints' bones. There was even a hymnbook. In 1641, Shakespeare's friend (and sometime rival) Ben Jonson said he "lov'd the man, and [would] honour his memory, on this side idolatry." By the 1760s,

England had crossed from this side of idolatry to the other. During his lifetime, Shakespeare had been appreciated. In the early eighteenth century, he had been admired, even adored. By the time of the Jubilee, Shakespeare was worshipped.

The Jubilee simply confirmed what was going on elsewhere in the culture. Readers and critics were starting to take Shakespeare seriously as a major author, but they were also turning him into a kind of god. That deification can be seen happening in a copy of a book now owned by the Rosenbach Museum & Library in Philadelphia. In 1691—near the beginning of Shakespeare's ascent—a critic named Gerard Langbaine published *An Account of the English Dramatick Poets*. To modern readers it's a dull book, filled with biographical trivia and literary analysis on dozens of now-forgotten English playwrights from William Alexander to Robert Yarrington. Langbaine was, though, one of the first writers to give critical attention to Shakespeare, whom he called "One of the most Eminent Poets of his Time." For the late seventeenth century, that was high praise indeed. Remember that, in 1692, Thomas Rymer could complain about Shakespeare, insisting that "in the *Neighing* of an Horse . . . there is . . . more humanity, than many times in the Tragical flights of *Shakespear*." Langbaine, on the other hand, had only good things to say: "I esteem his Plays beyond any that have ever been published in our Language." One would think "One of the most Eminent Poets of his Time" would be plenty for most Shakespeare admirers.

But not for the new breed of Shakespeare worshippers. An anonymous eighteenth-century reader decided that Langbaine's tribute wasn't extravagant enough and, in the Rosenbach copy of Langbaine's book, the entry has been defaced. With two pen strokes—canceling *One of* and the letter *s*—he corrected this copy to read, "the most Eminent Poet of his Time." Those two little pen strokes tell the story of Shakespeare's rise more eloquently than any number of analytical essays. Criticizing the Bard—even hinting that he was less than perfect—was becoming the literary equivalent of blasphemy.

This was a break from standard critical practice, at a time when virtually every work of literary analysis divided its coverage into "beauties" and "faults." Even Shakespeare was not immune from this sort of treatment; as Samuel Johnson wrote, "The observation of faults and beauties is one of the duties of an annotator." It was a duty he took seriously, because Shakespeare, for all his excellence, had faults that were "sufficient to obscure and overwhelm any other merit." The critic promised to discuss the playwright's flaws "without envious malignity or superstitious veneration," but he in-

William SHAKESPEAR.

~~One of~~ the moſt Eminent Poets of his Time; he was born at *Stratford* upon *Avon* in *Warwickſhire*; and flouriſhed in the Reigns of Queen *Elizabeth*, and King *James* the Firſt. His Natural Genius to *Poetry* was ſo excellent, that like thoſe Diamonds (¹), which are found in *Cornwall*, Nature had little, or no occaſion for the Aſſiſtance of Art to poliſh it. The Truth is, 'tis agreed on by moſt, that his Learning was not extraordinary; and I am apt to believe, that his Skill in the *French* and *Italian* Tongues, exceeded his Knowledge in the *Roman* Language: for we find him not only beholding to *Cynthio Giraldi* and *Bandello*, for his Plots, but likewiſe a Scene in *Henry* the Fifth, written in *French*, between the Princeſs *Catherine* and her Governante: Beſides *Italian* Pro-

In An Account of the English Dramatick Poets, *Gerard Langbaine declared Shakespeare "One of the most Eminent Poets of his Time." An anonymous early reader, unhappy with that faint praise, "corrected" the text to make Shakespeare "the most Eminent Poet of his Time."*

sisted that he could not in good conscience overlook them, since "little regard is due to that bigotry which sets candour higher than truth." With that "candour" always in mind, he pointed out a number of Shakespeare's lapses of judgment. Johnson disliked his many puns; he thought his plots were "often so loosely formed, . . . that he seems not always fully to comprehend his own design"; and he was bothered by Shakespeare's habit of "sacrific[ing] virtue to convenience." His style was "ungrammatical, perplexed and obscure." In chatting with Boswell, Johnson insisted that "Shakspeare never has six lines together without a fault."

For later readers, even Johnson's mild criticism rankled; it was becoming almost heretical for him to suggest that Shakespeare had faults. Even facetious criticism was inappropriate. Boswell reports on a bit of tomfoolery at the Jubilee, when "Mr. King, the comedian, got up to the orchestra, and gave us a smart ironical attack upon Shakespeare, in the character of a modern refined man of taste." The stunt was supposed to satirize modern dimwits who didn't appreciate Shakespeare's genius, but Boswell found it as inappropriate as jokes in church. "This might have gone very well on some other occasion," he wrote; "but, in my opinion, it had better have been omitted at this noble festival: it detracted from it's dignity; nor was there any occasion for it. We were all enthusiastic admirers of Shakespeare."

By the end of the eighteenth century, virtually everyone in the country was an enthusiastic admirer of Shakespeare. His were the most performed plays in the English theatre. He was also playing an increasingly large role in schools, as students began to study English works in addition to the Greek and Latin classics. Schoolboys were now expected to supplement their knowledge about Julius Caesar by reading *Julius Caesar*. Even girls were being introduced to English literature in private schools and academies, and the plays of Shakespeare made up a big part of their curricula. Admiration for Shakespeare was becoming a touchstone of taste:

anyone who thought him less than divine could not, by definition, have a refined sensibility.

This is clear in the reactions of the major literary figures of the early nineteenth century, the Romantic era. William Wordsworth proclaimed, in one of his most political poems, "We must be free or die, who speak the tongue / That Shakespeare spake." His friend and collaborator Samuel Taylor Coleridge referred to "myriad-minded Shakespeare," who "is of no age—nor of any religion, or party or profession"—he was truly universal. It was Coleridge who coined the word *psychoanalytical*, using it to describe the richness of character he found in Shakespeare's works. He also drew large crowds to a series of public lectures on Shakespeare's works he delivered between 1806 and 1819. Audience members included the poet Lord Byron, the philosopher William Godwin, and his young daughter Mary, who would later marry Percy Bysshe Shelley and go on to write *Frankenstein*.

Garrick had put Stratford-upon-Avon on the cultural map with his Jubilee, and as Shakespeare's reputation grew, writers began to see Stratford and especially the Birthplace as a kind of

The house in which Shakespeare was born began attracting tourists from around the world in the late eighteenth century. From the Gentleman's Magazine.

literary Lourdes or Mecca. The poet John Keats—who thanked God that he could "read and perhaps understand Shakespeare to his depths"—visited Stratford in 1818; he signed the visitors' book at the Birthplace and wrote his name on the wall of the Church of the Holy Trinity. A decade later the novelist Sir Walter Scott paid a visit to "the tomb of the mighty wizzard." Shakespeare had become the national poet. In Jane Austen's words in *Mansfield Park*, her novel of 1814, he was "part of an Englishman's constitution. His thoughts and beauties are so spread abroad that one touches them everywhere; one is intimate with him by instinct."

The Great Family

And not only an Englishman's constitution; Shakespeare's reputation was international. British colonial administrators brought the plays with them to India as early as 1607, making Shakespeare a central part of the cultural life in the Raj. English theatre troupes had begun performing the plays in Bombay by 1770, and English schoolmasters had their Indian students perform scenes from the plays in the 1820s. In August 1848 an Indian actor, Baishnab Charan Addy, played Othello professionally in Calcutta. Shakespeare was also important in Britain's other colonies in the age when the sun never set on its empire. When the artist Sydney Parkinson sailed to New Zealand on the *Endeavour* in 1769, a copy of Shakespeare's works came with him. *Henry IV* was featured at Robert Sidaway's theatre in Sydney, Australia, in April 1800; just over a year later, in September 1801, the African Theatre in Cape Town opened with the same play.

In America the admiration was even stronger. Puritan strongholds like Boston struggled to keep the theatres closed, but with little success. As early as the 1730s there were amateur productions of Shakespeare's plays in the colonies, and by the 1750s professional performances were becoming common in New York. The Southwark Theatre in Philadelphia, the first permanent theatre in America, regularly hosted Shakespeare productions. And the Englishman Lewis Hallam brought a troupe of British actors across the Atlantic in 1752 and included maybe a half dozen of Shakespeare's plays in their repertoire as they toured the colonies, making stops in Williamsburg, New York, and Jamaica. Hallam did not live much longer, but his family went on to become one of the first acting dynasties in America.

It's no surprise that Shakespeare should have been a favorite among Englishmen in the colonies. What is remarkable, though, is the way the great representative of Englishness remained a favorite even after America broke its ties with the mother country. After 1776 he belonged not to the English but to all English speakers,

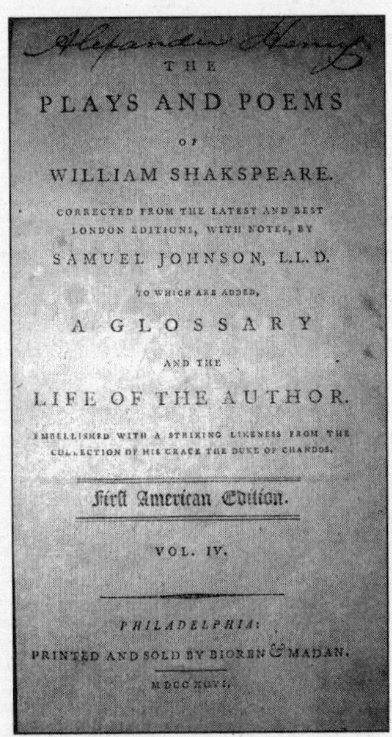

THE

PLAYS AND POEMS

OF

WILLIAM SHAKSPEARE.

CORRECTED FROM THE LATEST AND BEST LONDON EDITIONS, WITH NOTES, BY

SAMUEL JOHNSON, L.L.D.

TO WHICH ARE ADDED,

A GLOSSARY

AND THE

LIFE OF THE AUTHOR.

EMBELLISHED WITH A STRIKING LIKENESS FROM THE COLLECTION OF HIS GRACE THE DUKE OF CHANDOS.

First American Edition.

VOL. IV.

PHILADELPHIA:

PRINTED AND SOLD BY BIOREN & MADAN.

MDCCXCVI.

The British carried Shakespeare with them as their empire grew, but the newly independent Americans put their own claim on his works beginning in 1795.

and Americans were willing to ignore Shakespeare's English pedigree and focus on the self-made man who rose from humble origins. In nineteenth-century Boston, the Reverend James Freeman Clarke called on all "members of the great family which speaks the English tongue, to commemorate . . . the man who, in pure intellect, stands at the head of the human race." Noah Webster's famous *American Dictionary of the English Language*, which appeared in 1828, included plenty of quotations from Shakespeare alongside those from George Washington and Benjamin Franklin. And beginning in the 1830s, the Reverend William McGuffey's hugely influential set of *Eclectic Readers*—once used by four out of every five American schoolchildren—included generous selections from Shakespeare's works.

Among the many pilgrims who turned up in Stratford were a surprising number of Americans. John Adams and Thomas Jefferson, soon to be the second and third presidents of the United States, visited the Birthplace in 1786, shortly after the end of the Revolution. Washington Irving made the transatlantic voyage in 1815 and published his reminiscences four years later in *The Sketch Book of Geoffrey Crayon, Gent.*, the book that made him America's most famous writer. Alongside such classic stories as "The Legend of Sleepy Hollow" and "Rip Van Winkle," he printed a description of his Shakespeare-inspired journey: "I had come to Stratford," he wrote, "on a poetical pilgrimage. My first visit was to the house where Shakespeare was born." The Birthplace—"a small mean-looking edifice of wood and plaster"—was owned by an old woman, Mrs. Hornby, who "was peculiarly assiduous in exhibiting the relics with which this, like all other celebrated shrines, abounds." Irving knew perfectly well that most of the "relics" were bogus, but he enjoyed the tourist experience so much that it didn't really matter. "I am always of easy faith in such matters," he admitted, "and am ever willing to be deceived where the deceit is pleasant and costs nothing . . . What is it to us," he demanded of skeptical spoilsports, "whether these stories be true or false, so long as we can persuade ourselves into the belief of them and enjoy all the charm of the reality?" Such a willingness to believe quaint stories seems to have been the attitude of many American pilgrims, who have been eagerly pouring dollars into the Stratford economy ever since.

Some Americans went so far as to claim Shakespeare as distinctively American property. William S. Bartlet of Lowell, Massachusetts, for example, insisted that "Shakspeare is much more popular in the United States than he is in his native land. There are probably fifty readers of him in America to one reader in England." Another Yankee, Ralph Waldo Emerson, declared that "Shakespeare . . . drew the man of England and Europe; the father of the man in America." We live, breathe, and think Shakespeare whether we realize it or not: "Now, literature, philosophy and thought are Shakspearized. His mind is the horizon beyond which, at present, we do not see. Our ears are educated to music by his rhythm." He even raised Shakespeare above the rest of humanity, finding him "as much out of the category of eminent authors, as he is out of the crowd." Emerson's Shakespeare is "inconceivably wise," beyond even the most brilliant of mere mortals. "A good reader," he wrote, "can, in a sort, nestle into Plato's brain and think from thence; but not into Shakespeare's."

Shakespeare was becoming the transcendent author of the human condition. Even beyond the English-speaking world, many of the greatest writers were beginning to admire, even to worship, his insight into universal truths. Few French authors saw much to praise in Shakespeare, but in Germany he became a favorite; in fact, one of the oldest surviving Shakespeare societies in the world is the Deutsche Shakespeare-Gesellschaft. The poet and critic Friedrich Schiller, one of the most influential figures in German Romanticism, translated and adapted several of Shakespeare's works; he later visited Stratford and wrote his name on the walls of the Birthplace. He wrote to Johann Wolfgang von Goethe, now Germany's most revered author, "In the last days I have been reading the plays of Shakespeare . . . I am filled with true amazement." Goethe too adored Shakespeare; he declared 14 October 1771 "William's day" and called Shakespeare "my friend." In Russia Aleksandr Pushkin drew the inspiration for one of his most famous works, *Boris Godunov*, from Shakespeare and based his verse tale *Angelo* on *Measure for Measure*. Even Polish writers like Adam Mickiewicz and Juliusz Słowacki admired Shakespeare; the latter translated parts of *Macbeth* and *King Lear*, and even worked parts of his *Lear* translation into his own verse play, *Kordian*.

Many Thousand Lights

A religion needs a holy land and a set of rituals; it found both in Stratford. Garrick's original plan was to repeat the Jubilee either every year or every seven years. In 1770 he answered the Stratford town council's queries about how best "to celebrate the Memory of our Immortal Bard," advising, "the day (I think) should be on his Birth-day" and "the Bells should ring, & Bonfires should blaze, ye Ladies should dance, & the Gentlemen be Merry & Wise . . . There should be always proper Songs introduced at ye Table, & join'd with ye Hearts & voices of all ye Company in a feeling Enthusiastick Chorus." But he also remembered how ill-prepared Stratford was to host fashionable Londoners, accustomed to a certain degree of luxury, and he gave this advice to the town fathers:

> Let 'Em decorate ye Town, (y^{e} *happiest* & Why not y^{e} *handsomest*, in England) let your Streets be well pav'd, & kept clean, do Something wth ye delightful Meadow, allure Every body to Visit y^{e} *holy Land*; let it be well lighted, &

> clean under foot, and let it not be said . . . that the Town, which gave Birth to the first Genius since y[e] Creation, is the most dirty, unseemly, ill-pav'd, wretched-looking Town in all Britain.

His plans, though, never came to fruition; in fact Garrick never again returned to Stratford. He died in 1779, ten years after the Jubilee, and was buried with great pomp in Westminster Abbey at the foot of Shakespeare's statue.

Others, though, were eager to repeat the experience, but this time without the rain, without the ruined pageants, without the price gouging, and without the filthy streets. Wanting to repeat the Jubilee involved some selective memory. At the time many people ridiculed the whole affair. Garrick's friend Samuel Johnson didn't bother to show up. Others made the trip in a spirit of schadenfreude, hoping for the worst. At the Jubilee Garrick ran into Samuel Foote, a rival actor. "What do you think of the weather, Sam?" asked Garrick. "Think of it?" asked Foote in return. "What any sensible man would think of it. It is God's judgement on vanity and idolatry." Foote criticized the Jubilee for its "ode without poetry; music without melody; a dinner without victuals; lodgings without beds; a croud without company; a masquerade where half the people appeared barefaced; a horse-race up to the knees in water; fireworks extinguished as soon as they were lighted; and a boarded booth, by way of amphitheatre, which was to be taken down in three days, and sold by public auction." Even Garrick himself was disappointed with how the Jubilee came out, and was uncomfortable whenever anyone mentioned it to him.

But Foote's kind of cynicism, however widespread at the time of the Jubilee, quickly evaporated, and the celebration became ever more exalted in popular consciousness, ever more glorious. Even in 1771 the theatre manager Benjamin Victor called the

Jubilee "the most remarkable Event that ever happened in the Annals of Theatres, since the first Establishment of Dramatic Poetry in Europe, or, perhaps, in the known world." And by 1864 *The Official Programme of the Tercentenary Festival of the Birth of Shakespeare* noted that everything came off "to the complete satisfaction of all who engaged in it." Still, no one got around to organizing a second Jubilee until 1827, and then on a much smaller scale than Garrick's original. This time it was held on Shakespeare's (supposed) birthday, 23 April, which was also, by a happy coincidence, St. George's Day, honoring the patron saint of England. Another birthday celebration followed three years later, with royal patronage and a plan for triennial celebrations. But once again the idea was allowed to lapse, without another Stratford celebration until 1853.

This isn't to say that interest in Shakespeare was weak. Several private Shakespeare clubs began regular celebrations of the birthday in both Stratford and London beginning in the 1810s. When the Birthplace went on the market in 1847, the American circus impresario P. T. Barnum was eager to own it. But a committee raised money to buy it for the British nation, forming what has since become the Shakespeare Birthplace Trust, the organization that now manages all the Shakespearean properties in Stratford. (One of the most active campaigners to secure the house and restore it to its original state was Charles Dickens, a passionate reader of Shakespeare and a devoted performer of amateur theatricals.) And at the Great Exhibition of 1851, London's extravagant celebration of its own national and industrial pride, Shakespeare was conspicuous. Paintings and sculptures of Shakespeare and his principal characters abounded, and plaster copies of one of the statues of the Bard were available for sale.

In the early 1860s, as the three hundredth anniversary of Shake-

ON MONDAY EVENING, JUNE 5, 1848,

Will be presented Shakespeare's Comedy of

THE MERRY WIVES OF WINDSOR.

Sir John Falstaff .... Mr. MARK LEMON
Fenton .... Mr. CHARLES ROMER
Shallow .... (a Country Justice) .... Mr. CHARLES DICKENS
Slender .... (Cousin to Shallow) .... Mr. JOHN LEECH
Mr. Ford .... } Two Gentlemen Dwelling at Windsor { .... Mr. JOHN FORSTER
Mr. Page .... } Two Gentlemen Dwelling at Windsor { .... Mr. FRANK STONE
Sir Hugh Evans .... (a Welsh Parson) .... Mr. G. H. LEWES
Dr. Caius .... (a French Physician) .... Mr. DUDLEY COSTELLO
Host of the Garter Inn .... Mr. FREDERICK DICKENS
Bardolph .... } Followers of Falstaff { .... Mr. COLE
Pistol .... } Followers of Falstaff { .... Mr. GEORGE CRUIKSHANK
Nym .... } Followers of Falstaff { .... Mr. AUGUSTUS DICKENS
Simple .... (Servant to Slender) .... Mr. AUGUSTUS EGG
Mrs. Ford .... Miss EMMELINE MONTAGUE
Mrs. Page .... Miss KENWORTHY
Anne Page .... (her Daughter, in love with Fenton) .... Miss ANNE ROMER
Mrs. Quickly .... (Servant of Dr. Caius) .... Mrs. COWDEN CLARKE

The Costumes (of the Period of Henry IV.), by Messrs. Nathan, Titchbourne Street, London.

Charles Dickens, an enthusiastic amateur actor, appeared in The Merry Wives of Windsor *to raise money to buy the Birthplace.*

speare's birth approached, many people were convinced the event should be marked in the grand style. A committee of distinguished gentlemen from Stratford and London assembled early in 1863 "to suggest and carry out a scheme" for the upcoming anniversary. The first thing to be settled was the venue; there was some dispute over whether the tercentenary should be observed in Stratford or London, since both claimed Shakespeare as their own. As it happens, both places hosted celebrations, as did several other cities across the English-speaking world, including Boston and Lowell, Massachusetts. But the most important was in Stratford-upon-Avon.

Had the logistic problems that plagued Garrick's Jubilee not been worked out, London would almost certainly have won the day. But by now transport was much easier than it had been in Garrick's time; instead of two uncomfortable days in a crowded stagecoach, Londoners could choose from short, comfortable railway trips on either the Great Western or the London and North Western lines. Newspapers, magazines, and pamphlets offered suggestions on where visitors might stay; as *The Official Programme* pointed out, the usually "abundant and excellent" hotels in Stratford were not prepared "to meet the demands which such a gathering as the Tercentenary Festival of the birth of Shakespeare is likely to bring to his native town." This time, though, all such problems would be resolved. Victorian England prided itself on its projects for the public benefit, from lighting London's streets to compiling the *Oxford English Dictionary*; both were expressions of the spirit in which no obstacle was too great to get in the way of monuments devoted to the public good. As London's *Daily News* reported in 1863, "the Stratford authorities have undertaken an onerous and costly scheme in deference to the public voice of demand. It is also to be remembered that the matter will be discussed a hundred years hence, with sharp curiosity, to discern what the appreciation of Shakespeare really was about the year 1863."

This time a mere three days would not suffice; two full weeks were devoted to celebrating Shakespeare's three hundredth birthday. As tourists poured in, police were stationed throughout the town to keep an eye on thieves. Robert E. Hunter, the secretary to the organizing committee, kept his fingers crossed, admitting that "perfect success seemed ultimately to depend on but one contingency, the weather." This time, unlike in 1769, the weather cooperated, "and never was gala or festival so specially favoured in this respect as that at Stratford-upon-Avon in 1864." On 23 April—which Hunter noted was both "the day of 'our warlike champion, thrice renowned St. George,' and of our no less renowned Will Shakespeare"—the morning "dawned in splendour, and the day continued throughout brilliant . . . Thus did the propitious sky smile on the festival, from its commencement to its termination."

At noon came the erection of "a National Monumental Memor-

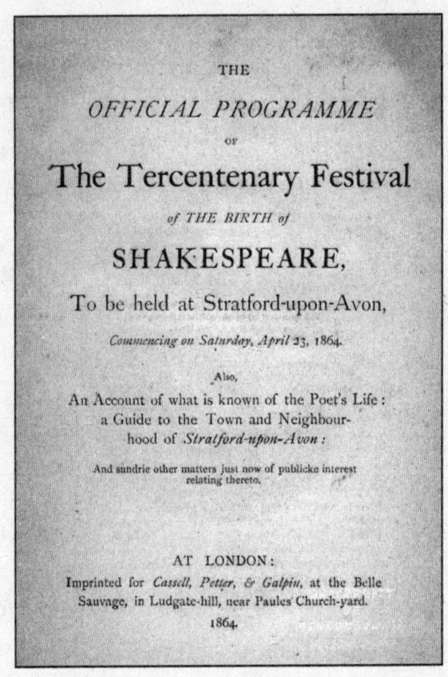

THE

OFFICIAL PROGRAMME

OF

The Tercentenary Festival

of THE BIRTH of

SHAKESPEARE,

To be held at Stratford-upon-Avon,

Commencing on Saturday, April 23, 1864.

Also,

An Account of what is known of the Poet's Life: a Guide to the Town and Neighbourhood of *Stratford-upon-Avon:*

And sundrie other matters just now of publicke interest relating thereto.

AT LONDON:

Imprinted for *Cassell, Petter, & Galpin*, at the Belle Sauvage, in Ludgate-hill, near Paules Church-yard.

1864.

By 1864 bardolatry was fully established, and a two-week celebration commemorated Shakespeare's three hundredth birthday.

ial," and at three o'clock a splendid (and expensive) banquet. "Ladies are particularly invited to attend," the program advised, "and the tickets issued will be strictly limited to the number of guests that can be accommodated with comfort." This intimate gathering featured some 750 guests, who enjoyed a Shakespeare-themed meal of many courses: boar's head (recalling the line "Like a full-acorn'd boar" from *Cymbeline*), York hams ("Sweet stem from York's great stock" from *1 Henry VI*), tongue ("Silence is only commendable in a neat's tongue dried" from *The Merchant of Venice*), and so on.

At nine o'clock on the first night visitors were treated to "a grand display of fireworks, by Mr. DARBY, the Celebrated Pyrotechnist." And grand it was: sixty-three separate aerial explosions, beginning with the ascent of two balloons, "each discharging an unique and beautiful Aerial display:—The first, 'Shakespeare,' Blue and White. The second, 'Stratford-on-Avon,' Pink and Blue." After that came dozens of displays—a "Royal Salute of Maroons, in imitation of Cannon"; a "Grand display of Bengal Lights"; "A display of Emerald Green Fire"; "A display of Crimson Fire"; and so on—ending with a "Grand concluding piece, made expressly for the occasion: 'The Vision of Shakespeare.'" The program gave the details of "The Vision," couched in the curious language of Victorian pyrotechnics. It was

> formed of many thousand Lights, and gigantic Transparent Effects, supported by Ornamental Pedestals in various coloured Fires, with Gerbes of the largest dimensions, interspersed with Showers of Pots d'Aigrettes, Mines of Saucissons, Girandoles of Coloured Rockets, forming a Bouquet of the most beautiful Fires known in the Pyrotechnic Art. During the exhibition of this superb piece, the grand *coup de feu* will take place, introducing showers of Streaming Stars, coloured Blossoms, and Saucissons, and the whole surmounted by the Prince of Wales's Plume.

This time there was no rain to ruin the fireworks, and the only complaint was that the exhibition was so spectacular that the resulting smoke made it difficult to see anything.

On the next day, a Sunday, came two sermons in the Holy Trinity Church, where Shakespeare was buried. The first was by Richard Chenevix Trench, archbishop of Dublin, who praised Shakespeare for "a healthiness, a moral soundness in all, or nearly all, which he has written," giving him the distinctively Victorian praise that "he dallies not with forbidden things"—there is little of the indecency that abounds in his contemporaries. What's more, Shakespeare gave portraits of women who embodied all the domestic virtues dear to a Victorian preacher's heart: "Surely if the woman be in God's intention the appointed guardian of the sanctities of home, the purities of domestic life," Trench declared, "we owe him much who has peopled the world of our imagination with shapes 'so perfect and so peerless' as are these." He invited his auditors to imagine a world in which Shakespeare had never existed: "Think how much poorer intellectually, yea, and morally, every one of us would be; what would have to be withdrawn from circulation, of wisest sayings, of profoundest maxims of life-wisdom, which have now been absorbed into the very tissue of our hearts and minds!" The afternoon's sermon was delivered by Charles Wordsworth, lord bishop of St. Andrews, who seconded Trench's proclamations: "it is not merely as a poet, or even as a poet who wrote, in a high and genuine sense of the word, religiously," said Wordsworth, "but as a man, a Christian man, that we, as a congregation of Christians, should be content to honour Shakespeare."

And so it went through the two weeks of celebration, an unmistakably Victorian blend of literary reverence, Anglican piety, and British nationalism. The third day featured a performance of Handel's *Messiah* by some five hundred musicians. (The *Times* of London granted that "It might be objected that there is little apparent connection between Shakespeare and Handel's 'Messiah,' " but justified the pairing because "the work which the English place at the head of musical classics may be reasonably thought worthy of association with the chief classic of English literature.") Later days brought excursions to places of Shakespearean interest in the neighborhood, dramatic readings from the plays, concerts, and something that was entirely overlooked during Garrick's original Jubilee: actual performances of Shakespeare's plays. But as at the other Jubilees, this time the play was not the thing, for these celebrations were directed not at the studious but at the fashionable. One of the highlights was a fancy dress ball, which began at nine o'clock on the seventh night and ran until five o'clock the next morning. Hunter gave some idea of what the costumes were like: "The pretty innocent Mirandas, and the gentle Desdemonas and fair Ophelias mingled with brigands, Zouaves, and bearded warriors. Benedict, Owen Glendower, a 'nutty' little jockey, Edgar of Ravenswood, and Harry the Eighth escorted Cordelia, Rosalind, Ceres, 'Spring,' Portia, Juno, Mrs. Ford, and Anne Page." Throughout the festivities the town hall was converted to a picture gallery, where nearly three hundred paintings of Shakespeare and Shakespearean scenes were on display. Once again commerce was close at hand: as one spectator noted, "The lower part of the Town Hall was let out in stalls for the sale of photographs, medals, badges, ribbons, statuary, and such wares as form the stock of fancy bazaars."

For two weeks, Stratford-upon-Avon was the center of the world. Those who were unable to attend sent their greetings. From Russia came a telegram: THE IMPERIAL UNIVERSITY OF MOSCOW, RECOGNISING THE GREAT INFLUENCE OF SHAKESPEARE ON THE RUSSIAN LITERATURE AND STAGE, THIS DAY PUBLICLY DECLARES THE THREE HUNDREDTH ANNIVERSARY OF THE BIRTHDAY OF THAT GREAT GENIUS, EQUALLY DEAR TO THE WHOLE CIVILISED WORLD, AND HEREBY CONGRATULATES HIS COUNTRYMEN ON THE OCCASION. Germany went one better, sending a delegation from Goethe's house to Shakespeare's house. "When honour was to be done to the memory of Shakespeare," the delegates said, "Germany could not be absent; for, next to Goethe and Schiller, there is no poet so truly loved by us, so thoroughly our own, as your Shakespeare." He was practically German property: "He has become of ourselves, holding his own place in the history of our literature, applauded in our theatres, and in our cottages studied, known and loved." The

German delegates concluded with a tribute to the playwright's tremendous stature: "As the height of the Alps is measured by Mont Blanc, let the greatness of England be measured by the greatness of Shakespeare." Even the usually skeptical French got in on the act, albeit a little late. Jean Baptiste François Ernest, the chevalier de Chatelain, composed a *Monument d'un français à Shakespeare, à l'occasion du 303ème anniversaire de la naissance du poète de l'Avon* (Monument from a Frenchman to Shakespeare, on the Occasion of the 303rd Anniversary of the Birth of the Poet of the Avon), though he missed the tercentenary by three years.

The Calendar of Obloquy

Shakespeare's fame spread not only across the world but from heaven to hell. Shakespeare had become the subject of religious adulation, and that religion now had a sacred Scripture, plenty of hymns and relics, a set of rituals, and pilgrimages to a holy land. The religion also found its devil in the Reverend Francis Gastrell, the man who had cut down the mulberry tree and knocked down New Place. The stories of his "desecration" of Shakespeare's tree and house continued to be told over the decades, becoming worse with each retelling. In 1789 a writer named John Adams told the story, declaring that "a man of taste in such a situation . . . would have congratulated himself on his good fortune, and have deemed himself the happiest of mortals." Perhaps in 1789, but not in 1752, when Gastrell moved in. But Adams could not conceive of a time when Shakespeare was anything less than divine; Gastrell must have been a moral monster. He marveled that "the luckless and ignorant owner" occupied Shakespeare's own house "without feeling those emotions which arise in the breast of the generous enthusiast." As a result, "the mulberry-tree, planted by the poet's own hand, became an object of dislike to this tasteless owner of it . . . In an evil hour, the unhappy priest ordered the tree to be cut down." According to Adams, "The people of Stratford, who had been taught to venerate every thing which related to the immortal Shakespeare, were seized with grief and astonishment when they were informed of the sacrilegious deed." In the ensuing lamentations, "the miserable culprit . . . was obliged at last to leave the town, amidst the curses of the populace, who solemnly vowed never to suffer one of the same name to reside in Stratford."

Over time, the stories were embellished to make the villain still more villainous. The *Official Programme* of 1864 compared the English clergyman both to the violent hordes that overran the Roman Empire and to an ancient critic who had the nerve to criticize Homer, denouncing him as "Gastrell, that Goth, deserving all the ignominy heaped upon the memory of Zoilus—who was the first infidel as regards the individuality of Homer." By 1864 Gastrell was long dead—it had been more than a hundred years since he knocked down New Place—but the worshippers of Shakespeare knew how to hold a grudge, and even to extend it into the next world. The writer's curse on the dead man's bones is remarkable for its vituperation, but not out of the mainstream of Victorian thought:

> If the Church has among her ceremonies any ceremony opposite to canonisation which might carry excommunication beyond the grave, and perpetuate the infamy of the sacrilegious, she out to have long since exercised it in respect of the Rev. Mr. Gastrell—(what a profanation of the word *reverend*!)—and placed his name first upon the calendar of obloquy.

In three hundred years, William Shakespeare the talented playwright and theatre shareholder had become Shakespeare the transcendent demigod. Beneath the ground, the remains of the fiendish

Gastrell were cursed. On the surface of the earth, some of the age's greatest preachers delivered sermons in which it was difficult to disentangle Shakespeare from Christ himself. And in the skies, Shakespeare's name was blazoned across the heavens in an elaborate fireworks display. The man had become the institution. Shakespeare had become Shakespeare.

Epilogue

THIS BOOK BEGAN BESIDE AN obscure grave where no one bothered to note Shakespeare's passing. It ends nearly 250 years later by surveying the entire globe: Boston, Bombay, Brisbane, and beyond. By 1864 the Shakespeare phenomenon was firmly in place, but the process of becoming Shakespeare still hasn't ended.

Four hundred years have now passed since his plays first appeared on stage, and Shakespeare continues to be performed, accounting for thousands of productions around the world every year. And where performances were once fleeting and transitory, they can now be preserved for posterity. In just the last dozen years have appeared big-screen Shakespearean performances by plenty of names one might expect—Kenneth Branagh, Emma Thompson, Helena Bonham Carter, Ben Kingsley, Ian McKellen, Derek Jacobi, Judi Dench—but also by less obvious performers like Laurence Fishburne, Al Pacino, Kevin Kline, Keanu Reeves, Leonardo DiCaprio, Claire Danes, even Billy Crystal and Robin Williams.

Shakespeare continues to be studied, with a whole sector of the publishing industry devoted to him. Many bookshops have only one section named for a single author, and that's Shakespeare. Every month countless pages of scholarship pour out of university presses, and Shakespeare's plays are floating on an ocean of commentary. *Richard II*, for example, was first published in a small pamphlet of seventy-six pages, but a recent annotated edition runs to more than six hundred. There's even a scholarly periodical devoted exclusively to *Hamlet*. Another learned journal is concerned just with Shakespeare in translation, and it should be no surprise, now that his works can be read in more than a hundred languages: at least one play or a volume of sonnets is available in translation in

> Afrikaans, Albanian, American Sign Language, Amharic, Arabic, Armenian, Assamese, Azerbaijani, Basque, Belarusian, Bengali, Bosnian, Bulgarian, Burmese, Catalan, Chinese, Croatian, Czech, Danish, Dutch, Esperanto, Estonian, Faeroese, Finnish, French, Gã, Georgian, German, Greek (both ancient and modern), Gujarati, Hausa, Hebrew, High Alemannic, Hindi, Hungarian, Icelandic, Indonesian, Interlingua, Italian, Japanese, Javanese, Kannada, Klingon, Konkani, Korean, Krio, Kuanyama, Kurdish, Ladino, Latin, Latvian, Letzeburgesch, Lithuanian, Macedonian, Malay, Malayalam, Maori, Marathi, Mauritian French Creole, Moldavian, Ndgonga, Nepali, Norwegian, Nzima, Ossetic, Panjabi, Pashto, Persian, Polish, Portuguese, Rhaeto-Romance, Romanian, Russian, Sanskrit, Sardinian, Scots, Scottish Gaelic, Serbian, Sindhi, Slovak, Slovenian, Sorbian, Sotho, Spanish, Sundanese, Swahili, Swedish, Tagalog, Tamil, Telugu, Thai, Tigrinya, Tswana, Turkish, Turkmen, Uighur, Ukranian, Urdu, Uzbek, Vietnamese, Welsh, Xhosa, Yiddish, Yoruba, Zulu.

And every year hundreds of Shakespearean delegates from around the world gather at meetings of the Shakespeare Association of America, the British Shakespeare Association, the International Shakespeare Conference, the Modern Language Association, and other professional organizations to trade ideas about his life and works.

Shakespeare continues to be improved. Today most people are hesitant to tinker with his sacred words, but many directors have no trouble with setting his plays in unfamiliar eras, or putting a white Othello in a Venice filled with black characters. And new plays on Shakespearean themes come out constantly—*The Comedy of Errors* recently became a hip-hop *Bomb-itty of Errors*, described by the *New Yorker* as "the Beastie Boys from Syracuse" and praised by London's *Independent* as "unexpectedly stonking"—and not only plays but short stories, novels, poems, and personal essays. John Gross's anthology *After Shakespeare* collects dozens of works inspired by the plays, and the book could have easily been stretched to twice its length, with works by Tom Stoppard, Jane Smiley, John Updike, and Jilly Cooper.

Shakespeare continues to be co-opted, often by the strangest of bedfellows. Early in the twentieth century he was a favorite of the Yiddish theatre and a favorite of the Nazis. During the cold war he thrived on both sides of the iron curtain. Today he's praised by cultural conservatives for holding back the flood of poststructuralism, feminism, and multiculturalism, and he's championed by the cultural left for his radical critiques of imperialism and his problematizing of sexual identity.

Shakespeare continues to be domesticated. Children's adaptations have been appearing steadily since the Lambs wrote two hundred years ago. And now that Shakespeare is a standard part of every school curriculum in the English-speaking world, editions with notes suitable for young readers are a steady source of new revenue for textbook publishers. Not all of those schoolbook versions give the plays in quite the way Shakespeare wrote them, though; the Bowdlers are alive and well, whether they actually edit the text of the plays or, less obtrusively, leave the naughty parts unexplained with notes.

Shakespeare probably continues to be forged, though by the nature of the crime no one can know the extent of it. It's safe to bet that many minor "discoveries" published in respectable journals are based on shoddy scholarship, wishful thinking, even outright fabrication; but the world may remain in the dark about them forever, or at least until some twenty-first-century Edmond Malone does the necessary investigative work. No one in the last hundred years has had the moxie of William Henry Ireland, discovering previously unheard-of plays. Once a decade or so, though, another little-known work is attributed to Shakespeare—in 1990 a handwriting expert claimed *The Second Maiden's Tragedy* was really the lost *Cardenio*, and others have credited Shakespeare with obscure plays like *Edward III* and *Edmund Ironside*—and with each new attribution the scholarly world goes into overdrive. The corridors at academic conferences buzz with chatter, and long exchanges in the *Times Literary Supplement* and the *New York Review of Books* take up the question: is it or isn't it? That's not the same thing as creating new plays and poems from whole cloth, but skeptics aren't above hinting that their opponents are arguing in bad faith, and tempers often flare. When, in the 1980s, the scholar Donald Foster suggested a long-forgotten poem called "A Funerall Elegye" was by Shakespeare, Brian Vickers responded with a broadside of nearly six hundred pages with the evocative title *"Counterfeiting" Shakespeare*, and accused Foster "not only of arrogance but of pervasive dishonesty." Foster responded that Vickers suffered from "an inattention to facts that would not be tolerated in an undergraduate student." The quotations could almost have come out of an exchange between Edmond Malone and William Henry Ireland two centuries earlier.

And of course Shakespeare continues to be worshipped. Today the Jubilee is a nonstop event. Stratford-upon-Avon invented the business of literary tourism, and it's very big business indeed. Stratford is the second-most-visited town in England, behind only London itself, and it draws nearly four million tourists every year. The Birthplace Museum on Henley Street is the ancestor of all modern cultural attractions—whether Charles Dickens's house on Doughty Street in London, Mark Twain's house in Hartford, Connecticut, or the Emily Dickinson Homestead in Amherst, Massachusetts.

And the process by which Shakespeare became, and is still becoming, Shakespeare doesn't stop there. This story encompasses dozens more chapters: "Composing Shakespeare," on musical adaptations from Henry Purcell's baroque opera *The Fairy Queen* to *West Side Story*; "Illustrating Shakespeare," on the drawings and paintings of scenes from his works; "Portraying Shakespeare," on portraiture from the title page of the First Folio to the hologram on modern British check guarantee cards; "Chronicling Shakespeare," on the attempts to tell his life story; "Fictionalizing Shakespeare," on the many novels where the Bard features as a character; "Questioning Shakespeare," on the bizarre efforts to attribute his works to someone else—the list could go on.

It's worth ending with a question about the nature of genius. Few people thought highly of Shakespeare in the 1630s and '40s; as his reputation rose in the 1670s and '80s, he still lagged behind Ben Jonson and John Fletcher; and even after he was widely celebrated as a great genius, he was still a genius badly in need of tidying up. It all seems agonizingly wrongheaded to us: how could generation after generation be so foolish? But it's too simplistic to dismiss thousands of editors, actors, critics, readers, and auditors as being stupid and tasteless for two centuries. Something else must have been going on. My argument here is that they were largely right: Shakespeare *was* merely "very good" by the standards of his own age and the age that followed. He became "great" only later.

Does this mean that I'm taking anything away from his achievement? In fact I think it's a further tribute to his stature.

Imagine someone with the power to summon up all the best critics of literature from 1650—and, since this is pure fantasy, imagine they've been divested of all their personal biases, prejudices, and hang-ups. Now imagine asking them to create a balance sheet showing Shakespeare's strengths and weaknesses. They'd probably begin with the faults: his plots could be poorly constructed; he had no respect for the unities of time, place, and action; he was too fond of puns; he had no sense of poetic justice; his notion of decorum was inadequate; he mingled comic and tragic scenes willy-nilly; he was poorly educated. And now his strengths: he was a master of characterization, letting his audiences look into the depths of his characters' minds; he had a knack for certain kinds of language and imagery; having been an actor himself, he was able to write lines that actors could memorize easily and speak well; he appealed to all levels of society, whether royal or common, scholarly or "unlettered." When these critics came to reckon the bottom line, they'd almost certainly decide that Shakespeare was a good poet and playwright, but far from perfect. On his final report card he might earn a B-plus—maybe an A-minus if the critics were feeling generous.

Later ages didn't change their minds about these failings. Instead, they began to pay less attention to the things Shakespeare did badly and more to the things he did well. Granted, he ignored the Aristotelian unities—but maybe the unities weren't as important as everyone had assumed. Granted, he was unlearned—but that just meant he was an untutored genius. Once it had been high praise to say that a writer followed classical precedents and an insult to say he was an uneducated rube; eventually it became an insult to say that a writer was bound by arbitrary rules and high praise to say he was a natural prodigy. Before Shakespeare's elevation, "natural genius" was something to be explained away; afterward it was to be celebrated as a writer's greatest recommendation. As John Dryden put it, right around the time the balance was beginning to tip in Shakespeare's favor, "Those who accuse him to have wanted learning, give him the greater commendation: he was naturally learn'd; he needed not the spectacles of Books to read Nature; he look'd inwards, and found her there."

Eventually the things he did poorly were dismissed as unimportant, and the things he did well came to set the standard for artistic excellence. The kinds of language and imagery at which he excelled became the standard by which language and imagery were to be measured ever after. It's no real exaggeration to say that Shakespeare wasn't great because he drew convincing characters; drawing convincing characters became great because Shakespeare did it. The rules for literary excellence had changed, and Shakespeare was the one who changed them. The critic Jonathan Bate makes the point forcefully: we can be sure that he was a genius "*Because 'genius' was a category invented in order to account for what was peculiar about Shakespeare.*"

Shakespeare was unappreciated not because the world was stupid, unable to understand his true greatness until centuries passed. By the standards of 1650, Shakespeare really *did* deserve his B-plus, and not much more. But as he worked his way into millions of minds around the world in the centuries after his death, he somehow managed to revise those standards. He turned "unschooled" from an insult into a compliment and "rule-bound" from a compliment into an insult. He was there at the beginning of the modern idea of genius, when "neoclassical" ideas about propriety and decorum gave way to "Romantic" ideas about individual expression and unbounded passion.

It's a pity that most of this history has remained unknown to most readers, that the adaptations have stayed off the stage for two hundred years, that the editorial decisions are usually kept hidden from people who read Shakespeare in print. Understanding Shakespeare fully means knowing not only the works he wrote but what happened to them in the years, decades, and centuries that passed after his death. Our story is about the long process that turned a very competent playwright into a demigod who transcended the human condition. It didn't have to happen that way; had history turned out just slightly differently, his name might be no more familiar today than Francis Beaumont's or Philip Massinger's. But something happened during Shakespeare's afterlife, something that changed the way the world has thought about genius ever since. The biggest testimony to Shakespeare's greatness may be that he changed what it meant to be great.

Acknowledgments

THE ARGUMENT OF THIS BOOK is that Shakespeare didn't do everything by himself, that it took the concerted efforts of many people to turn Shakespeare into the cultural figure he has since become. And if Shakespeare couldn't do it alone, what chance do I have? It's therefore a pleasure to acknowledge the help I received from many people along the way.

This project began in 2002 as an exhibition called "Making Shakespeare" at the Rosenbach Museum & Library in Philadelphia, and many of the materials here are drawn from that collection's astonishing treasures. Michael Barsanti first encouraged me to do a project along these lines, and I'm grateful not only to him but to the director, Derick Dreher, the librarian, Elizabeth Fuller, and the entire staff at the Rosenbach for patiently guiding me through their holdings.

Although this book wasn't written for professional academics, I benefited from both the works and the acquaintance of many fine scholars: Nicolas Barker, Jonathan Bate, Brycchan Carey, Margreta de Grazia, Steve Ferguson, Arthur Freeman and Janet Ing Freeman, Michael Gamer, Nick Groom, Rachel Hadas, David Hoddeson, Peter Holland, Andrea Immel, John Logan, Nora Nachumi, John Pollack, Eric Rasmussen, Lana Schwebel, Tiffany Stern, and Dan Traister all offered valuable tips. Kevin Cope allowed me to rework some material that originally appeared as "*King Lear* and 'the Taste of the Age,' 1681–1838," in *1650–1850:*

Ideas, Aesthetics, and Inquiries in the Early Modern Era 10 (2004): 285–303. It's been a treat to work with George Gibson and Michele Amundsen at Walker & Co. I'm only sorry that Paul Korshin didn't live to see the completion of this project, since twenty years ago he first drew my attention to many of the stories that have fascinated me ever since.

Organizations provided other kinds of help. At Rutgers University, the David Hosford Scholarship, the Trustees Research Fellowship Program, and two semester-long sabbaticals furnished both the time and the money to finish this book. The Raymond K. Denworth Fellowship allowed me to spend several months in the Rosenbach Museum & Library, and the Richard H. Popkin Travel Fund Award from the American Society for Eighteenth-Century Studies supported a research trip to London, Oxford, and Edinburgh.

Every researcher knows, though few will admit, that one of the functions of an acknowledgments page is to boast about all the wonderful places we've been able to visit. The scholarships, fellowships, and sabbaticals mentioned above let me work in some of the finest libraries in the world, and I'm pleased to make others jealous by listing them. In addition to the Rosenbach and the Dana and Alexander libraries of Rutgers University, I did my work in Firestone Library of Princeton University, Van Pelt Library of the University of Pennsylvania, Bobst Library of New York University, Butler Library of Columbia University, the John Hay Library of Brown University, the Beinecke Library of Yale University, the Houghton Library and the Theatre Collection of Harvard University, the Library Company of Philadelphia, the Athenæum of Philadelphia, the Free Library of Philadelphia, the New York Public Library, the Boston Public Library, the Pierpont Morgan Library, the William Andrews Clark Memorial Library, the Huntington Library, the Folger Shakespeare Library, the British Library, the Shakespeare Birthplace Trust Records Office, the Bristol Central Library, the University of Edinburgh Library, and the National Library of Scotland. Finally, Gabriel Austin of Four Oaks Farm gave me access to some of the remarkable materials in that collection. I thank him and the late Lady Eccles for their generosity.

Further Reading

THERE'S NO SHORTAGE OF PUBLISHED material on Shakespeare. If you search for the keyword *Shakespeare* in the Library of Congress's online catalog, the message comes back, "Your search retrieved more records than can be displayed. Only the first 10,000 will be shown." And those 10,000 books only scratch the surface. The Folger Shakespeare Library in Washington, D.C., holds more than a quarter of a million volumes. A typical year now sees around 1,500 new articles, 650 new books, 200 new editions, and 100 new doctoral dissertations devoted to Shakespeare. To look at it another way, by my rough estimate, that's around 750 new pages published every day, or 30 pages an hour, twenty-four hours a day—another page comes off the press every other minute. And these figures probably underestimate the true amount of publication, since many foreign books and small-market periodicals never make it into the databases. In the time it takes you to read this book, dozens of newer books about Shakespeare will have appeared. Not even the most devoted expert can keep up with all of it.

This section therefore lists only those books that might be helpful to what the First Folio called "the great Variety of Readers." The focus is on titles that are still in print, that are likely to turn up in public libraries, or that can be had secondhand for a reasonable price. Also included are a few books written with academic specialists rather than intelligent lay readers in mind, and they are identified as such.

First, though, I should note my debt to a few monumental reference works. They're not available outside big research libraries, but I drew on them so much that they deserve particular mention. The first is the *Oxford Dictionary of National Biography*, 60 vols. (Oxford: Oxford University Press, 2004), which I used for much of my biographical information (and which I consulted to settle the form of names that have been spelled various ways, like Heminges and Ralegh). More detailed biographical information often came from *A Biographical Dictionary of Actors, Actresses, Musicians, Dancers, Managers & Other Stage Personnel in London, 1660–1800*, ed. Philip H. Highfill Jr., Kalman A. Burnim, and Edward A. Langhans, 16 vols. (Carbondale: Southern Illinois University Press, 1973–93). And for the nature of the stage in the Restoration and the eighteenth century, and for lists of performances, no one can do without *The London Stage, 1660–1800: A Calendar of Plays, Entertainments & Afterpieces, Together with Casts, Box-Receipts and Contemporary Comment: Compiled from the Playbills, Newspapers and Theatrical Diaries of the Period*, 6 vols. in 12 (Carbondale: Southern Illinois University Press, 1960–79).

General

I begin with general accounts of Shakespeare that may be of interest to many readers. Biographies abound, though they range widely in quality. Samuel Schoenbaum's *Shakespeare: A Documentary Life* (Oxford: Clarendon Press, 1975) may deserve to be placed at the head of the list for reliability, since he resists the urge so many biographers feel to fill gaps in the record with idle speculation and to take legends for fact. Schoenbaum also produced a shorter version of the book called *Shakespeare: A Compact Documentary Life* (New York: Oxford University Press, rev. ed. 1987), which focuses on the more important documents.

A few recent books on the life and times are worth careful

attention. I had originally planned to use *Making Shakespeare* as the title to this book, but Tiffany Stern beat me to it. Still, *Making Shakespeare: From Stage to Page* (London and New York: Routledge, 2004) is so good that I'm *almost* prepared to forgive her for getting there first. Frank Kermode, *The Age of Shakespeare* (New York: Modern Library; London: Weidenfeld and Nicolson, 2004), offers a brief and readable take on the theatrical culture of Elizabethan London, along the way offering short comments on most of Shakespeare's plays. Stephen Greenblatt's *Will in the World: How Shakespeare Became Shakespeare* (New York: Norton, 2004) is a fascinating account of Shakespeare's life and times and the way he transmuted biography into art. Though Greenblatt often lets speculation run away with him, his insightful readings of the plays may let us excuse some of the flights of fancy. And James S. Shapiro's *Year in the Life of William Shakespeare: 1599* (New York: HarperCollins, 2005)—published in the United Kingdom as *1599: A Year in the Life of William Shakespeare* (London: Faber, 2005)—is a superb example of how meticulous historical knowledge can bring literature to life. Shapiro focuses on the single year in which *Henry V*, *Julius Caesar*, *As You Like It*, and *Hamlet* were written, and discusses the way the external world touched on Shakespeare's creative process.

Books on Shakespeare's afterlife aren't common, but they do exist. One of the earliest is George C. D. Odell, *Shakespeare from Betterton to Irving*, 2 vols. (New York: Scribner's, 1920), an account of the stage practice and the major actors from the Restoration to the end of the Victorian era. Ivor Brown and George Fearon traced the rise of bardolatry in *This Shakespeare Industry: Amazing Monument* (New York and London: Harper and Bros., 1939). F. E. Halliday did something similar in *The Cult of Shakespeare* (London: Duckworth, 1957), as did Louis Marder in *His Exits and His Entrances: The Story of Shakespeare's Reputation* (Philadelphia and New York: J. B. Lippincott, 1963). All four of these works are now too old-fashioned to satisfy experts—too many discoveries have occurred since they were written—but they can still be enjoyable. More up-to-date is Stanley Wells, *Shakespeare for All Time* (London: Macmillan, 2002), an entertaining and illustrated account of the history of Shakespeare's reception from his time to ours. Gary Taylor, Wells's coeditor on the Oxford edition (cited below), discusses what "Shakspeare" meant in six periods in *Reinventing Shakespeare: A Cultural History, from the Restoration to the Present* (New York: Weidenfeld and Nicolson, 1989). His tone is light, even irreverent. Similarly iconoclastic is Terence Hawkes, who contributes the first essay to a section called "Shakespeare's Afterlife" in *Shakespeare: An Oxford Guide*, ed. Stanley Wells and Lena Cowen Orlin (Oxford: Oxford University Press, 2003). Jonathan Bate, in *The Genius of Shakespeare* (London: Picador, 1997), argues that "the genius of Shakespeare is not co-extensive with the life of William Shakespeare," and that "a knowledge of the 'pre-life' and the 'after-life' of his art is essential to an understanding of his power." The second part of the book, "The Shakespeare Effect," describes Shakespeare's posthumous fate. Finally, there's Samuel Schoenbaum, *Shakespeare's Lives* (Oxford: Clarendon Press, new ed. 1991), which sets out to describe the many efforts to write Shakespeare's biography over the centuries, but has many fascinating things to say about other topics along the way.

It's also worth mentioning a few collections of essays that approach Shakespeare from different angles. A series of books in the Cambridge Companion series, cited in the appropriate places below, offers collections of essays by leading scholars, and many of them are useful introductions for those new to the field. *The Oxford Companion to Shakespeare*, ed. Michael Dobson (Oxford: Oxford University Press, 2001), is an encyclopedia rather than a collection of essays; it includes more than three thousand entries on Shakespearean topics.

Finally, a note on editions of Shakespeare's works. Chapter 3 of this book tries to make clear just how much disagreement there is over exactly what Shakespeare wrote. I usually quoted *William Shakespeare: The Complete Works*, ed. Stanley Wells and Gary Taylor (Oxford: Clarendon Press, 1986), published in a slightly revised edition in 2005. The Oxford *Works* is the product of prodigious research, but many of its readings, while thought-provoking, strike most critics as idiosyncratic, even perverse. It also lacks interpretive footnotes. More traditional texts, accompanied by more thorough annotation, can be found in *The Complete Works of Shakespeare*, ed. David Bevington, 4th ed. (New York: Longman, 1997), and *The Riverside Shakespeare*, ed. G. Blakemore Evans, 2nd ed. (Boston: Houghton Mifflin, 1997). There are many series of single-volume editions of the plays, including the Pelican Shakespeare, the Folger Library Shakespeare Editions, and the Norton Critical Edition; all offer clearly printed texts and notes accessible to the nonprofessional. Two other series offer copious annotations for specialists: the Arden Shakespeare and the New Variorum Edition of Shakespeare.

1. Reviving Shakespeare

Even experts have a hard time negotiating their way through the extensive library on Britain's complicated political and military history in the seventeenth century, but a few works are suitable for novices. The classic short history is Maurice Ashley's *England in the Seventeenth Century* (London: Penguin, 1952), vol. 6 of the Pelican History of England. Many developments have changed our understanding since it was first published, but later revised editions take some of these discoveries into account. Ashley also wrote a very readable book, *The English Civil War: A Concise History* (London: Thames and Hudson, 1974), focusing on the political and military crisis at the center of the seventeenth century. Another concise and accessible history, more up-to-date and with a broader scope than Ashley's, is Robert Bucholz and Newton Key, *Early Modern England, 1485–1714: A Narrative History* (Oxford: Blackwell, 2003). It goes back to the beginning of the Tudor period and therefore includes Shakespeare's lifetime along with the first century after his death. Newcomers to British history might find Barry Coward, *The Stuart Age: England, 1603–1714* (London and New York: Longman, 1994), the best short overview.

For a colorful "you were there" description of Restoration London, the diary of Samuel Pepys can't be bettered. Pepys began his journal in January 1660, shortly before Charles II was restored to the throne, and he covered nearly a decade of social life in the metropolis. Pepys adored the theatre and left notes on the dozens of productions he saw. He also left shockingly frank notes on his various love affairs and medical infirmities. The complete modern edition of the diary stretches to eleven fat volumes, but there are many abridgments, including *The Shorter Pepys*, ed. Robert Latham (Berkeley: University of California Press, 1985). Be careful, though; many editions published before the 1970s, even ostensibly "complete" editions, omit the racier passages. Claire Tomalin's biography, *Samuel Pepys: The Unequalled Self* (London and New York: Viking, 2002), is also worth reading.

Nell Gwyn's life is the stuff of fairy tales, and she is therefore well served by biographies. Both Charles Beauclerk, *Nell Gwyn: A Biography* (London: Macmillan, 2005; published in the United States as *Nell Gwyn: Mistress to a King*), and Graham Hopkins, *Nell Gwynne: A Passionate Life* (London: Robson Books, 2003), are entertaining and sympathetic, and depict Gwyn against the background of Restoration London.

2. Performing Shakespeare

Many amusing theatrical stories are collected in *The Methuen Book of Shakespeare Anecdotes*, ed. Ralph Berry (London: Methuen,

1992). For those interested in a more connected history, Tiffany Stern describes the conditions of the Elizabethan and Jacobean stage in *Making Shakespeare* (cited above), and the most accessible overview of stage practices from Shakespeare's day to the present is *Shakespeare: An Illustrated Stage History*, ed. Jonathan Bate and Russell Jackson (Oxford: Oxford University Press, 1996). Lois Potter, "Shakespeare in the Theatre, 1660–1900," appears in *The Cambridge Companion to Shakespeare*, ed. Margreta de Grazia and Stanley Wells (Cambridge: Cambridge University Press, 2001). And George C. D. Odell's *Shakespeare from Betterton to Irving* (mentioned above) collects plenty of information on the major figures, though it can be slow going.

Contemporary accounts are harder to come by outside university libraries. Pepys's diary, cited above, includes many of his reactions to plays from the 1660s. *An Apology for the Life of Colley Cibber* first appeared in 1740, and it's available in a number of cheap modern reprints. William Hazlitt's *Characters of Shakespeare's Plays* was first published in 1817 and has been reprinted countless times. It offers valuable insights into Romantic-era performance styles.

A pair of books in the same series—*The Cambridge Companion to Shakespeare on Stage*, ed. Stanley Wells and Sarah Stanton (Cambridge: Cambridge University Press, 2002), and *The Cambridge Companion to Shakespeare on Film*, ed. Russell Jackson (Cambridge: Cambridge University Press, 2000)—collect a wide range of essays on Shakespeare in performance. The first includes chapters on stage practice from the sixteenth to the twentieth centuries.

3. Studying Shakespeare

Most of the early editions of Shakespeare's works are now available only in academic libraries, but a few publishers have issued inexpensive facsimile reprints of the First Folio for those who can't afford the three million pounds or six million dollars that the real thing commands at auction.

Tiffany Stern offers a gentle but accurate introduction to the process by which Shakespeare's works first saw print in chapter 7 of *Making Shakespeare* (cited above). The most thorough recent survey of the long history of Shakespeare editing is Andrew Murphy's *Shakespeare in Print: A History and Chronology of Shakespeare Publishing* (Cambridge: Cambridge University Press, 2003); it's written for academics but, since it's both encyclopedic in scope and the only comprehensive book on the subject, it's worth reading. A briefer account is Barbara A. Mowat, "The Reproduction of Shakespeare's Texts," in *The Cambridge Companion to Shakespeare* (cited above). And for those interested in the often complicated and technical process by which modern editors try to turn the early quarto and folio texts into readable and actable plays, a useful reference work is *William Shakespeare: A Textual Companion*, ed. Stanley Wells and Gary Taylor (Oxford: Oxford University Press, 1987; reprinted New York and London: Norton, 1997). It describes many of the decisions Wells and Taylor had to make in producing their edition of the *Complete Works* in 1986. The early chapters of Ron Rosenbaum's *Shakespeare Wars: Clashing Scholars, Public Fiascoes, Palace Coups* (New York: Random House, 2006) offer a personal, passionate, sometimes even breathless account of the major editorial and critical debates of the last few decades. A more scholarly overview of the critical topics that interest modern Shakespeareans is *The Cambridge Companion to Shakespeare* (cited above), a collection of essays by leading figures in the field.

The early editions and older works of criticism aren't easy to come by, though John Dryden's *Essay of Dramatick Poesie* and Samuel Johnson's preface to his Shakespeare edition are widely reprinted. Johnson's *Dictionary of the English Language* contains around ten thousand quotations from Shakespeare. The abridged version I edited, *Samuel Johnson's Dictionary: Selections from the*

1755 Work That Defined the English Language (New York: Walker & Co., 2004; London: Atlantic, 2005), contains about 3,100 of the original 43,000 entries, and includes an index to all the Shakespearean quotations. Alexander Pope's edition of Shakespeare can't be had easily, but his own poetry, including his attack on rivals like Lewis Theobald and Colley Cibber in *The Dunciad*, is available in many editions.

A few anthologies of important early critical works on Shakespeare make some rare material accessible. Brian Vickers's monumental six-volume *Shakespeare: The Critical Heritage* (London and Boston: Routledge and Kegan Paul, 1974–81) is a great place to begin, and Arthur M. Eastman's *Short History of Shakespeare Criticism* (New York: Random House, 1968) puts all the comments in context. And although it's not concerned exclusively with Shakespeare, the Folger Collective on Early Women Critics offers a valuable collection called *Women Critics, 1660–1820: An Anthology* (Bloomington: Indiana University Press, 1995).

4. Improving Shakespeare

Surprisingly little has been written on this subject for common readers. Most accessible is *Shakespeare Made Fit: Restoration Adaptations of Shakespeare*, ed. Sandra Clark (London: Dent; Rutland, Vt.: Tuttle, 1997), an inexpensive anthology that includes Cibber's *Richard III*, Davenant and Dryden's *Tempest*, Dryden's *All for Love*, Tate's *King Lear*, and Lacy's *Sauny the Scot* (based on *The Taming of the Shrew*). *Shakespeare Adaptations from the Restoration: Five Plays*, ed. Barbara A. Murray (Madison: Fairleigh Dickinson University Press, 2005), is similar in design, though it collects less familiar titles. More wide-ranging is *Adaptations of Shakespeare: A Critical Anthology of Plays from the Seventeenth Century to the Present*, ed. Daniel Fischlin and Mark Fortier (London and New York: Routledge, 2000), which includes a dozen plays adapted from Shakespeare, from John Fletcher and Nahum Tate in the seventeenth century through Philip Osment and Djanet Sears at the end of the twentieth.

Several of the books mentioned above, including Odell's *Shakespeare from Betterton to Irving*, Brown and Fearon's *This Shakespeare Industry*, and Halliday's *Cult of Shakespeare*, discuss the adaptations, though they spend much more time wagging fingers than trying to understand the attractions of the rewritten versions. More solid and respectable is Michael Dobson's *Making of the National Poet: Shakespeare, Adaptation, and Authorship, 1660–1769* (Oxford: Clarendon Press, 1992), one of the most intelligent and influential surveys of Shakespeare adaptations. It's clearly written but assumes a fair amount of knowledge about seventeenth- and eighteenth-century politics; nonspecialists may want to approach this one only after reading a few of the other titles here.

5. Co-opting Shakespeare

Shapiro's *Year in the Life* (cited above) includes a good account of the Essex affair and how it played out in 1599. Dobson's *Making of the National Poet* (also mentioned above) is the best overview of the ways Shakespeare's plays were rewritten to serve political ends in the Restoration and eighteenth century. A pair of books—Richard Moody, *The Astor Place Riot* (Bloomington: Indiana University Press, 1958), and Richard Nelson, *Two Shakespearean Actors* (London: Faber and Faber, 1990)—provide the background on the riots of 1849.

Political interpretations of Shakespeare's works are now very common in the academy, but not much of that criticism is accessible to nonspecialists. An exception is Jan Kott's seminal *Shakespeare, Our Contemporary*, trans. Boleslaw Taborski (Garden City, N.Y.: Doubleday, 1964), which discusses the uses to which the plays were put during the cold war. In 1990 a number of critics revisited the topic in *Is Shakespeare Still Our Contemporary?*, ed. John Elsom (London and New York: Routledge, 1990).

6. Domesticating Shakespeare

The best account of Shakespeare's racier passages is Eric Partridge, *Shakespeare's Bawdy: A Literary and Psychological Essay and a Comprehensive Glossary* (London: Routledge, 1947), often reprinted. More recently, Stanley Wells wrote *Looking for Sex in Shakespeare* (Cambridge: Cambridge University Press, 2004). *The Family Shakspeare: In Which Nothing Is Added to the Original Text, but Those Words and Expressions Are Omitted Which Cannot with Propriety Be Read in a Family* first appeared in its full edition in 1818; it has since gone through countless editions. Even though no one has reprinted it in decades, many libraries carry it, and secondhand copies from the Victorian era aren't difficult to find, often for surprisingly little money. The standard history of bowdlerization is Noel Perrin, *Dr. Bowdler's Legacy: A History of Expurgated Books in England and America* (New York: Atheneum, 1969). It begins with a survey of expurgation before the Bowdlers and continues well into the twentieth century. An updated edition appeared in 1992, this time with the story of a censored edition of Ray Bradbury's classic attack on censorship, *Fahrenheit 451*.

There are few good histories of early children's books. The standard account is F. J. Harvey Darton, *Children's Books in England: Five Centuries of Social Life*, 3rd ed. (Cambridge: Cambridge University Press, 1982), which looks back to the Middle Ages and forward to the twentieth century. Also valuable is Peter Hunt's *Introduction to Children's Literature* (Oxford: Oxford University Press, 1994), which takes a similarly long view. *Reimagining Shakespeare for Children and Young Adults* (New York and London: Routledge, 2003), a collection of thirty-one essays, offers various perspectives on adapting Shakespeare for children.

Tales from Shakespear: Designed for the Use of Young Persons first appeared in two small volumes in 1807 and, like *The Family Shakspeare*, has been reprinted dozens of times. Inexpensive paperbacks are still easily available. A recent biography—Susan Tyler Hitchcock's *Mad Mary Lamb* (New York: Norton, 2005)—tells the story of Charles and Mary Lamb, including the infamous murder, their work on *Tales from Shakespear*, and their long "double singleness." Other children's versions of Shakespeare go in and out of print fairly quickly, but most big bookshops will include a few in their children's section, and a few minutes' browsing the big online booksellers will turn up possibilities, including Marchette Chute, *Stories from Shakespeare* (Cleveland: World Publishing, 1956, often reprinted).

7. Forging Shakespeare

There's no comprehensive biography of William Henry Ireland, and while many have told the story in outline, only a few works in the last hundred years have been based on original research. Two twentieth-century biographies focus on the forgery episode but provide little more information on the rest of Ireland's life: John Mair, *The Fourth Forger: William Ireland and the Shakespeare Papers* (London: Cobden-Sanderson, 1938), and Bernard Grebanier, *The Great Shakespeare Forgery: A New Look at the Career of William Henry Ireland* (New York: Norton, 1965). The most accessible short account appears in Samuel Schoenbaum, *Shakespeare's Lives* (cited above). Jeffrey Kahan retells the story of the *Vortigern* episode for scholars in *Reforging Shakespeare: The Story of a Theatrical Scandal* (Cranbury, N.J.: Associated University Presses, 1998). Most recently Nick Groom devotes a provocative chapter to Ireland in *The Forger's Shadow: How Forgery Changed the Course of Literature* (London: Picador, 2002). There are many other accounts of Ireland's life, but, with a few exceptions, most simply rehash the research in Mair, Grebanier, and Schoenbaum. The most recent full-length account is Patricia Pierce, *The Great Shakespeare Fraud: The Strange, True Story of William-Henry Ireland* (Stroud: Sutton, 2004). Among my own future projects is a full-scale biography of Ireland.

John Payne Collier, though he has attracted fewer commentators, has ended up being much better served thanks to a monumental biography and bibliography: Arthur Freeman and Janet Ing Freeman, *John Payne Collier: Scholarship and Forgery in the Nineteenth Century*, 2 vols. (New Haven: Yale University Press, 2003). The Freemans have spent many years examining the records related to Collier, and their definitive account is the most thorough and balanced assessment of Collier's life and career ever attempted.

8. Worshipping Shakespeare

The best book on the Jubilee is Christian Deelman, *The Great Shakespeare Jubilee* (London: Michael Joseph, 1964)—a volume that has the rare distinction of being meticulously scholarly and perfectly readable at once. A more imaginative take on the same event is Peter Barnes's play, *Jubilee* (London: Methuen, 2001). Stanley Wells's *Shakespeare for All Time* (cited above) includes much discussion of the reception of Shakespeare, and the way he became the central figure in English literature. And Samuel Schoenbaum's *Shakespeare's Lives* and Gary Taylor's *Reinventing Shakespeare* (both cited above) include much on the development of the cults of Shakespeare in the eighteenth and nineteenth centuries.

Index

A Note on the Author

Jack Lynch is a professor of English at Rutgers University and a Samuel Johnson scholar, having studied the great lexicographer for nearly a decade. He is the editor of *Samuel Johnson's Dictionary* and *Samuel Johnson's Insults*, and the author of *The Age of Elizabeth in the Age of Johnson*. He has also written journal articles and scholarly reviews addressing Johnson and the eighteenth century, and hosts a Web site devoted to these topics at http://andromeda.rutgers.edu/~jlynch/18th/.